CONFLICT IN URBAN DEVELOPMENT

Conflict in Urban Development

A Comparison Between East and West Europe

Arie Dekker
Henri Goverde
Tadeusz Markowski
Maria Ptaszynska-Woloczkowicz

*a*SHGATE

© A. Dekker, H. Goverde, T. Markowski, M. Ptaszynska-Woloczkowicz 1992

All rights reserved. No part of this publication may be reproduced, stored in a retrieval system, or transmitted in any form or by any means, electronic, mechanical, photocopying, recording, or otherwise without the prior permission of the publisher.

Published by
Ashgate
Ashgate Publishing Limited
Gower House
Croft Road
Aldershot
Hants GU11 3HR
England

Ashgate Publishing Company
Old Post Road
Brookfield
Vermont 05036
USA

A CIP catalogue record for this book is available from the British Library and the US Library of Congress.

Printed and bound in Great Britain by
Billing and Sons Ltd, Worcester

ISBN 1 85742 040 3

Contents

Preface		viii
Foreword		x
1	**Study of urban conflicts; scope, approaches and methodological aspects** *Henri Goverde*	1
	Introduction	1
	The scope of the study	2
	Urban conflict and its management	3
	Three analytical approaches	4
	Methodological aspects	6
2	**Urban conflicts reflect policy-networks, the theoretical framework** *Henri Goverde*	10
	Introduction	10
	The theoretical framework: analysis of policy networks	10
	Operationalization of the theoretical framework	13
	Elements for comparative analysis and evaluation	13

3	**The two policy systems in relation to urban questions** *Arie Dekker and Adam Kowalewski*	19
	Introduction	19
	Policy systems concerning land use and locational questions	23
	The Netherlands	23
	Poland	30
	Decision networks	39
	The Netherlands	39
	Poland	40
	Performance of the systems	41
	The Netherlands	41
	Poland	43
	A comparison between the two systems	45
	General description of the policy system concerning the cases	47
	The Netherlands	47
	Poland	47
4	**The cases** *Tadeusz Markowski, Barrie Needham, Aleksandra Jewtuchowicz,* *Arie Dekker, Maria Ptaszynska-Woloczkowicz, Leo van der Meer*	52
	Introduction to the cases	52
	The choice of a waste disposal site	55
	Poland (Lodz)	55
	The Netherlands (Beuningen, Borne, Nistelrode)	68
	Environmental nuisance of a large industrial plant	80
	Poland (Polonit, Lodz)	80
	The Netherlands (DSM, South-Limburg)	88
	Large scale urban expansion	103
	Poland (Stara Milosna)	103
	The Netherlands (Duiven-Westervoort)	117
5	**Analysis of the cases** *Arie Dekker*	130
	Introduction, synopsis and quantitative analysis of the cases	130
	Qualitative analysis of the cases	133
	Comparative analysis of the cases	136
	Evaluative aspects	138
6	**Urban conflict-management at work:** **conclusions and recommendations** *Henri Goverde*	142
	Introduction	142
	The case studies in the light of the theoretical framework	143
	Lessons from the cases	148
	Performance of the Dutch and Polish political administrative systems	150
	A contribution to the theory of urban conflicts	153
	Conclusions	157

Epilogue 161
Henri Goverde

Appendix 167

List of abbreviations 178

About the authors 180

Preface

How does physical planning function in practice when reconciling clashes of interest and in solving conflicts? And how does physical planning function under divergent political systems?

These intriguing questions have been considered by academics from the University of Lodz and the Polish Academy of Science (Warsaw) and the Catholic University of Nijmegen. In a co-operative project under the title PONECOS (Poland-Netherlands Comparative Study) they carried out a study into the conflict solving capacity of the administrative systems in both countries.

In three pairs of case-studies with comparable problems in each of the two countries, the conflict solving process was examined. As part of that, the formal and informal means that the parties used in the course of the conflict were studied. The cases deal with the location of a large waste disposal site, urban development in the environmental shadow of an industrial plant, and urban expansion in a metropolitan region.

The cases have been set in the context of the policy systems of both countries. It is for that reason, that the study also includes comparative descriptions of the policy systems with regard to spatial and urban questions at the time the case studies were examined, which was over the period 1970-1989.

The studies are preceded by a methodological chapter and a chapter concerning policy networks as a theoretical framework. A comparative analysis of the cases ends with conclusions regarding the theory and the management of conflicts.

This book therefore offers an important insight into how conflicts originate and develop and how to deal with conflicts with a complex character.

We warmly welcome the publication of this study and would like to stress the extra significance of this book in view of the dramatic changes that took place in Poland in 1989. The lesson that can be learned from a comparison of two regimes which, until recently, were so different, have now acquired even more relevance.

The Ministry of Housing, Physical Planning and Environment of the Netherlands is glad to have supported this study, which fits in with the "Declaration on Co-operation in the field of physical planning" signed between the two countries.

J.G.M. Alders,

The Minister of Housing, Physical Planning and Environment of the Netherlands

A. Kowalewski

The Deputy Minister for Spatial Economy and Architecture of Poland

July 1991

Foreword

The idea of the research project reported in this book arose in 1987. Two networks of contacts brought together academics and people from practice in Poland and the Netherlands. People from the Department of Urban Economics of the University of Lodz, the Department of Regional Economics of the Polish Academy of Science in Warsaw, the Department of Urban and Regional Planning and the Department of Administrative and Policy Sciences of the Catholic University of Nijmegen, the National Physical Planning Agency (the Hague) and the Provincial Physical Planning Agency of Gelderland (Arnhem) started their co-operation in the end of 1987 and from the beginning contributed to the project. Two seminars and two editorial meetings were held. People invited from outside took part in the seminars, so as to broaden the discussion and to bring the researchers in contact with people actually involved in the policy-making processes which were being investigated.

In both networks Professor Dr. Jerzy Regulski was the central person and this particular comparative research project was one of the series which he has stimulated. His interest in local democracy was a driving force to promote international contacts, which could produce possibly useful knowledge and capabilities from the other countries.

When the project was halfway, Professor Regulski had to terminate his contribution to it, so as to enter the Polish political scene in the period of the dramatic shift.

We are grateful to him for his part in the initial stage of the project and believe that, as it developed, it reflects his ideas about international co-operation.

Numerous persons and bodies have helped us during the research project. We would like to thank all of them and to mention some of them especially.

The voivodship of Lodz, the provinces of Limburg and Gelderland, the municipalities of Duiven, Geleen and Westervoort, the Department of Safety and Environment of DSM, and the Agency of the Environment of the Ministry of Housing, Physical Planning and Environment, contributed in various ways. We are grateful to have received their co-operation and hospitality.

The National Physical Planning Agency supported the project financially. Drs. Rob Kragt was responsible for the fruitful relation with the Agency and took part actively in various activities during the project. The Department of Urban and Regional Planning of the Catholic University of Nijmegen and the Foundation for Research and Consultancy concerning Administrative and Policy Affairs (BOA) supported a seminar in the Netherlands financially. The University of Lodz and the Academy of Science in Warsaw financed a seminar in Sulejow and an editorial meeting in Warsaw and Lodz respectively.

On the Polish side, researchers were involved who do not appear as authors of this book. We thank Dr. Piotr Bury, Dr. Iwo Byczewski, Stanislaw Furman Msc, and Dr. Janusz Kot for their contribution. Mrs. Maria Horbaczewska provided organisatorial assistance for the seminar in Poland.

On the Dutch side two students took as their graduation thesis the cases of Duiven-Westervoort and DSM-Geleen respectively: Roel Winkelhuyzen and Cecile Gribling. The latter helped us to organize the seminar in the Netherlands.

Mrs. Angela Needham-Houghton corrected the use of English in the text. Mrs. Annie van Bergen-Hendriks and Mrs. Willy Verheijen-Verkroost of the Secretariat of the Faculty of Policy Sciences of the Catholic University of Nijmegen word-processed the text of the book and accomplished a complicated job. Mr. Paul Wissink of the Section Cartography of the A-Faculties of the same university drew the maps and diagrams skilfully.

Chapter 1

Study of urban conflicts; scope, approaches and methodological aspects

Henri Goverde

Introduction

This study is an attempt to improve our understanding of public policy-making in Poland and the Netherlands concerning the management of conflicts in urban development at the local level. Although this is a topical subject for many countries, it is of special interest to those countries in Eastern and Central Europe which have embarked on the tremendous task of reforming their political systems at the local level.

This chapter will present in outline the scope of the study, the concept of conflict used, and some methodological aspects.

The research took place in the period 1988-1990. Researchers from the following institutions were involved:

Poland:
- Polish Academy of Sciences, Institute of Economic Science (Warsaw)
- University of Lodz, Department of Urban Economics

The Netherlands:
- Catholic University of Nijmegen, Department of Urban and Regional Planning and Department of Administrative and Policy Sciences
- National Physical Planning Agency (Ministry of Housing, Physical Planning and Environment, The Hague)
- Regional Physical Planning Department of the Province of Gelderland (Arnhem)

The scope of the study

Before describing the framework within which the project operated, it will be necessary to outline its goals.

The aim of the project

The aim of the project was twofold
1. to improve insight into the performance of the Polish and Dutch policy-making systems, especially those concerning conflicts in urban development at the local level;
2. to contribute to the theoretical understanding of urban conflicts.

To realize the first aim, the research design has to include a multi-level comparison.
 A distinction was made between two levels:
- the level of the Dutch and Polish policy systems; an overview of the main characteristics of both systems will be given, concentrating on land use and locational questions (chapter 3);
- the level of the selected case-studies; in this project three pairs of comparable case-studies have been selected (see chapter 4)).

The realization of the second aim needs a common theoretical framework concerning the management of conflicts in decision-networks. This is necessary also for formulating the main criteria for the selection of the cases and for comparing the selected pairs of cases (see chapter 5 and 6).

The scope of the project

The study was restricted by the following:
- the subject: the performance of the policy-systems of Poland and the Netherlands was studied in the field of urban development alone;
- the theoretical approach: the development of power relations in policy-networks (chapter 2);
- the research design: multiple case-studies.

The strength of analyses using the network approach is that it gives insights into the dynamics of policy-processes, starting from the relationship between variables such as power and influence on the one side, and on the other side the goal-oriented actions of individuals, groups and organisations involved. This approach also has its weaknesses. The insight remains at the level of very complicated relationships which cannot easily be translated into clear and testable propositions. Therefore, although this type of analysis often produces a picture of policy-making within which many politicians can recognise themselves or their field of action, it cannot convince all academics because the material of the analysis cannot be always tested scientifically. Nevertheless, information about the functioning of policy-networks on selected political issues is the basis for finding tools for effective consultancy and recommendations. This information is a precondition for advising actors how to realize common decisions and for preventing serious problems being dominated by power-games.

Urban conflict and its management

Dahrendorf (1959; cited by Porter and Taplin, 1987, p. 4) succintly stated: 'Not the presence, but the absence of conflict is surprising and abnormal, and we have good reason to be suspicious if we find a society or social organization that displays no evidence of conflict.'

Gresch and Smith (1985) mention many words synonymous with "conflict" such as clash, competition, struggle, contest, fight, battle, warfare, collision, etc. However, these terms do not all have the same meaning or emotional value and the character of conflicts can differ.

A conflict emerges whenever two or more people (or groups) seek to possess the same object, occupy the same space or the same exclusive position, play incompatible roles, maintain incompatible goals, or engage in mutually incompatible means for achieving their purposes (North, 1968, part 3, p. 226). In fact, conflicts are always social conflicts (see the next section point 2).

Characteristics of spatial conflicts

Physical planning is concerned with the management of conflicts that are presented in a spatial form. Although spatial conflict has been studied only little (Gresch and Smith, op.cit., p. 159), it is quite evident that the increasing competition for the use of scarce land makes conflict management a major issue in urban and regional planning.

Generally speaking a spatial issue has three characteristic, which are relevant for physical planning (Van der Cammen, 1979, pp. 19-24):
- it concerns processes of development, which together constitute a dynamic system (Steigenga, 1973; Dekker, 1975; Ganzevles c.s., 1975);
- it concerns spontaneous as well as publicity initiated developments (Wissink, 1982 a,b)
- it concerns a mutual interdependence between the physical and the societal component (Rouge, 1947). Both can in turn be dominant and adaptive (Foley, 1964).

So, urban conflicts are social conflicts and include some elements of spatial issues. Urban conflicts often show the following combination of elements:
- property rights are always involved;
- property rights are not always congruent with the right to decide about the function of the property (e.g. in the general interest, a government can give another function to a specific location and expropriate the owner of his property);
- such decisions generally produce a lot of externalities which cause many new actors to enter the political arena of this urban and/or environmental issue;
- externalities produce new conflicts, which require new political choices to be made.

In chapter 6 an attempt will be made to improve the understanding of urban conflicts using the results of the case-studies in this book.

Traditionally, physical planning includes methods for managing conflicting claims on physical space (e.g. cost-benefit analysis, the planning balance sheet, multi-criteria analysis). However, these methods do not always consider social aspects adequately when weighing those claims one against the other. In centrally organized and planned economies, these methods were often not used at all, because the planning system accepted only presupposed conflicts (i.e. the conflict between capital and labour) and avoided making conflicts explicit. Nevertheless, in those countries physical planners have recently tried to learn from information gathered about organizations and their environment. They are especially interested in conflict management within and between organizations.

In order to analyse these conflicts, the concept of policy-networks is often introduced. If this concept is to be applied in order to steer societal development, this is much more difficult and remains in this study a theoretical challenge. Although this challenge will not be gone into here in its entirety, chapter 5 will look at and evaluate the techniques of conflict management used in the case-studies worked out in chapter 4.

Three analytical approaches

Conflict can be studied in different ways. Here, a distinction is made between three approaches:
1. conflict as an inevitable concomitant of the use of urban space;
2. conflict as a strategy of one or more actors in a process of decision-making;
3. conflict as a result of the dynamism of a policy-network.

approach 1: conflict as a characteristic of urban space (land economics)
It can be argued that the very characteristics of land itself make conflicts in urban development inevitable. The physical space is a limited resource which cannot be replaced. Land and the environment as an economic resource is always used under conditions of an imperfect market. Economically, the physical space has the character of a natural monopoly. In practice, the importance of this monopoly will increase the more environmental destruction continues.

The conflict is locational (Cox, 1973, pp. 3-15) in the sense that it results from a conflict between the utility-maximizing goals of the individual decision-making units and their allocative behavior with respect to other decision-making units, either on the same geographical scale (e.g. between households or between municipalities) or on different geographical scales (e.g. between a household and the municipality in which it is located). If locational conflicts are resolved by either private locational strategies or by private bargaining, these private solutions tend to be sub-optimal. Externalities will remain and cause residual localized stress. Further, co-ordination by collective control of some of the individual decision-making units' property rights could make one unit better off without making another worse off. However, when conflicting interests are at stake in a situation of mutual interdependency, the decision by collective control may be optimal. Nevertheless, this kind of locational conflict together with regulations to pursue the common interest have given rise to public law concerning land use, property rights and expropriation.

approach 2: conflict as an actors' strategy (the actor oriented approach)
To characterize conflicts it is not necessary to include the locational context. For example van der Knaap (1987) gives the following preconditions for a serious conflict:
- more than one party is involved;
- the parties have a key-position in the policy-making process;

- there is no consensus about goals and means;
- there is a situation of scarcity;
- parties/actors should have a serious interest in solving the conflict, i.e. in getting the planned project realized;
- the existence of conflicts is indicated by deadlocks which no one knows how to break. It is relevant that deadlocks do not exist at the start of a policy process; there is often consensus at the beginning, but the actors produce the conflict during the course of the process.

In policy analysis, strategies are understood as being the ways in which actors try to influence the creation of a collective will, as well as being the results of this process (policy-making). The main strategies of actors in policy-making processes are conflict, negotiation, making coalitions and threatening sanctions. Actors use different arguments to start or to keep a conflict going. For instance, one actor can believe that showing his strength will produce some movement in the position of other actors. Another case is when an actor believes that his aspirations will be realized by taking the issue to a higher level in the hierarchy (Leemans, 1978, pp.105-106). So, conflict can be perceived as a special strategy which actors can use to move the policy-network (i.e. all the actors involved in a particular policy issue) in a direction more favourable to them. Approaching conflict as the strategy of an actor is important, not only for distinguishing conflict from other behaviour of actors in policy-making, but also for making clear what the management of urban issues means. In essence, management of conflicts in urban development should encourage actors to use all types of strategies except conflict, as that could produce deadlocks too easily.

approach 3: conflict as the result of the dynamism of policy-networks

This perception of conflict emphasises the unplanned character of social processes. When every actor operates appropriately to his position in the policy-network, the outcome of the process can be - and often is - contrary to the goals and wishes of all participants (Elias, 1970).

Many case-studies worked out using the network approach have demonstrated that the dynamism of the network itself often dominates the goals of the actors involved and is also one of the main reasons why the network started. Very often the actors in networks act to diminish the power of the other actors, although the network was started for co-operation in order to solve common problems. With this approach, it is important to know how policy-networks can work effectively, how organisations can reach common decisions, and how serious problems dominated by power games can be prevented.

The concept of conflict in this study

In this study all three approaches to conflicts are followed. The first because it gives information about questions in urban development such as those studied here. It gives a practical description of the field within which the performance of the Polish and Dutch policy-making systems are studied. The second and third approaches give the theoretical basis for the selected case-studies and the foundation on which practical recommendations are built.

All three approaches are based on the idea that decisions concerning urban developments are made in a situation within which the actors are interdependent. Interdependence means that the results of any actor's activity are influenced by the actions of other relevant actors (van Asperen, 1986, p. 11). The action can produce co-operation or conflict. More precisely, within the interdependence of the actors involved in the policy process, strategies of conflict or of co-operation can become dominant.

In this book the central focus is on conflicts and the cases have been selected for this. Nevertheless, our main interest was to discover and to analyse how conflicts are managed, if and how co-operation was arrived at in order to tackle the spatial issue.

Methodological aspects

This section includes some methodological remarks concerning cross-national comparative studies, basic assumptions of the study, the research design, the selected cases, and the research methods.

Cross-national comparative studies

The following methodological principles are important concerning cross-national comparative studies:
- the scope of a study must be broad enough to cover not only the phenomena analyzed but also the external frameworks of the field of research (the national political culture; patterns of national traditions; the dominant ideological framework; the level of social-economic development; geographical location; international dependence);
- if external frameworks differ, a research design must be chosen which is based on a common theory or theoretical orientation in order to get phenomena which can be compared;
- special care is needed to create a common understanding among the national teams involved (Jensen and Regulski, 1988).

Assumptions

No researcher can make a proposal for a research project without having some assumptions in his mind concerning the topic and the expected outcome of the project. The basic suppositions in this study are that:
- every society has some urban conflicts, whatever the character of the political system;
- it is possible to compare urban conflicts in different social and political systems;
- cross-national urban comparative studies can help one to find useful academic hypotheses;
- cross-national comparative studies can help to expose the policy choices in a society.

Research design

Cross-national comparative research often uses the case-study method. This project did the same. After setting out the research steps, we will look at the methodical aspects of this method and at the selection of the cases.

Research steps These were three research steps:

1. the creation of the research design: production of a theory/ hypothesis/ or theoretical notion; selection of the cases and the variables which could be used for comparative case-study research;
2. data-collection and analysis of the different cases; the empirical inquiry was made for every selected case and a separate report made for every case;
3. the comparative analysis: selected cases were compared, conclusions drawn, the theory modified and recommendations formulated.

After each research step a conference was held: Sulejow (Polen, 1988); Nijmegen (Holland, 1989); and Warsawa (Poland, 1990).

Multiple case-study research According to Yin (1981, p. 23) a case-study is an 'empirical inquiry', that (1) investigates a contemporary phenomenon within its real-life context, when (2) the boundaries between phenomenon and context are not clearly evident, and in which (3) multiple sources of evidence are used.

Multiple case-study research follows the strict pattern:
1. a theory is developed;
2. the theory is used as a basis for the selection of the cases and also for studying them;
3. the study of the cases produces a basis for comparing the selected cases;
4. the results of the comparison are used for adapting or developing the theory.
5. the study of the cases together with the adapted theory give some ideas for policy recommendations.

Selection of the cases Operationalising the theoretical-analytical framework helped the research-team to select case-studies, which could be expected to be feasible within the very limited research capacities (manpower, money, time, and access to empirical data). So figure 2 (see chapter 2) has, in fact, three functions:
- an instrument to find feasible case-studies;
- an instrument for the selection of the relevant data per case-study;
- a framework for the descriptive analysis of the cases.

Much time in the first Ponecos conference (Sulejow, 1988) was spent finding suitable case-studies.

Two criteria had to be fulfilled:
1. they had to be studied with the human figuration approach (see chapter 2);
2. they had to give insight into the functioning of the conflict-solving mechanisms in both countries, in the fields of urban development and environmental management.

Three pairs of cases seemed to fulfill both criteria:
- economic development and environmental zoning: the issue of large polluting industrial complexes (Dutch States Mines, DSM-Geleen; and the packing and asbestos plant 'Polonit' in Lodz);
- the location of waste disposal sites (region Arnhem/Nijmegen; and the region Lodz);
- new towns and new urban extensions in relation to political-administrative management (Arnhem-Duiven/Westervoort; and low rise residential areas in East-Warsaw, Stara Milosna).

In 1989, the chosen cases were studied in detail.

Research techniques   Not many resources were available for this project. Therefore, to keep the project feasible it was decided to use where possible existing or empirical work done by researchers outside the Ponecos-team (e.g. waste disposal sites in the Netherlands). For most of the other cases the formal documents were relatively easily available and this made it possible to decide whether or not the decision-network approach could be used. Special empirical research was necessary for the following case-studies: DSM-Geleen (Gribling, 1989); Arnhem-Duiven/Westervoort (Winkelhuyzen, 1989); 'Polonit'; and the waste disposal site at Lodz.

The main research techniques used in the case-studies were the analysis of formal documents, and open interviews with key-participants in the selected cases. In Poland the empirical matter was mainly restricted to public sources such as newspapers, television broadcasts and so on, and was supplemented by research into the files of public authorities.

References

Asperen, G.M. van (1986) *Tussen coöperatie en conflict* Inleiding in de sociale filosofie, Assen/Maastricht.
Cammen, H. van der (1979) *De binnenkant van de planologie*, Muiderberg.
Coser, Lewis A. (1968) Conflict: social aspects, *International Encyclopeadia of the Social Sciences* Crowell, Coltier and McMillan Inc., New York, part 3, pp. 232-236.
Cox, Kevin R. (1973) *Conflict, Power and Politics in the City: a geographic view* McGraw-Hill, New York etc.
Dekker, A. (1975) *Planningmethodiek* 1e deel, Algemeen ruimtelijk planningkader, studierapport RPD, nr 5, Ministerie van VRO, 's-Gravenhage.
Elias, N. (1970) *Wat is sociologie?* Utrecht/Antwerpen, Aula 462.
Foley, Donald L. (1964) 'An approach to Metropolitan Spatial Structure', *Explorations into Urban Structure* Philadelphia, pp. 21-78.
Gresch, Peter and Smith, Bryan (1985) 'Managing Spatial Conflict: The Planning System in Switzerland', *Progress in Planning* vol.23, Pergamon Press, Oxford, pp. 155-251.
Ganzevles, M.G.J. (et all) (1975) 'Enige beschouwingen over procesplanning' *Stedebouw en Volkshuisvesting* nr 7/8, pp. 251-255.
Gribling, C.C.M. (1989) Milieuzonering rondom DSM, Nijmegen (PIN).
Jensen, H.T. and Regulski, J. (1988) 'Introduction', in Regulski et al.(eds) *Local Government and Decentralization: A Danish-Polish Comparative Study in Political Systems* Universities of Lodz and Roskilde.
Knaap, J.W.M. van der (1987) 'Leren van conflicten. Over conflicten bij het realiseren van regionale afvalverwerkingslokaties', *Tijdschrift voor Openbaar Bestuur* vol. 13, nr 7, pp. 140-144.
Leemans, A.F. (1978) 'Het bepalen van overheidsbeleid', in: A. Hoogerwerf (ed), *Overheidsbeleid* Alphen ad Rijn, pp. 87-107.
North, Robert C. (1968) 'Conflict: political aspects', *International Encyclopeadia of the Social Sciences*, Crowell, Coltier and McMillan Inc, New York, part 3, pp. 226-231.
Porter, Jack Nusan and Ruth Taplin (1987) *Conflict and Conflict Resolution* A sociological introduction with updated bibliography and theory section, Univ. Press of America, Lanham/London.
Rouge, M.F. (1947) *La géonomie ou l'organisation de l'espace*, Paris.

Steigenga, W. (1973) *Planologie in beweging*, Amsterdam.
Winkelhuyzen, R. (1989) Beschrijving van het beleidsproces Duiven-Westervoort, Nijmegen.
Wissink, G.A. (1982a) *Ruimtelijke ordening als mensenwerk* Assen.
Wissink, G.A. (1982b) 'Het krachtenveld van de ruimtelijke ontwikkeling' in: D.B. Needham en G.A. Wissink (eds), *Ruimtelijke planning en ruimtelijke ontwikkelingen: een gespannen verhouding*, Assen, pp. 4-14
Yin, R.K. (1981) 'The case study as a serious research strategy', *Knowledge*, vol 3 pp. 97-114.
Yin, R.K., (1981) 'The case study crisis: some answers', *Administrative Science Quarterly*, 26, pp. 58-65.

Chapter 2

Urban conflicts reflect policy-networks, the theoretical framework

Henri Goverde

Introduction

In this chapter the analytical framework of the study is explained. The first section concerns the policy networks approach. What is its theoretical basis? What are the main concepts and how are these concepts related? How is this analytical framework operationalised? The second section gives two sets of variables which will be used to compare the Polish and Dutch cases. One set concerns the role of the state, the other gives a list of criteria for evaluating policy-making in the cases.

The theoretical framework: the analysis of policy networks

As stated in the third section of chapter 1, conflicts in urban development are mainly social conflicts which arise because of the spatial characteristics of the conflict. These social conflicts reflect the activities of and the interactions between individuals, groups and institutions. These activities and interactions can together be considered as a dynamic inter-organisational human figuration, i.e. a decision- or a policy-network (Baaijens, 1988; Kickert, v.Vught, 1984).

This starting-point implies that:
1. Each urban question reflects such a decision network. There is no one social-political system that covers all urban questions.
2. The concept of dynamic decision-networks includes the idea that the actors in the network are mutually interdependent. Therefore, in general,

no one single actor is able to control the network.
Using this starting-point it is easy to understand that research which attempts to recommend management of urban questions should start with the descriptive analysis of policy-making in the decision networks involved. This analysis should:
- use the different participating actors and their conflicts of interests as the starting point;
- give special attention to the distribution of power resources;
- focus on the interactions between the participants (inter-organizational perspective; the development of the power balance in the decision-network);
- enable the formulation of strategies for conflict-solving [1].

Policy networks in action: the development of the power balance

In all urban questions it is possible to distinguish participants who share the location of the problem (e.g. residents in a neighbourhood through which a new freeway is planned) and participants who have no direct locational connection to the issue (e.g. national leaders of trade unions in building construction). Together they make the human figuration involved in the urban question. In studying this figuration one should look at the interactions between the participants. This interdependence and how it develops influences the distribution of power resources and hence the power balance in the figuration. These factors are of particular significance because they will, in the end, be reflected in the policy-making process and also in the final decision-making.

Positions of power and power resources

For a powerful position one needs control of power resources. Power resources can be put into four categories. The control of:
- the means of production (e.g. land, capital, labour, machinery, distribution systems, public finance, the physical environment);
- the means of coercion (e.g. physical force, weapons, police, army, prisons);
- the means of orientation (e.g. ideology, religion - expressed in 'labels', 'symbols' and 'rituals' - science and scientific research, education, values, norms);
- the means of organization (e.g. the organization and management of the loyalty of supporters of the interest groups; the competence to recognize institutional arrangements; the control of (planning)procedures; the control of and access to the mass-media).

The competition to gain control of power resources is not open and equal. All participants have to enter a political arena in which the power resources are already divided. The participants do not therefore start from equal positions. The competition cannot be perceived as a strictly pluralistic one. But the competition for power resources is not a pure zero-sum game either. Although the assets of one actor can imply the same quantity of liabilities for another (power relations are per definition relative), studies of long-term policy processes in particular demonstrate that new power resources are developed during these processes.

The creation of new power resources by one or a number of actors produces a demand for these resources from other actors. It is precisely this creation of and demand for new power resources which gives the balance of power perpetual instability. This characterizes the dynamics of the human figuration and the decision-network. In other words, there is a dialectical dimension to the mutual interdependence between the participants. The network reflects the power relations but, at the same time, attempts are made to change it.

Conflict management: uncertainty and strategy

Because of the interdependence between the actors in the network, one single actor cannot control the process. Therefore, it is wrong to assume that a single actor or institution can solve a conflict in a specific urban question. Elias (1970) added the proposition that the higher the number of participants, the less the entire process can be controlled by any one of them. Therefore, it is difficult to predict what will be the final decision resulting from the process of policy formation in complex human figurations, nor its effects.

Control of the rules of the game

Nevertheless, differences in power between individuals as well as constant interaction between individuals, groups and institutions can reduce the unpredictability of the process as a whole. In these interactions certain routines can develop. The participants can learn what to expect from each other and what not. Progress in developing these habits and expectations can produce rules for behaviour and norms which can even be written down (laws, rules of the game). Of course, the control of the 'rules of the game' is itself an important resource of power. Therefore there is constant pressure to change the rules. The rules which diminish the predictability of the policy-making processes (e.g. rules concerning public participation) are often subject to the interactions of different actors, who want to change mutual interdependence in such a way that the outcome of the game becomes more predictable for them. The mutual interdependencies then reflect the power relations between the participants, whilst these interdependencies are constantly under stress because of the changing assessment of power resources by individual actors, groups and institutions.

Uncertainties

In this framework, the uncertainties in the process of policy-formation are perceived as a reflection of the ever-changing interdependencies between the actors in a decision network. For policy-makers it is particularly interesting that the concept of power is related to the concept of uncertainty. Increase of power and reduction of uncertainty are essential aspects of strategic acting. According to Crozier and Friedberg (1977) actors have a power-strategy, which means that they:
- try to keep and to enlarge the fields in which they make decisions by themselves;
- try to limit the predictability of their behaviour;
- try to increase their control over all variables which can influence the realization of their goals.

Power strategy

In this power strategy, the control of the sources of uncertainty is important for two reasons;
1. certainty is directly related to rational behaviour because it makes decision making easier and it increases the chances of making the right decision;
2. the control of the sources of uncertainty indirectly influences rational behaviour: it is a resource of exchange which can stimulate other actors in negotiations to deliver the certainties which are as yet beyond their control. In this process of negotiation, the actor can use his control of those sources of uncertainty which are important to the other actor.

This is the reason why the control of the sources of uncertainty can be interpreted as a matter of power. Crozier and Friedberg add that actors not only use their power to get certainties which they need immediately, but they try to safeguard their position in the future too. For this reason, they generally do not give priority to resources such as 'physical force', 'money', 'knowledge' or 'goods', but they try primarily to influence the use of resources in the future. So actors use their power in interactions mainly to reconstruct the power relations for the future in a way favourable to themselves.

Summary

The theoretical-analytical framework (the analysis of policy networks: the relationship between the development of the power balance and conflict management) has been constructed in order to gain a better understanding of how urban issues are produced by human beings as individuals or as participants in organizations. Further, the dialectical dimension of the framework is important when making practical recommendations for managing urban conflicts

Operationalization of the theoretical framework

The theoretical framework is worked out in a 10 step schedule which combines an actor-oriented and an inter-organizational approach. Together with the series of research steps (chapter 1) it produces a research method which can be characterized as a qualitative power analysis in human figurations i.e. decision/policy networks (Table 2.1).

Method of comparative analysis and evaluation

The analytical comparison of the cases is based on the following:
- the operationalization of the theoretical framework (Table 2.1);
- the various roles of the state;
- the general standards for the evaluation of policy-making in both political systems.

Table 2.1 Operationalization of the theoretical-analytical framework

I   ACTOR-ORIENTED: GOALS-MEANS APPROACH

1. (neutral) character of the environmental problem
2. who is involved? actors/participants
3. what are their interests? public/private
4. what is the initial policy of the public authorities if any?
5. what are the policy instruments? power resources (especially control over means of orientation and organization)

II INTER-ORGANIZATIONAL APPROACH/ NETWORK IN OPERATION

6. operationalization of 'mutual interdependency' (formal and informal position of the actors / map of inter-relations / developments : who is dependent on whom?)
7. is the dependency of an actor congruent with his goals/instruments?
8. who has to change his power position? who needs a shift in the power balance in order to realize his goals?
9. which strategies / games / dimensions of interaction are used by the actors to change the position of the power balance / to steer the network?

9.a. strategies: (design of a course of action by an actor with a view to the goals which he wishes to attain)
    - the maintenance or increase of power
    - the maintenance or increase of certainty
    - the purposeful running of risks
    - the avoidance of power and responsibility
    - the maintenance of established social constructions and value-oriented action
9.b. games: co-operation/ coalition/ competition/ limitation of competition/ open conflict/ avoidance/ merger/ (bureaucratization)
9.c. general dimensions of interaction: communication/ negotiation/ exchange/ decision-making

10. types of available power resources not used (recommendations/ ex post)

In fact the authors of the case-studies used the 10 step schedule when selecting information and when interviewing. Table 2.1 contains several steps by which the character of the conflict can be made explicit. For example step 5 includes all types of power resources. If the means of coercion are used by any of the actors the issue will contain conflict. If actors use mainly resources like 'the control of means of organization and orientation' (in fact they follow the process of mutual argument), then there is still a conflict but the chances of co-operation will be much greater. Step 9 gives a view of the intensity and the scope of the conflict by showing the strategies, the games and the general dimensions of the interaction used by the actors in the policy-network. In step 9 all types and means of conflict solving are relevant. According to Porter and Taplin (op.cit., chapter IV) the main means in this respect are:
- avoidance,
- conquest,
- education and contact,
- spontaneous remission,
- transactional resolution (direct negotiation, mediation),
- arbitration,
- judicial decision and
- non-reconciliation.

Using different means of conflict solving implies diverse political and administrative costs. For example, the coercive aspect is low in the first items on the list and high in the later items. The political and administrative costs are low at the top and high at the bottom of the list. The voluntaristic aspect, however, is high at the top and low at the bottom, whilst the satisfaction is the other way around: high at the beginning and low at the end of the list. So, to assess the means of conflict solving in concrete urban issues, knowledge of the side-effects of using the different resources is very relevant.

Insight into another aspect concerning the resolution or avoidance of a conflict is gained by identifying the different functions of a conflict. In the theory of social conflicts Porter and Taplin (op.cit., p. 4) found, in the work of Coser and Simmel in particular, several functions of conflicts:
- establish unity and cohesion;
- produce stabilizing and integrative elements;
- ascertain the relative strength of anatagonistic interests within the structure;
- constitute mechanisms for maintenance and/or readjustment of the power balance;
- produce associations and coalitions;
- help reduce social isolation and unite individuals;
- maintain boundary lines between new associations/ coalitions;
- act as a 'safety-valve' to reduce frustration and aggression;
- produce situations for consensus.

So, a conflict can be very functional in finally getting the right policy output. In chapter 5 the relationship between the schedule (table 2.1) and the case-studies is made explicit. Chapter 5 and chapter 6 will look at the functional aspects of the selected conflicts as well.

The other two dimensions of the cases (the various roles of the state and the overall standards for evaluating policy-making) will be dealt with later in this section. These dimensions will mainly be used in chapter 6.

The main aim of the comparative analysis was to find similarities and differences in policy-making in the two political systems. By gaining insight into the policy-making mechanisms it is believed that tools will be found which can produce better management of policy processes.

The role of the state

Poland and the Netherlands have different political systems. The Polish system is changing fast and significantly at this very time. The Dutch system has been fairly stable for many years. In the Netherlands also the role of the state is an important political issue. There is strong pressure to diminish the intervention of the state in many fields. Further, the Netherlands is involved in the '1992' operation of the European community i.e. the opening of the social-economic markets throughout the 12 member states. This is expected to have a major impact on Dutch society in general but especially on political and administrative relations between governmental institutions (Home Office, 1990).

Whatever the actual continuities and changes in both systems, we can distinguish at least five roles of the state:
- supplier of general interest facilities: army, police, courts, schools, roads, airports, tele-communication;
- (re-)distributor of goods and services: rights, privileges, passports, standards of living, school-milk, land, health controls (persons, imported goods);
- guardian of the interests of the public administrative institutions: employment, careers, income;
- arbiter, the ultimate authoritative decision-taker;
- manager of social-political tensions: prohibitor of destructive conflicts between individuals, groups and institutions (actors).

All these roles can be discovered in the policy-networks concerning urban development. Generally, the role of arbiter is difficult to play when the governmental institutions involved in an issue are mainly pursuing their own institutional interests. The role of arbiter needs a lot of authority, which, in essence means legitimised, widely accepted power. Such authority is generally not part of the executive but of the judicial powers of the state.

The role of manager of social conflicts is becoming more important. This is easier to play if the state is only slightly involved as an initiator and intervener in societal fields. However, when the executive part of the government is a major participant in the social conflict, the role of manager of these conflicts is quite often allocated to the judicial power, to the court. The managers' role can also result in the state becoming a partner in public-private partnerships. This is especially relevant in the context of urban development.

Evaluative aspects

Although the study is not a policy evaluation, it has an evaluative aspect, that it searches for criteria for 'better management' of urban conflicts. To set standards for better management, it is necessary to relate them to the main characteristics of the political system within which they will be used. The criteria are mainly intended for the interventions of governmental participants in policy networks. This implies that the recommendations have

a limited scope: they are mainly for the governmental actors. Of course these actors have special relevance, because they are the main actors who have to accept responsibility for improving policy-making. For the Dutch political system (a decentralized unitary state based on a constitutional monarchy with a parliamentary democratic system) the following global standards can be used to evaluate the policy-making process:
- effectiveness: does the policy realize its goals?;
- efficiency: are the goals realized using as few means as possible (finance, time, manpower, space)?;
- taking account of interests: are all relevant interests seriously taken into account before a definite decision is made?
- autonomous position of different governmental levels: are decisions made at the lowest possible level?; does the necessary co-ordination lead to effective co-operation?;
- position of the elected state organs: is it really the national parliament, provincial and municipal councils which are taking decisions?;
- position of the individual citizen in relation to the state: is he really able to participate in the policy-making and how strongly is the protection of his legal rights organized and guaranteed?

As mentioned above the Polish state was organized very centrally. The main methods of governing were one-sided, rigid central distributive mechanisms. The centralised one-party system could not deal with conflicts openly. The only conflict which was acceptable was the class struggle, which was managed by giving almost absolute priority to public interests. Deficiencies in the impartiality of judicial protection were another source of conflict but these also were neglected.

The political system of Poland is in transition. As yet, no one knows when this process will end. Nevertheless, looking at the intentions of the recent Polish cabinet, the global standards mentioned above can be used for the evaluation of the policy networks in Poland as well.

Notes

1. Recently a theoretical-analytical framework for the analysis of policy formation in decision networks based on the following social scientific orientations has been suggested (Goverde, 1988.a/b):
   - mutual interdependencies in human figurations (N.Elias,1939,1970; J.Goudsblom, 1974,1987);
   - the inter-organizational dimension in organization theory (Friend, Power, Yewlett, 1974; Scharpf,1978; Mayntz, 1978);
   - the network approach in public administration (Bekke/Rosenthal, 1984; Kickert/v.Vught,1984; Baaijens,1988)
   - the idea of the dialectical relationship between the actors and the social system (Crozier, 1963; Crozier and Friedberg, 1977; Godfroij, 1981).

References

Baaijens, J.M.J. (1988) *Beleidsnetwerken in actie*, Deventer.
Bekke, A.J.G.M. en Rosenthal, U. (eds) (1984) *Netwerken rond het openbaar*

bestuur, Ver. Bestuurskunde, congrespublikatie 1983, Samsom, Alphen aan den Rijn.
Crozier, M. (1963) *Le phénomène bureaucratique,* Paris.
Crozier, M. and Friedberg, E. (197) *L'acteur et le système,* Paris.
Elias, N. (1969) *Uber den Prozess der Zivilisation* Soziogenetische und psychogenetische Untersuchungen, (2 Banden) (1939), Bern.
Elias, N. (1970) *Wat is sociologie?* Utrecht/Antwerpen, Aula 462.
Friend, J.K., Power, J.M. and Yewlett, C.J.L. (1974) *Public planning: the inter-corporate dimension* Tavistock.
Godfroij, Arnold (1981) *Netwerken van organisaties. Strategiën, spelen, structuren,* 's-Gravenhage.
Goudsblom, J. (1987) *De sociologie van Norbert Elias. Weerklank en kritiek/ De civilisatietheorie,* Amsterdam.
Goudsblom, J. (1974) *Balans van de sociologie,* Aula 518, Utrecht/Antwerpen.
Goverde, H.J.M. (1988a) *A theoretical-analytical framework within which to compare the Polish and Dutch Planning Systems on Urban Questions,* (paper presented at the Sulejow Conference), Nijmegen.
Goverde, H.J.M. (1988b) *Power and International Environmental Management. Some theoretical and practical aspects of an ongoing line of research* (paper presented in the IPSA Study Group 'Political Power Analysis', Washington DC), Nijmegen/Oslo.
Home Office (Ministerie van Binnenlandse Zaken) (1990) Nota *Binnenlandse Zaken en de Europese Integratie,* Den Haag.
Kickert, W. and Vught, F.v. (1984), 'Beleidsnetwerken en maatschappelijke sturing', in A. Bekke and U. Rosenthal, *Netwerken rond het openbaar bestuur* Ver. Bestuurskunde congrespublikatie 1983, Samsom, Alphen aan den Rijn.
Mayntz, R., 'Intergovernmental implementation of environmental policy', in Hanf, K. and F. Scharpf (eds) (1978) *Interorganizational policy-making; limits to co-ordination and central control* London/Beverly Hills, pp. 37-55.
Porter, Jack Nusan and Ruth Taplin (1987) *Conflict and Conflict Resolution. A sociological introduction with updated bibliography and theory section,* Univ. Press of America, Lanham/London.
Scharpf, F.W. (1978) 'Interorganisational policy studies: issues, concepts and perspectives', in: K. Hanf and F. Scharpf (eds), *Interorganisational policy--making; limits to co-ordination and central control* London/Beverly Hils, pp. 345-370.

Chapter 3

The two policy systems in relation to urban questions

Arie Dekker and Adam Kowalewski

Introduction

In this part of the study an overview is given of the policy systems for urban questions in both countries. As urban questions themselves are complex and diffuse, so are the policy systems complex and diffuse. A complete description is beyond the scope of this study; a selection has had to be made. We focus upon questions in which locational and land use decisions dominate. This does not imply that other aspects are unimportant but that they are taken into account only in as far as they play (or should play) an explicit role. There are no unambiguous criteria for delimiting the area of interest. The purpose and analytical framework of the study can be added as a criterion. This means that the very existence and tackling of conflicts, the operation of decision-networks, and the understanding and appraisal of the cases are guiding factors. The delimitation is based upon the expert knowledge of the authors, tested by the other researchers.

The level of description can be defined as intermediate, i.e. higher than the cases and lower than the principles of the state, administrative structure and general legislation.

The description of both policy-systems serves as a context for the cases. Some of the phenomena which are described in the cases can be explained to a greater or a lesser extent by elements of the respective policy systems. This will be part of the analysis in chapter 5 and chapter 6.

We start with some remarks about the principles and structure of the state in both countries.

The Polish policy system is in a stage of dramatic change [1] after a period of transition from 1980 until 1989. Until 1980 the administrative system of Poland was built upon the principle of full centralization and a hierarchical subordination of all tiers of administration to the central government. Each upper level supervised the lower one, legally and functionally.

Three types of powers existed at all levels: political parties, the legislature, and the administration, the latter subordinated both to political parties (in practice) and to the legislature (nominally). At all levels, since 1945 elections have been manipulated by the communist party which was the only real ruler of Poland until 1980. Consequently, all important decisions, budgetary policy, political nominations, taxation-systems etc., were at the total discretion of central government, although some ritual forms of public participation in politics were established in the fifties and applied subsequently.

The foundations of the socialist administrative model were supported by three axioms:

a. The decisive and predominant role of planning, instead of market forces (Decree of 1946, and several subsequent legal documents) in the management of the national economy.
b. The unified system of public power introduced by the "Territorial Agencies of Unified State Authority Act" (March, 1950). The local legislatures and the administration belong to a "unified system of public power". The essence of this "unified" system is the Leninist doctrine which, simplified, says that in a socialist system there is unity of goals and interests, conflicts are nonexistent and therefore the Montesquieu 'three powers' model must be replaced by an integrated system of authorities.
c. The leading role of the communist party (PZPR - Polish United Workers' Party), granted formally in the Constitutional Law of 1978 (but factually, by the Soviet Union's domination in the Eastern Europe) to Polish communists. This was carried out by the 'nomenclatura' system, i.e. the obligatory acceptance of all candidates for managerial posts by an appropriate Party Committee, before they could be formally appointed.

The administration of the Netherlands is based upon the principle of the decentralised unitary state: each tier of government has autonomous powers, which are only limited by the explicit policies of higher authorities and by certain basic legal principles. On all levels of government, elected bodies have discretionary and legislative powers: the Parliament, the Provincial Council and the Municipal Council. The executive bodies of the provinces and municipalities form part of the respective councils. At all levels, elections are held in a multiparty system.

In terms of personnel and budget, the national and municipal governments exceed the powers of the provincial government by far. The latter is rather a co-ordinating, advisory and supervisory tier than an executive and spending one.

According to the Joint Regulations Acts, municipalities can establish a public body which takes over certain municipal tasks. The establishment of a joint regulation needs the approval of the Provincial Executive Council. Such bodies now exist all over the country and carry out tasks concerning the processing of waste, the ambulance and fire service, and so on.

For some policy fields the provinces and municipalities serve as executive bodies with regard to national policies. This is reflected by the fact that the central government grants to the provinces and municipalities are for 70% earmarked allowances (e.g. for public housing, education, urban renewal and social security). The power of municipalities and provinces to raise taxes is very limited: they raise only 8% of their revenues. The remaining part is granted from central government according to a fixed scale.

The distribution of responsibility varies from policy field to policy field. To give some examples: the financing of public housing, education and rural land consolidation is centralised, whereas land use planning, and nature and landscape protection are more decentralised. An interesting feature is the range of powers of government in general in each policy field in terms of financial arrangements, binding regulations and ordinances, approval or permit procedures, consultation, information, organisational capacity and expertise. In many policy fields, the different tiers of government have at their disposal a part of this range of powers. There is a great variety of public/private decision-packages.

To make the picture complete, apart from the territorial tiers there is another functional authority viz. the Water Boards. Water Boards are public bodies responsible for the management of water quality and quantity in the area of their jurisdiction. The provincial government has supervisory powers over water authorities. The council and executive are elected, but not in a multi-party election system.

Productive forces in Poland were mainly in hands of the state. The share of the private sector (1988) in total industrial production was approx. 2 per cent, in handicraft approx. 3 per cent, only in agriculture did it dominate and amount to approx. 80 per cent (an exception in socialist European countries).

In the production sector, industry directly owned by the state accounted for 85 per cent of the total output, social-cooperatives approx. 13 per cent and other social organizations approx. 2 per cent (all figures from 'Decentralization and Local Government' (1988).

Productive forces in the Netherlands are in general the prime responsibility of the private sector. State ownership of and State participation in enterprises is exceptional. The private sector also contains many societal organizations for all kinds of purposes and representing different societal outlooks. Some of these organizations are interwoven legally or informally with the policy system (see further).

The concept of pluralism is basic to the Dutch political system. This is visible vertically (national-provincial-municipal) as well as horizontally (within one tier of government). One part of this pluralism is the relative autonomy of the provincial government and, especially, of the municipal government. A consequence of pluralism is the great variety of policy styles and traditions within government. Pluralism is visible in the embedding of public administration in other institutional frameworks. Three types are to be seen:
- intermediate organisations
- semi-public bodies with a public task
- pressure or interest groups.

These types interact with each other, and the intermediate organisations and semi-public bodies act as pressure groups as well. Semi-public organisations are often financially dependent on public administration and must operate in accordance with government standards, but they possess extensive discretionary power to a larger or smaller extent. Examples are to be found in housing, education, social work, and in nature and landscape protection. The intermediate organisations consist of representatives of societal organisations and act as advisory bodies to the - usually national - government or as pressure groups.

It is interesting that some bodies stem from societal movements, which in the past were linked with certain political parties - mainly the christian-democratic party and the socialist-democratic party. Examples are to be found in the fields of housing and education. Active and influential pressure groups are to be found among environmental and agricultural organizations. The latter is traditionally well organized and has many personal linkages with the christian-democratic party and the liberal-conservative party. The environmental groups are more issue-oriented or situation-oriented task forces. Their rather loosely organized umbrella organisations act now as permanent pressure groups.

The texture of the societal organisations is complex and criss-crosses the boundaries of the political parties. This leads generally to a rather unpredictable power-structure and adds to the unpredictability of conflicts.

Whereas pluralism is the main feature of the State, internal and external consistency of behaviour of State bodies has only limited significance.

Within this complex system, the principle of the legal protection of the citizen is pervasive. This is to be seen in the system of objection, appeal, compensation and consultation incorporated in almost every law. During the seventies, public participation developed in many policy fields. In general citizens and public bodies can appeal against a decision of a public body by addressing the Council of State, Administrative Disputes Department; and of course Civil Law applies to relationships between public bodies and citizens.

In Poland political opposition and the private sector of the economy were destroyed in 1949, and pluralism was eliminated from politics, from economics and from the societal sphere. In the eighties, pluralism again became an important issue but its full restoration is a matter for the future. In some areas, such as the activities of the Catholic Church, political opposition, professional and societal organizations, pluralism was already visible in Poland in the seventies, but it was not legally accepted as a political reality before 1989.

In the system of socialist urban policy, the public interest is formally protected. It is a separate question, who defines this interest and why, but its formal and legal priority is nevertheless guaranteed.

In the urban policy system the rights and position of an individual are protected formally. Private ownership (land, property, means of production) is guaranteed and protected by the Polish Constitutional Law. There is also legal protection of private rights of an owner, citizen or entrepreneur. Three institutions were created in the urban policy system to safeguard the rights of individuals. In the sixties, public hearings was introduced and the right of appeal was legally established. Next, in the seventies, the administrative courts were constituted, primarily for the protection of public enterprises and companies, but later, they started to serve as courts for personal cases as well. But generally, the problem is very complex even though the priority of public interest is still an official goal. Also, the strong position of the state and the local administration is a real challenge to the private proprietor or small businessman. Nevertheless, the latter came to political prominence in the eighties.

Although at the intermediate level in both countries the public administration is relatively stable, attention has to be given to the dynamics of the systems. In both countries a tendency to decentralisation and privatisation is to be seen, albeit beginning from totally different starting points.

In the Netherlands a moderate move toward decentralisation from central government to the provincial and municipal level is visible. In some fields (education, arts, health, housing) a more distant style of public involvement is being developed, which implies more freedom for societal bodies and the private sector. Grants from central government to the provinces and municipalities are being made more general. These tendencies, however, are not unambiguous. Environmental policy is developing fast, measured by legislation, expenditure and professional expertise. In this field governmental involvement is increasing rapidly. Privatisation has, up till now, been limited to the delivery of certain kinds of services which used to be provided by government agencies. Services which have been privatised are, for example, engineering, research, consultancy, catering, printing and so on.

In Poland the situation has been in a process of rapid change since March 1989. The round table talks, the elections and the establishment of a new government launched privatisation and decentralisation of which the final result is impossible to predict. It seems that the turbulence of the last decades in the Polish system has been greater than in the Netherlands. That is why, in the next chapters, much attention is paid to the historical account of the Polish situation.

To conclude, some remarks about public planning within the two policy systems. In the Netherlands planning has primarily been associated with physical planning many plans for which (see the subsequent sections) have legal status. In other fields, planning as a vehicle for policy making has been developed only recently, for example in traffic and transport, environmental affairs and water management. Public plans in these fields are gaining more and more legal status. Economic planning is restricted to public finance and global forecasting of private production and employment. Regional economic planning is very limited in scope and in the instruments of policy. The ambitions of public planning, which were quite high in the seventies have been reduced since then.

In Poland public planning has primarily been associated with productive forces, and in that way, with a large part of society. Planning had a decisive role in the management of the national economy. In Poland the urban policy system is associated with both the productive and the physical sphere. In long-term strategy, physical planning and urban policy dominate.

Policy systems concerning land use and locational questions

The Netherlands

Historical background

In the Netherlands, land use and locational questions are primarily regulated by physical/spatial planning. This policy field developed relatively fast in terms of its own institutions after 1960. Many of this issues are older (Kreukels, 1980):
- development and management of reclaimed land (polders)

- water management, which has been a well developed public task for centuries, with far reaching physical planning consequences
- housing which became a public issue at the end of the nineteenth century
- town planning as a professional activity which developed particularly in the twenties and thirties
- land consolidation in rural areas, which developed rapidly after 1945
- infrastructure planning, which became important after 1960
- promotion of regions with a weak economic structure (from 1955)
- urban renewal, recognised as a matter of public concern since 1965

All these factors have resulted in the steady development of the physical/spatial planning system based upon a widespread acceptance of public involvement in land use and land management. Although issues, approaches, strategies and policy instruments have changed over time, the legal framework and organizational setting have developed relatively steadily. Over time, much attention was given to improving the co-ordination between physical planning policy and other policy fields and between the policies of different layers of government.

Stable elements in physical planning policies have been:
- providing good locations for the rapidly increasing housing stock and for industrial sites, for instance by designating growth cities [2] which should take the overflow from the larger cities;
- safeguarding the quality of the environment of the larger cities so as to avoid urban sprawl and to keep the cities economically healthy;
- safeguarding the countryside from being eaten into, by the establishment of zoning systems;
- linking locational decisions and decisions concerning transport facilities

As mentioned before, physical planning became the leader among public planning. Because of this its goals tended to be ambitious, especially in the sixties and the early seventies. Since around 1975 the leading position was lost and since 1980 in all levels of government, staff expenditure for physical planning has been cut. The present position is in part the result of a general discussion about the role of government and about the level of public expenditure.

A striking phenomenon of the last decade is the rapid increase of court cases concerning physical planning.

By and large, physical/spatial planning has been a fairly stable issue in Dutch politics during the last decades. Shifts in political power have only had slight influence.

To conclude with some observations about the planning profession. It was in the context of the origins of physical planning as mentioned above that the planning profession developed. Initially town planners, geographers and lawyers dominated. Later on civil engineers, landscape architects, sociologists, regional economists and policy scientists entered the scene. During the sixties and the seventies the research and survey approach of planning was predominant, complemented with design methods. Later, social interaction-approaches gained significance. By and large there is no dominant profession in the field now, and even a full time course in physical planning has been available only since 1982.

Legislation

In the last 15 years, legislation concerning land use and locational questions

has become increasingly complex. The various laws are based upon different doctrines. They differ for example in terms of the following:
- the intensity of public intervention
- the degree of centralisation
- the degree of public participation/consultation and the possibilities of objection and appeal
- the degree of binding regulations laid down in the law itself or in the bylaws
- the degree to which financial arrangements are part of the law
- the way the relationships between the different tiers of public administration are dealt with
- the way plans and planning are seen as policy devices.

Two kinds of regulations can be distinguished:
- location-specific
- functional

The location-specific regulations will be outlined first. The backbone of the legal system concerning land use and locational affairs is the Physical Planning Act of 1962 (revised in 1986). The Act (Brussaard, 1981) specifies the legal powers of each tier of public administration, the organisational network of public bodies dealing with physical planning, the procedures of different location-specific plans, an elaborate system of vertical relations throughout public administration, and an extensive system of public participation and consultation, objection, appeal and compensation. The latter, together with the provision for compulsory purchase, is a quasi-financial arrangement of the Act. The Act also stipulates that a land use plan should be financially feasible and that every Municipal Council should establish a Land Development Ordinance. In such an ordinance the conditions are established under which the municipality will co-operate in the development of land designated for building on in the near future.

All the regulations of the Physical Planning Act are location-specific:
- national physical planning key decisions (national government) [3]
- regional physical plans (provincial government)
- structure plans (municipal government)
- land use plans (municipal government)

The 'pièce de résistance' of the Physical Planning Act is the municipal 'land use plan'. Hardly any locational or land use decision can be implemented unless it has been included in a land use plan, nor can any building or construction activity be allowed unless it is in accordance with the land use plan. The land use plan is binding upon all citizens.

The Municipal Council [4], the elected body at local level, is the body which decides upon the land use plan. This gives municipalities a strong position in locational and land use affairs with respect to other tiers of public administration and with respect to citizens and private institutions. The Municipal Council can establish a structure plan as well but this is general and non-binding. Land use plans can be provided with a system of exemptions. Deciding on exemptions is the responsibility of the Municipal Executive which operates, within the limits objectively specified by the land use plan itself.

The national and provincial governments have generally only corrective and constraining directive powers with respect to the municipalities. The Minister of Physical Planning and the Provincial Executive can issue directives concerning land use plans, based upon national physical planning key decisions and regional physical plans respectively. Land use plans (and exemptions) have to be approved by the Provincial Executive.

Citizens can lodge objections against draft land use plans by the Municipal Council and, where necessary, appeal to the Provincial Executive and the Crown. The latter is a constitutional body at central government level and serves in part as a body of jurisdiction in public law. The Council of State advises the Crown in such cases.

National physical planning key decisions are prepared by the ministers in the relevant field(s) and the Minister of Physical Planning is always informed. The Second and First Chamber of Parliament [4] have to approve the key decisions. The Minister of Physical Planning can issue a directive concerning the content of a regional physical plan to the provincial government, based upon an explicit policy laid down in a national planning key decision or based upon an explicit physical planning decision approved by the Second Chamber of Parliament.

The Provincial Council [4] decides upon regional physical plans. Regional physical plans and structure plans need no formal approval from the respective higher authorities.

Two other locationally-specific intervention systems have to be mentioned:
- land consolidation in rural areas
- urban renewal

The laws concerning land consolidation and urban and village renewal contain financial arrangements, and national government provides extensive grants for land consolidation projects and urban renewal. Expenditure with regard to land consolidation is project-specific. With regard to urban renewal, approx. 95% is paid to municipalities according to certain objective allocation rules.

The Land Consolidation Act prescribes a complex system of plan preparation, decision making and public participation, objection and appeal. Although the implementation is carried out by a task group with local members, the Act is in fact a centralised system in which the main powers (finance and expertise) are with the Ministry of Agriculture and to a lesser extent the provincial governments.

In contrast, the Act on Urban and Village Renewal provides the Municipal Council with the main powers, apart from the aforementioned financial arrangements. The system of local urban renewal plans is in fact an application of a land-use plan in specific urban renewal situations. Two types of regulation are possible in such areas:
- the urban renewal plan, which is the equivalent of the land use plan and has the same procedures;
- the regulation concerning living conditions, which is a less rigorous type of intervention system and has more simple procedures.

Apart from the above mentioned locationally specific regulations, several laws contain functional regulations influencing land use. Examples are: (here N = National Government, P = Provincial Government, M = Municipal Government)
- the Nature Conservation Act, which allows designation of specific areas to be protected (N);
- the Act concerning Noise Abatement, which prescribes a zoning system in areas where the noise level exceeds a certain standard. This zoning system is explicitly related to the municipal land use plan (M, P). This Act provides provincial governments with the power to designate 'silent areas'

(P) and to designate zoning systems around large industrial plants (P);
- Acts concerning roads, railroads, energy supply, water supply, air transport and so on, which give different tiers of government the power to designate areas for functional purposes (N, P), to be realised by government or bodies answerable to government;
- Acts concerning nuisance abatement, soil protection, manure disposal, water management and soil excavation, which give different tiers of government the power to forbid or restrict particular land uses under certain conditions (N, P, M);
- the Act concerning the Protection of Monuments (M).

Five additional observations can be made.
1. For the majority of the above mentioned regulations, appropriate additional regulations in a municipal land use plan are a necessary condition for implementation. According to the Housing Act, a building permit can be granted by the Municipal Executive Council only if the application is in accordance with the land use plan.
2. The Compulsory Purchase Act, in combination with the Physical Planning Act, gives the municipalities a strong position in the land market. A regulation in a land use plan is a legal entitlement to apply the Compulsory Purchase Act. On the other hand land or property taxation plays a negligible role in spatial planning.
3. While the Physical Planning Act is a decentralised type of Act, other legislation gives rise to increasing intervention by provincial and national government in land use and locational affairs. All the Acts have their own provisions for decision, advice and objections. The complexity of the institutional network is increasing.
4. An increasing number of laws establish an explicit relationship between the regulations according to the Physical Planning Act and the regulations of the law itself.
5. In the period 1970-1990 much attention has been paid to legislation [5] concerning the environment and water management. This legislation involves many aspects also regulated by the Physical Planning Act. One regulation concerns Environmental Impact Assessment. Important decisions concerning building sites, waste disposal sites, industrial areas, infrastructure, recreational sites and so on must be preceded by an Environmental Impact Assessment. This Assessment must be carried out by the body responsible and submitted to an independent committee for advice.

Organisational aspects: the actors

The agencies and advisory bodies concerned with physical/spatial planning are the core of the organisational network involved in land use and locational questions. Some of them are bodies provided for in the Physical Planning Act, namely:
- the National Physical Planning Agency
- the Inspector of Physical Planning
- the National Physical Planning Committee
- the Physical Planning Advisory Council
- the Provincial Physical Planning Committee

It has to be stressed however, that all formal powers mentioned in the Physical Planning Act are vested in the elected bodies (Parliament, the

Provincial Council and the Municipal Council) or the respective executive bodies (i.e. the Minister, the Provincial Executive Council, and the Municipal Executive).

Apart from having to have a Provincial Planning Committee, the provincies and municipalities are free in how they organise their work in physical/spatial planning, provided that the legal procedures are respected.

The National Physical Planning Agency and Provincial Physical Planning Agencies have existed since the Second World War. The larger municipalities have a Physical Planning Agency at their disposal. Over time all these agencies have developed into bodies with a high standard of expertise in different fields such as urban design, civil engineering, geography, law, sociology, economics and policy sciences (see the previous section). In general terms the number of people involved in physical/spatial planning grew rapidly from 1960 - 1975, decreased in the period 1980 - 1987 and is now relatively stable.

All tiers of government have other agencies and advisory bodies which are involved to a greater or lesser extent in locational and land use questions. The complexity of the legislation is reflected in the organisational network.

Generally speaking, the organisational units which have a primary task in physical/spatial planning spend money only on staff and on research. They spend little public works or subsidies. In contrast, the agencies involved in urban and village renewal, land consolidation, housing, technical infrastructure, education and health-care spend large amounts on investment, operational costs and subsidies for physical facilities. It has to be added that some public facilities are self-supporting e.g. electricity supply, gas supply, water supply, water management, sewerage and waste disposal. The costs are recouped by charging for these facilities. In the following paragraphs a short description will be given of each of the three tiers of government.

The municipalities Most municipalities have an organisational unit in charge of physical/spatial planning. This unit is responsible for the preparation and in part for the implemention and enforcement of structure plans and land use plans (including the granting of exemptions). In general this unit is part of a larger agency in charge of public works, housing, urban or village renewal and land management. It is these other units which spend the money. In other words, part of the implementation is undertaken by other organisational units. The land (estates) department deserves special attention. This department plays a crucial role in the implementation of land use plans by purchasing, holding, selling or leasing land. The active role of municipalities in the land market in urban development and urban renewal processes is considerable and gives them a reasonably strict control of land prices. In most municipalities, environmental affairs, parks, open space and recreation, and economic and social affairs are tasks of agencies other than the ones mentioned above. It is not difficult to see that the unit (and the member of the municipal executive who is primarily responsible for physical/spatial planning) has to have many contacts with other units.

In most municipalities interest groups of various kinds are active.

The provinces All provinces possess a unit responsible for physical/spatial planning. This unit is generally part of a larger agency with responsibility for housing, urban and village renewal, recreation, agriculture and land

consolidation, and nature and landscape protection. For example, in the province of Overijssel (an typical example) the number of professional staff involved in the different tasks is (1989):
- physical/spatial planning: 50
- housing and urban and village renewal: 13
- agriculture and land consolidation: 5
- recreation: 7
- nature and landscape protection: 11
- environmental policy: 50-60
- traffic and transportation policy (exclusive of construction, management and maintenance): 50

The Provincial Physical Planning Committee consists of public officials representing more than 10 ministries and of members from societal organisations. The committee advises the Provincial Executive about all physical planning decisions, including approvals of municipal land use plans. It is noteworthy that national agencies play an advisory role to the Provincial Executive.

At the provincial level, interest groups in the fields of agriculture, the environment, social work and culture are active.

National government Three bodies have already been mentioned and will now be described in more detail. The National Physical Planning Agency is an organisation of a high professional standard which is responsible for the preparation and implementation of the national physical/spatial policy. The agency is part of the Ministry of Housing, Physical Planning and Environment. It has about 300 staff. Some of them work outside the capital, such as the Inspectors of Physical Planning and their staff. They represent the Ministry in the Provincial Physical Planning Committees. Some of the staff of the central organisation are involved in research. In addition there is an annual budget for external research of $ 3 m. Although the agency as such has no budget for public works or subsidies, it has a large influence on the subsidies given to cities which are designated in the national spatial policy as "growth cities" and on the urban and village renewal fund. This influence is realised by inter-organisational linkages.

The other agencies of most significance for this chapter are:
- the Agency for Housing and Urban and Village Renewal (R)
- the Land Consolidation Agency (R)
- the Agency for Transport and Water Management (R)
- the Agency for Public Transport (R)
- the Agency for Nature and Landscape Protection (R)
- the Agency for Outdoor Recreation (R)
- the Agency for Land Management in Rural Areas (R)
- the Agency for Environment (R)
- the Agency for Regional Economic Policy

(R): agencies with regional offices.

The agency for land management in rural areas is interesting. Whereas the municipalities are active in the urban land market (the land department), in rural areas a national agency is the most important public body in the land market. This agency is part of the Ministry of Agriculture.

All kinds of societal organizations and interest groups attempt to influence national policy making.

There is a need for co-ordination and in this respect the National Physical

Planning Committee plays an important role. This committee consists of public officials of the relevant agencies (approx. 20) and provides the Minister of Physical Planning with advice on various topics concerning spatial policy. These topics are not only related to issues about spatial policy in the strict sense but also to other policy fields with a spatial component.

The Physical Planning Advisory Council is a legally established body with representatives from various organisations such as labour unions, employers' organisations, building companies, agricultural organisations, organisations for environmental protection, transport organisations, the association of provinces, the association of municipalities, and the academic world. The Council gives advice upon the main policy documents to the Minister in charge of physical/spatial planning. It has the right to give advice on its own initiative as well as upon request. The Council is an example of an intermediate organisation between public administration and societal organisations. A specific feature is that most members of the Council represent such an intermediate organisation active in other fields. This reflects the fact that in most policy fields, societal organisations or action groups with different interests are active. They are involved in policy processes in both regular and incidental ways.

Poland

Without the presentation of its historical background, an explanation of the Polish policy system in the field of urban policy is not possible.

The historical background of the present urban policy system

The history of Polish socialist urbanism and the history of its policy model, can be divided into three periods characterized by different urban models, distinct urban policies and various phenomena of urban development :
- the rebuilding of the country in the years 1945-48. The urban development and urban plans then represented the Modern Movement philosophy mixed with typical socialistic ideas and principles;
- the full domination of the socialist doctrine in urban policy in the short period of 1949-55. This short period totally changed the concept of urban development;
- the years of modern urban policy from 1956 until the end of the seventies are represented by several planning documents.

Then came the fourth period, the decade of the eighties which were in general terms the years of severe crisis in urban planning and in the articulation of the policy of the socialist city, too.

The first years after the Second World War (1945-1948) were the years of civil war, political struggle and rebuilding the country after the disastrous losses of war. The Communist Party was consolidating its position, but a multi-party system was still operating and the private sector of the economy was still strong. It was a period of reconstruction and these were years when architects and urban planners in Poland were in a powerful position. The unity which existed between political, social and professional aims for urban policy created favourable circumstances. The ideology of socialism in its idealistic version of the forties was consistent with the old, totalitarian dreams of Polish 'progressive' urban planners and architects.

In the next period, the years 1949-55, Stalinism changed concepts, approaches and priorities, in politics and in urban policy. The new doctrine in Poland of 'socialist-realism' imported from the Soviet Union, urbanization as a political aim, and the centralized model of management, reshaped urban policy and its model. And the roots of those changes were political.

These were hard times in the economy and in political and social life. The costs of the Cold War and the growing inefficiency of the socialist managerial system halted economic progress, depressed living standards and diminished the enthusiasm of the people.

The post-war period initially brought a rapid growth in Polish cities. In those years the implementation of urban projects was generally according to plan and complete. It was a unique period in the recent history of Polish urbanism, when housing districts were built together with streets, shops, services, educational and cultural facilities. It was a period when conflicts were non-existent or hidden. Measured by present standards the planning approaches in this period were very rigid, they also imitated the methods of architectural design. But those methods exactly fitted the socialist system of management of that time and, therefore, the urban planning system worked efficiently. The high degree of effectiveness of the system was supported by the centralization of political and administrative power. Nobody could 'disturb' politicians and planners in their implementation of new visions of society and cities. Local government had already been abolished and real democracy was simply non-existent. Political opposition had been crushed.

The political equilibrium reached in the first half of the fifties was weakened at first by the performance of the Polish economy and finally, shattered by the turbulent year of 1956. A kind of democratization became a political issue in socialist Poland for the first time. The 'Polish Spring' of 1956 had an important impact on the development of the planning system, which was seen by leaders of those days as one of the means for successful decentralization of less significant decisions, without losing control over the national economy, the Polish people or local institutions. But the political events of the year 1956 did not essentially change the urban planning and urban policy systems. The "Polish Spring" had a serious impact only on the aesthetic aspects and some functional aspects of architecture and urban planning, without changing its essential features. And it was in the next fifteen years that the legal and institutional system of urban policy was constructed. By 1964, the construction was complete and later, it could be seen that it was only an evolution of the same model, operating in corresponding political and economic environments. Despite promising beginnings, the relaxed economy of the 'Polish Spring' 1956, and increased freedom, this period again ended in failure and in economic stagnation, which resulted finally in a rigid and unsuccessful economic policy.

The next period of the seventies was very important, not only for the further evolution of the political system in Poland, but also as a new political basic for its urban policy model. In those years not only were the roots of the 1989 Polish crisis planted, but also the basis for a radical reform of the socialist system. Several political and economic reforms were initiated, and, according to the excellent analysis made by Staniszkis (1984), it was the evolution '...from a totalitarian to an authoritarian-bureaucratic regime (which) was more responsible for the events of August 1980 than was the worsening economic situation. The dynamics of the political system in Poland in the last decade were marked by the appearance of new elements not encountered on such a scale in other East European countries. There was a limited, non-responsible, 'lame' pluralism... (in which political opposition had a peculiar, a-legal status but possessed no institutional channels to reach the mass of the population); well-developed corporatist techniques of interest articulation... and, last but not least, a peculiar crisis-oriented philosophy of rule...'. The beginnings of the seventies did not bring anything importantly new to Polish urban planning policy, its methods of implementation, the instruments used and the institutions involved. What was new was an ambitious policy of fast economic and spatial development, promoting an urban growth which was again to be achieved through huge investment programmes, based on "Western" credits and technologies. Several new social and economic issues and problems which affected the national economy also changed the 'environment' of urban policy. Urban plans and urban policies were still directed towards creating and presenting a picture of future happiness. There was a strong belief still in existence that administrative measures, supported by a powerful state and the party, would be adequate for the implementation of accepted policies.

After several years of 'dynamic development', the Polish economy showed itself to be incapable of satisfying growing social expectations. Finally, inflation and a severe shortage of food and industrial consumer goods brought down the standard of living of the population - approx. 25-30 % in 1981 when compared with 1978.

Since 1980 Poland has been in crisis and in transition. After nine tumultuous years, its economic recovery is still in the distant future. The crisis of 1980 also shattered the urban policy and planning systems, which cannot deal with new issues, future problems or satisfy new demands. And in nearly all professional discussions, four factors crucial for contemporary Polish physical planning and urban processes are usually mentioned:
- lack of a concept for regional and national spatial policies; regional development is unplanned; urban policy on a national scale is non-existent; regional inequalities are growing fast; areas of "social depression" have become a national issue;
- the decline of Polish cities is a fact, and the location of physical development is unplanned. The latter brought strong conflicts and tensions into land management policy;
- pollution of industrial regions;
- the crisis of confidence in urban planning which stems partly from the political "connections" of urban planning in the past, but is also an outcome of the low efficiency of urban planning and of a general desire for democracy in Polish cities.

Legislation and organization

The Polish legal system was constructed to be formally and factually subordinate to ideological principles. The urban policy system was one of the elements, performing many vital functions for the socialist ideology.

The main legal steps in the development of the economic and urban policy systems are given by the following important decisions and dates :
- in November 1945 - by the Decree of the Polish Provisional Government, the Central Planning Office (CUP) was established (its main task was to make planning proposals for the allocation of available resources). In March 1946 the Office presented its first programme of economic

development;
- in April 1946 - the Decree introduced the planning system in Poland and, since then, physical planning as a part of the planning system has been a mandatory and guiding element of the national economy;
- 1946-1948 a network of physical planning institutions was constructed, the most important of which were: the Central Planning Office, the Regional Planning Directorates (RDPP), and the City or District Urban Offices (MUPP);
- in April 1949 the Central Planning Office was abolished and replaced the following year by the State Committee for Economic Planning (PKPG). But the new role of planning, more political than managerial, and the economic tools were to have catastrophic effects first on the national economy and later on urban planning;
- in December 1950 the State Committee for Urbanism and Architecture was established and its main task was supervising the physical planning system and establishing standards, norms and methods for physical planning. Almost exactly ten years later (June 1960) the building industry also was included under the remit of the Committee;
- in January 1961 the Physical Planning Act passed the Polish Sejm. This Act still has a fundamental significance for Polish urban planning, since all subsequent laws followed its ideas and spirit. The last version of the Physical Spatial Planning Law was approved (by the Sejm) in 1984 and the last important amendments were made to this Law in 1988. The Physical Planning Act of 1961 is a very foreward looking legal document;
- in February 1964 the State Committee for the Building Industry, Urbanism and Architecture was abolished, the supervision of physical planning activities at the local and regional (voivodship) levels was transferred to the Ministry of Building Industry and to the Ministry of the Communal Economy;
- in February 1964 the network of Regional Physical Planning Offices was founded; since then they have served as a link between physical and economic planning.

After 1964, the urban policy and planning systems were developed, but this process could be seen, until the eighties, to be the evolution of the existing model, operating in a corresponding political, social and economic environment. And as long as this model could operate as a normative type of planning and as a part of a socialist, centralized management system, its efficiency was high.

The legal framework of the present (1989) urban policy system was founded on numerous legal Acts of different sorts and of various importance. The legal core of the system consist of:
- the Planning Law (1982), defining the problems of social and economic planning in Poland,
- the Act on the System of Peoples' Councils and Local Self-Government (1983), as a basis for local governments,
- the Act on Spatial Planning (12 July 1984), prescribing the tasks and the structure of the physical planning system,
- the Land Use Act (1978),
- the Act on the Shaping and Protection of the Environment (1980),
- the Location Act,
- the Building Law (1974),
- the Law concerning Administrative Procedures (1960),

- the Law concerning the Conservation of Nature (1949).

In addition, there was a stream of legal regulations created by the Sejm, the Prime Minister of Poland, Council of the Ministers, Ministries, Regional Councils etc. A description of the legal system and urban law in Poland would needed several volumes but what has to be said is that the legal system in socialism is generally very confusing and is the root of many present urban conflicts and problems. Urban laws and the whole socialist legislation had until the eighties to serve exclusively the politicians and the communist party. The legislation was officially declared as an instrument of socialist justice. Therefore, the legal Acts and instructions are vague, unclear, contradictory, sometimes very general and sometimes very detailed. The whole system is incoherent and full of legalized exceptions.

Urban planning belongs formally to the system of local planning, and urban planners and urban authorities are obliged to co-ordinate their activities with:
- social and economic planning at the local level (which are practically absent)
- the upper levels of planning (regional and national), in both the socio-economic and physical planning field.

In comprehensive socialist planning three types of plan exist: long term (strategic or perspective) plans, Five Year Plans and short term (one-two year) plans. The last type includes a wide spectrum of different policy documents serving as an operational basis for everyday decisions. In addition to those types of plans, there are other planning and financial documents, elaborated and accepted by different governmental bodies, committees, companies, social and professional organizations and often irrelevant for planning.

Summarizing this very general and simplified picture, we can describe physical urban planning in a socialist system as, essentially, a local, long term (perspective) planning, elaborated by the municipalities, co-ordinated by regional authorities, approved and implemented by the City (County or District) Councils and their executives.

Legally, the land use plan is the basis for all location decisions: according to present legal practice (verdicts of the Supreme Administrative Court), no one (no institution) can dispute the decisions of a formally approved local physical plan. Amendments to plan decisions can be introduced by exactly the same procedure as the approval of the plan.

Local authorities in Poland (Voivodship, commune, city and district legislatures and administration), acting in two capacities, as the "plenipotentiary" of central government and as local communities' representatives, are responsible for the implementation of urban policy (for a presentation of this issue, see: Regulski et. al., 1988). They are equipped with several, traditional urban policy instruments:
- Planning instruments (Act on Spatial Planning); physical development plans for urban areas (cities, agglomerations), which usually employ traditional land-use techniques. For replotting and land consolidation procedures, a specific type of urban planning, 'detail planning' is employed;
- Location instructions (Location Act); local administration can offer public or private developers and investors an attractive new location or can reject proposals submitted by them to the municipal authorities. The Location Act includes instructions which have to be followed by developers;

- Building permit (Building Law), which is issued by the Voivodship's Architect or by District's Architect, on the condition that all requirements of the Location Act and obligatory instructions have been strictly followed;
- Utilization permit, given by the administration when the project is completed, on condition that all obligatory standards and codes have been satisfied;
- Taxes and fees, which are largely irrelevant to physical planning;
- Permits and licenses, not exploited in a serious form for urban policy enforcement.

Categories of actors and institutions

At first the formal bodies will be listed.

Local level At this level the following actors are relevant:
- local (town, commune, district) and regional (voivodship) people's councils, spatial policy commissions of the councils,
- local and regional administration (President of Region and his office, President or Head of Municipal unit, County or District); chief architect's office, planning commission and other functional departments of administration (town hall or regional office), regional planning agency (directly or non-directly) subordinate to the local administration,
- communist party (PZPR) at the regional and local level (executives),
- functional agencies (district or regional branches of Ministries and Chief National Offices),
- land use problems and location decisions are primarily the responsibility of the Chief Architect's Office (voivodship or town, commune and district) and Planning Commission (voivodship or town, commune or district), supervised by the Presidium of the Council (voivodship, town, commune or district) and the Physical and Economic Development Commission of the Council (all levels, respectively). At the central level all actors are supervised by the Ministry of Spatial Economy and Building Industry.

It has to be stressed that in Lodz and Warsaw, where the Polish cases are located, the cities have the formal status of voivodship.

National level The relevant actors at national level are:
- Council of Ministers, Ministries and Central Planning Commission (CUP);
- political parties, leading role of communist party;
- functional agencies and central offices (Environmental Protection, Sanitary Inspection, Supreme Chamber of control, Central Office for Water Economy, and several others of different rank and size);
- physical development policy, planning, legislation which is the responsibility of the Central Planning Commission (which directly supervises regional, i.e. voivodship planning, issues recommendations for spatial distribution of crucial capital investments) and the Ministry of Spatial Economy (Physical Planning) and Building Industry (the methodology of local planning, supervision of Chief Architect's Offices, appeals against the decisions of local and voivodship administration).

Bodies of justice and arbitration Since the seventies, administrative courts have been established at both the national and district level. In addition the

Ombudsman can be addressed if the law seems to be out of touch or if public bodies seem to act without due care.

Other actors The following actors are indirectly involved:
- societal organizations,
- clients (developers, owners, users),
- the Catholic church.

They will be described in subsequent paragraphs.

The actor-oriented approach to the studies on urban theory could, for political reasons, never have been accepted in Polish research. A proper understanding of the real nature of the main actors on the urban scene, their goals and motivations, formal and real positions and power, areas of influence, performances and inter-relations, are still a matter for future investigation. This approach was nevertheless chosen for the PONECOS programme. Three groups of actors in the Polish political-urban system were to have been defined: (a) rulers, (b) activists (co-rulers) and (c) society (opposition). This classification left out social groups, individuals and private citizens, since these groups or persons were practically excluded from decision making in the political-urban system until the eighties.

What made this investigation very difficult is the great gap which exists between formal (legally described) structures and the real network of (practical) decision making. Nevertheless, the brief functional characteristics of different groups of actors can be given. To start with the actors called, in this classification, rulers:
- Political (three political parties with the Communist Party in a dominant position, plus Democratic and Peasant Parties) and governmental administration (central, voivodships and local governments and their professional agencies) and finally, "ad hoc" but long lived bodies such as the Council of National Alliance. The system is strictly hierarchical. In the field of urban policy this group of actors undertakes all important decisions regarding strategic issues. Their political power in urban questions and political control over urban development is total (or was until 1989) and was very effective in practice.
- The legislature which is formally superior to the first group of rulers but which, for forty years, had been used as a rubber stamp for Party decisions. There is also a specific internal conflict in the Party, a contradiction between socialist (elected) legislature and the executive (nominated) part of the establishment. For decades a Party bureaucracy (non-elected nominated members of executives, secretariats, etc) was practically ruling Poland. In the last years, however, elected members of Party Committees, formally superior to the Party administration and formally authorized as the only group for making policy in Poland (also in the area of strategic, urban decisions), has begun a political struggle for real power. And this type of conflict is a structural feature of many political institutions in Poland.
- Planners, (central, regional and local planning institutions) should be listed in the same group. The position of a planner in a conflict is very specific. Most of the planners came to the profession in the fifties and sixties and were motivated by a sense of public service, having a genuine interest in urban issues. They were elevated by the system to prominent and powerful positions. They wanted to contribute to the public good and their motivations were idealistic. We have to accept that ideas do matter

in urban planning, but in the end, planners faced enormous difficulties converting their high-minded goals into pragmatic and working programmes and schemes, and many of the conflicts in urban life originated at the planner's desk.

In the second group called activists (co-rulers, but with no clearly defined power) on the urban scene, we include organizations, institutions and social groups which are usually not fully controlled by the Party and even sometimes (albeit seldom) are really independent of its ideological influence but which accept pragmatically the socialist system for the time being. These are primarily: the Catholic Church, a very powerful [6] institution active from the mid seventies in the field of urban policy; a private sector of the economy (land-owners, farmers, manufacturers, small commercial organizations, shop owners and services); a co-operative sector of the national economy (in housing, commerce, services and in small scale industrial production). Without exception, all members of this group are, both ideologically and practically, important actors on the urban scene and enjoy great influence usually without political responsibility.

The third group, society, includes all social and political forces and groups which oppose communist rulers and aim at the radical reconstruction of the Polish political model. The presence of this group in Polish life was a reality at first in the forties and again in the seventies, but only in 1980 could its members act openly. Martial law, imposed in December 1981, again suppressed the activity of the political opposition in Poland but after slow recovery in the eighties an organized opposition was finally legalized and active. It has been formally accepted as a part of the Polish political environment.

There is another social group, i.e. the citizens of Polish cities. It is potentially the following actor in urban life but it has an unpredictable future. Characteristic of this last group is that it was never vitally interested in urban issues or in the problems of local government. The Solidarity movement started discussions in 1981 on housing problems (millions of young Polish families wait for years for their own apartment), but even this organization never properly understood urban issues. Nevertheless, this group also is potentially an important actor on the urban scene.

Institutional network The institutional network of urban policy is well developed and includes several institutions.

At national level, it is the State Planning Commission (from 1988, again Central Planning Bureau, CUP), which elaborates national physical development plans which should then be submitted for approval to the Sejm. Preparation of this plan is an obligatory task of the Commission and from the mid-sixties several were elaborated (the latest in 1987) but no single National Physical Development Plan was ever formally approved.

At the regional level, preparation of the plans (the Voivodship Socio-Economic Perspective Plans and since 1984, the Regional Development Plans) is a duty of voivodship's administration. These plans are usually elaborated and revised by the voivodship's agencies, next sent to the Planning Commission for an opinion, and recommended by the Mayor of the city to the Voivodship Council for approval.

The organization of planning at the regional (voivodship) level is complicated, even confusing in some details. It reflects the complexity of formal and informal systems of government in Poland. The regional planning office is usually a public enterprise. Nevertheless, it is not directly financed from the city's budget, but it operates as a self-financing company, on the basis of commercial contracts with communities or regional public institutions. The managing director of the Office is appointed by the city Mayor and is directly subordinate to him. The regional planning offices usually carry out most urban planning tasks both at regional and at local level. This means that the Warsaw Development Planning Office, for example, has to serve the entire Warsaw Voivodship (which includes seven city districts and 54 towns and rural communes).

At the local level (of commune, town, city or city district) planning institutions are virtually absent, while the most important planning document at this level is the economic [7] Five Year Plan, which serves as a policy document for current development decisions. Long term spatial development planning includes all strategic proposals both for physical and for social and economic development. The preparation of local physical plans is obligatory and is a task of the local administration. The plans (master plans for the city, detailed plans for an action area) are approved by the City or County Councils. This level of planning represents a classical land use plan and it is the main area of interest to urban and city planners in Poland.

Elements of city planning are also included in development programmes and projects, especially when these are large scale ventures, conceived by the city administration (housing projects, industrial parks, major transport facilities etc).

To summarise the six actors playing a decisive role in the distribution of resources related to urban space we have:

1. The central political power, (the Party and the National Government) which exercised control over general policy questions but often concerned itself with the details when it decided that the details were important. This group was usually supported by experts, planners, "ad-hoc" groups etc. It also created the political strategy for distribution. The distributive policy was also decided at this level, the inter-regional balances, allocation of investment funds among regions and cities, communal budgets of all administrative units in Poland, the scope and range of private ownership: all these large and small issues were decided centrally in the socialist system.

2. The legislature (the Sejm) which formally approves all important strategic documents and proposals. This political group still distributes more than 80 percent of national financial resources and 100 percent of all rationed goods and resources. This level also creates an institutional and legal network of distribution and allocation systems and justifies the political decisions.

3. The local political bodies, legislature and administration (Party Committees, local Councils and administration) which, until the eighties, could be seen as a coherent block ruled by local communist party organizations. In practice, they were and still are responsible for the detailed decisions and for the distribution of goods and funds already allocated to them.

4. Local lobbies and various social groups of different sort which in certain periods of modern Polish history have achieved great influence at a local or even a national scale. In the eighties, the activity of informal and semi-formal social groups, the legalized political opposition or re-established trade unions, was already strong and directed toward urgent issues such

as ecology, housing problems, democracy and civil rights.
5 The owners of the land and the tenants of public housing, who are very active. Nevertheless, the practical influence of this group on planning decisions is still very limited.
6 The demanders and potential consumers of goods and services, a social group which includes people waiting for new bus-lines or for schools to be built in their district. It also includes the members of new housing co-operatives in quest of new locations, and many other groups including dissatisfied citizens. These groups can sometimes be very aggressive and influential, their actions can result in alterations to urban plans or to urban policy. These effects are not always positive.

Decision networks

The Netherlands

The sections concerning legislation and organisation give an outline of how decision networks can be looked at. Some common features are visible in locational and land use questions in general and the cases of this study in particular:
a. In almost every situation several laws are applicable, regulating strategic powers or supervisory or operational tasks,
b. In almost every situation agencies at all levels of government (including the Water Boards) are involved,
c. Depending on the situation, several agencies at this same level are involved,
d. In some situations, advisory bodies or special task forces, consisting of members of different agencies, play a role,
e. In all situations, societal organizations and/or interest groups are potentially active,
f. In almost every situation, many regulations concerning public participation, objection and appeal are applicable.

The objection and appeal procedures of the Physical Planning Act were used in all three cases studied. Bodies which play a role in objection and appeal procedures are:
- The Municipal Council
- The Provincial Council
- The Provincial Executive
- The Council of State, Department of Administration Disputes
- The Council of State, Department of Jurisdiction.

In all cases the different bodies have different packages of instruments at their disposal:
- planning
- statutory
- financial
- organisational
- supervisory

The bodies use these instruments as sources of power. They can be used for taking an initiative, giving an incentive, constraining decisions of third parties, exercising a veto and giving a final decision.

These points lead to the conclusion that in hardly any situation does one body or agency have the exclusive power to decide or the exclusive right to initiate or co-ordinate. In relation to the theoretical-analytical framework, the decision-networks are complex and unclear.

It has to be stressed, however, that apart from the formal rules and powers, informal networks can be influential. These networks follow political party lines, linkages between societal organisations and political parties, and personal relationships.

Poland

There are two groups of functions performed by socialist urban policy: the formal functions, declared and legally defined, and the real functions, not always declared, but executed by the city urban plans and by urban planning policy. This influences the decision networks.

The formal functions of urban policy are specified by the Planning Law and are filled in by political parties, politicians, government and its agencies. They are directed, according to the Act on Spatial Planning (1984), toward: '...increasing the standard of living and the environmental quality of cities and regions, for the benefit of society...in accordance with the existing economic conditions and requirements of the national economy...'. Following this goal, physical plans formulate the aims of urban development policy and describe a long-term, strategic picture of the socialist city inhabited by the future socialist society.

The real, not always fully visible, functions of urban policy in the socialist system are connected with the ideological, political and economic functions of socialist economics and its distributive aims. Ideologically, urban policy should serve in Poland as an instrument for shaping future socialist society, for the creation of a "socialist" spatial order of the cities. These cities should promote, by their physical features, a new economic order.

The planning system as a whole and urban planning in particular play three practical and fundamental roles in a socialist economy:
1. it serves as a basic tool for the sectoral and spatial distribution of products, goods, standards of living, rights and privileges;
2. it creates a formal (legal) system of institutions and a network of functional connections for the execution of a chosen urban development policy;
3. it offers an important tool for "ideological battles", playing effectively the role of a propaganda vehicle.

But its first task as a distributor is the real essence of socialist planning and urban policy. Urban policy in socialist Poland was always an important element of the distribution system. And it is still distributing: land (the right of use and type of use), programmes of development (concerning public facilities, communication etc.), activities and the rights to them, the standard of living and quality of life. It also creates the economic value of the land and the rent of land. It also support the social and economic sphere in performing its distributive functions in a spatial context. The economic or social aspects of distribution in territorial planning was, however, never a real interest of practitioners or researchers of urban policy. The task of urban policy was an "adequate spatial distribution and allocation of resources". The next aim was an "optimization" of the distributive decisions and spatial structures. The problem of private ownership and distributive effects of the plan decisions were totally ignored. The urban plan and its implementation were to be the tools for promoting ultimate "socialist justice" and should finally create a socialist town benefiting all its citizens. In the end it turned out to be a dream never to be fulfilled.

So, decision networks concerning urban planning are diffuse and complex, with a formal structure and a powerful informal structure. Within these structures many implicit or explicit ideologies, attitudes, approaches, procedures and processes are to be distinguished. The roles of administrative bodies are not always clear and are often even ambiguous. In this way the picture of a centralised state with a unifying ideology and power structure becomes less clear and even confusing in practice.

In the distributive system of socialist urban planning, the positions of society and the public interest are formally and practically protected. It is quite another and a very interesting question who defines this interest and why, but its formal and legal priority is, nevertheless, guaranteed. Formally, the rights and position of an individual also are protected in the urban policy system. Private ownership (of land, property, the types of production) is guaranteed and protected by the Polish Constitution. Legal protection also exists for the private rights of an owner, citizen or entrepreneur. Three institutions were created in urban planning, to ensure the rights of individuals (public hearings, the right of appeal to the upper level of administration and the establishment of the administrative courts. As has already been explained, the first two institutions helped little. In the courts, however, ca. 30% of the winning cases at present are those sent by private citizens.

Today, when a conflict starts, nobody can predict who will be a winner, when an important interest is at stake. A procedure which involves a random selection of all participants is also unpredictable. In practice, formal procedures fail to work.

The performance of the systems

The performance of the two systems will be illustrated by the three pairs of cases. In this section on policy systems a preliminary impression will be given. This impression is based either upon comparable research or upon a qualitative appraisal of the situation.

The Netherlands

As this research project is based upon an actor-oriented and inter-organizational approach, we are able to refer to comparable research which has already been completed (de Koningh, 1985).

From 1982-1985 research took place concerning the co-ordination between public bodies at different levels with regard to spatial planning issues. Five cases of a somewhat complex character were investigated. All cases involved conflict such as conflicts of interests, many parties were involved, and interest groups were active. The efficiency and effectiveness of the decision-making process were assessed according to criteria such as duration, costs, coherence, implementation, and the degree of consensus. In addition, criteria concerning the weighing of interests, the role of public bodies (including

elected bodies) and legal protection and public participation were used.
The cases were:
- a large sand excavation
- land consolidation
- a regional waste disposal site
- an urban renewal project in a city centre
- the design and construction of a highway which bordered residential areas and also an area of outstanding natural beauty.

The conclusions of the research were as follows:
- when conflicts of interest are at stake, the decision-making process takes a long time;
- the weighing of interests one against the other is often questionable; this is mainly because in a certain case most parties have only partial powers and there is rarely any party which is responsible for the project in all its aspects;
- legal protection is unsatisfactory. Although the system of legal protection is extensive (see the introductory section) in practice there are problems [8];

As the cases show how the system - or rather parts of the system - work in practice, it is not necessary that the system at the meso-level is subject to the same critical examination.

The question of whether to improve fundamentally the co-ordinating mechanisms of the Physical Planning Act in relation to legislation concerning facilities such as roads and other (semi-)public works has been asked. Up till now the official conclusion has been, that improvement must be sought in how parties use their powers rather than in the power-structure itself. In the meantime the cross-relations between legislation are being developed gradually so as to promote co-ordination (see the introductory section).

On a more general level, the effectiveness of physical and urban planning has been questioned. Whereas parts of the physical planning policy have been successful (e.g. the policy concerning "growth cities"), the goals put forward by authorities at different levels of government have tended to be too ambitious and have over-estimated the steering capacities of government bodies. Part of the ineffectiveness is caused by differences in view between the various levels of government, concerning either goals or policy instruments. In a way, the processes which take place between governmental bodies show many of the features of a market: bidding, negotiation and contracting.

There is a tendency for decentralisation to be seen as a consequence of control from a higher level of administration being often ineffective and inefficient due to lack of information and due to the rigidity of centralised systems.

The Dutch experiences shows that there are different kinds of conflicts:
- conflicts within the administrative system
- conflicts between a public body/ies and a societal group, enterprise or citizen.

The first kind is quite varied in character:
- conflicts between different layers of administration
- differences in the views of different political parties
- conflicts about the power structure as such
- conflicts about the use of power in single cases.

By and large there are three systems within which the conflicts are handled:

- the political system
- the administrative system
- the system of legal protection.

These three systems differ from each other in the rules of the game. In the cases studied here all three systems will be visible, with the emphasis upon the administrative system.

As mentioned before the number of cases which are taken to court is increasing rapidly. Most of these cases stem from a citizen, firm, organisation, or public body believing that the rights to use an area of land have been violated by a public policy or by the action of someone else. Moreover, environmental issues in themselves are increasing rapidly as a cause of dispute. As far as conflicts between governmental bodies are concerned, most disputes are related to the autonomy of the lower tiers of government.

Poland

In the previous sections, ample attention has been paid to the performance of the system in several post-war periods. This shows that the performance of the system has been poor and is open to severe criticism. We will now give a brief analysis of the main sources of conflicts concerning socialist urban policy, urban economies, the costs of urban development and land management problems. Economic costs and economic instruments of socialist urban policy have been issues which, although investigated by urban theory, have never been properly investigated within the practice of socialist urban policy. Firstly, there is a conflict between the budget allocation mechanisms and urban development policy. One impact of central budget policy on regional and urban issues, and on declared spatial policy, is mostly a result of a contradiction which exists between the declared goals of those spatial policies and budget decisions implemented in practice. The latter, which include the allocation of funds from the central budget between different sectors of the economy and between different regions and cities, usually allocate funds and investment goods - machinery and all rationed resources - to the sectors of the economy which are unfavourable according to physical policy principles and plans (as e.g. heavy industry) and to already developed industrial regions and cities. This economic strategy invariably favours congested and polluted regions affected by shortages of labour and not able to function properly. At the same time areas recommended by urban strategy for new development, characterized by strong economic potentials and designated by physical plans for economic revitalization, are neglected in the budget policy process.

The second group of problems is created by the influence which tax policy and tax instruments exercise on urban development and growth. In a socialist system, taxes are used to maximize, the state's revenues not for implementing urban or regional development policy goals. Nevertheless, the impact which tax systems have on urban development is enormous in its scale and profound in its scope. Since bargaining is a normal procedure in a socialist tax system, sectors of the economy which are politically strong and institutions or regions which are economically strong are in an advantageous position. The same applies to regional tax policy. In the eighties, a local tax system was introduced in Poland but in the case of urban policy it is insignificant.

The third problem is that of calculating costs in urban policy and urban planning.

Land management and urban land policy in socialist cities are a specific source of conflicts. Since the majority of land in Poland has remained privately owned, it should have been tackled explicitly. However, after a short discussion, the problem disappeared since neither urban planners nor politicians were interested in making an issue of ownership. Policy for urban land had been influenced by three important factors since 1945. First, there was the ideological dogma of the public ownership of land and the means of production (which resulted in the nationalization of factories, larger estates and farms; housing stock and the land in CBDs' were also communalized in some Polish cities in the forties and fifties). Secondly, there was the existence during the whole post-war period of a private land market. In some periods this was illegal. Today nearly 80 per cent of farm land, 60 per cent of built up areas in cities and more than 25 per cent of afforested land belong to private owners. Thirdly there is the ruling position of The Plan, which was established in 1946 and which was important in the creation and execution of urban development policy and subsequently of urban land policy and land management.

The most important problem from the very beginning was that of (the level of) rent paid for land, and from the very beginning this problem was not tackled adequately. Rent was non-existent for ideological reasons and the politically established priority of social goals and the public good, were strongly confronted by the private market, private ownership, the private interests of individuals and by the real value of the land. Until the sixties, the problem was concealed, but today a strong and effective protection of private ownership creates one of the greatest constraints on urban policy.

Urban policy also neglected the existence of land prices and the problems of land values, and enormous areas of land were frozen by urban plans as a result of land use zoning. Many of the actual owners could not properly utilize their plots as the urban plan designated them for a public use. The city usually has no funds, however, for public investment, and the land and its owner could wait twenty years or more, paying taxes, for the moment when the city would be ready to implement a plan for a new school or shopping centre. This meant that a land owner had to carry the costs of urban land policy. But the eighties brought a new approach to these issues in Poland. The land market was revitalized and the purchase value of the land now reflects its location and real desirability. In Warsaw city, the highest tender (April, 1989) for a small building plot in a fashionable district of Warsaw (Stary Zoliborz), was won by a purchaser who offered 850 mln. zloty (approximately 120 thousand US dollars) for a 440 Sq.M. parcel. In the eighties, local governments were made responsible for land management problems, and communal ownerships was formally re-instated. A strong and very effective protection of agricultural land has been introduced and the constitutional rights of private owners have been established. Finally the housing stock has also been almost completely denationalized.

Summarizing the main causes of conflicts in the field of urban development are:
1. The one-sided, rigid central direct distributive and allocation mechanisms with regard to production, which neglect indirect methods of governing inherent in urban planning.

2. The large gap between the formal policy system and the world of ideology and declamation expressed officially on the one hand, and the real world of operational decisions and pragmatic policy on the other.
3. The ideological content and function of planning in general and urban planning in particular.
4. The neglect of land values and interests in land as crucial factors in urban policy.
5. The incapacity of a highly centralised one-party policy system to admit of and deal with conflicts in an open way. This applies to conflicts between various governmental bodies as well as to conflicts between governmental bodies and citizens or private organisations. The "class-struggle" was the only acknowledged source of conflicts and the "public interest" was declared superior to individual rights and interests.
6. The deficiencies of impartial judicial protection in contentious questions.

A comparison between the two systems

We will take the period up till 1989 for making comparisons.

Similarities

1. The policy system concerning urban (development) questions is extremely complex in both countries. Although physical planning agencies and legislation concerning physical/spatial planning play an important role, this role is performed within a complicated network of legislation from other fields and of bodies with partial responsibilities in the questions concerned. This means that it is very difficult for citizens to understand the system and to know to where to apply when they wish to be informed or to be involved.
2. In both countries there seems to be a relative monopoly of public bodies in the field of physical/spatial planning as far as long term urban planning is concerned. In both countries the pretentions - and influence! - of the bodies concerned have decreased over time. The effectiveness of comprehensive long term planning is questioned in both countries.

Differences

1. Although public spending between the different tiers of government does not suggest much difference in the financial power of local government in the two countries, the Polish policy system is basically centralised and the Dutch system a mixture of centralised and decentralised. In urban questions such as those of land use and land management, the power of municipal government in the Netherlands is strong, although constrained by the explicit policies of the national and provincial government and in some respects dependent on the financial support of higher authorities (such as for housing and urban renewal).
2. In Poland the management of productive forces is a public affair. Central planning is primarily economic planning. Physical planning is part of the economic planning system, or at least strongly related to it. This means that locational, land use and zoning questions relating to firms and industrial sites are subject to agencies concerned with production as well

as to agencies in the field of physical/spatial planning. In this respect, territorial co-ordination is a question to be answered within the public administration. The same applies to amenities such as school and hospitals. State enterprises often serve as the nucleus of territorial and functional power and influence.

In the Netherlands, productive forces are largely in private hands. Locational, land use and zoning questions are primarily discussed between the municipal government and the citizens and firms concerned. As far as hospitals, schools and similar amenities are concerned, municipalities mostly have to deal with private organisations which are relatively autonomous in their locational decisions. Physical planning in the Netherlands has its own status, with no predominant dependency on other fields of planning. Relations with housing policy, land management and environmental policy are relatively strong.

3. Within the monolithic system of Poland, the style of government can be characterised as legalistic and bureaucratic, whereas in the Netherlands more open and flexible arrangements are to be seen.
4. Somewhat in contrast to the previous point, the distance between formal and informal arrangements seems to be greater in Poland than in the Netherlands. This is due to the exclusive relationship between the communist party and public administration. Due to the multi-party system and the relative ease with which the private sector can approach public bodies, the learning capacity of the Dutch system seems to be greater, causing a smaller distance between formal and informal arrangements. As a consequence, the possibilities for objection and appeal which apply in both systems seem to be more effective in the Netherlands.
5. In urban questions in the Netherlands, the power is predominantly in the hands of elected bodies or agencies answerable to elected bodies (national government, Provincial Executive and Municipal Executive). In Poland public officials play a relatively important role as a part of a bureaucratic system.
6. Although discontinuities are visible, the development of the Dutch policy system concerning urban questions is more stable and continuous than the Polish one. The changes in the economic situation and in the general political situation in Poland have run parallel with sudden and frequent changes in the policy system of urban planning, although up till the eighties the principles of the state remained the same. It is striking that the frequent change of coalitions in the Netherlands is coupled with less societal changes than the change of governments in Poland.

To conclude, can we comment upon the two policy systems concerning urban questions in the light of the theoretical and analytical framework?

In both systems, decision networks are visible as well as attempts to steer such networks. The networks differ in structure and especially in their openness towards society. In the Netherlands, interactions between the policy system and societal groups and citizens are more frequent, intensive and influential than in Poland. This theme will be elaborated upon in chapters 5 and 6.

General description of the policy system concerning the cases

In the previous sections, a general description of the legislation and organisational framework concerning land use and locational questions was given. Parts of the system are relevant to the cases studied here. To understand these cases some elements will have to be elaborated upon. These have been put into the form of a diagram for both countries, which reflects the general structure in force when the cases were developing.

Important changes which occurred in the relevant period are mentioned.

The Netherlands

In Figure 3.1 the main powers and formal relations concerning land use and locational questions are shown. Parts of this diagram (bodies, powers and relations) are applicable in all the cases. In the cases concerning waste disposal sites and environmental zoning, the lower parts are most important. Along the physical planning line, the national bodies play only a secondary role. In the case concerning an urban extension (Duiven-Westervoort), national government urbanisation policy and national policy instruments are relatively important.

In the general picture, the relative autonomy of the provincial government and especially of the municipal government has to be stressed, although many vertical lines of consultation, advice and supervision are visible, as well as specific procedures for objections and appeals against local land use decisions in addition to general administrative appeals. It is remarkable that the influence of central or national government can be exercised by a formal appeal or objection procedure by a national agency against a municipal land use plan decision or against a provincial decision concerning a regional physical plan, rather than by an approval procedure.

The only binding regulation is the municipal land use plan. National physical planning key decisions and provincial regional physical plans have only a indicative status. Societal groups are represented in the Physical Planning Advisory Committee.

In the sections where the cases are described, the general diagram is complemented with specific powers and relations applicable in the case. In the case of the waste disposal sites, the bodies of collaborating municipalities which are responsible for waste management in their area, will be mentioned together with other regulations of the Waste Products Act. In the case of environmental nuisance around an industrial area (DSM), acoustic zoning (Noise Nuisance Act) and allocation of housing subsidies are relevant. In the case of an urban extension (Duiven-Westervoort), legislation concerning changes in administrative boundaries and the national policies and specific instruments concerning 'growth cities' will be added to the general picture.

Poland

The formal relations of the Polish system in the period of the cases are shown in Figure 3.2. In all cases, the power of the voivodship authorities is predominant. Both in the Lodz and Warsaw area, the voivodship authorities serve as metropolitan bodies as well. The local communities have only very

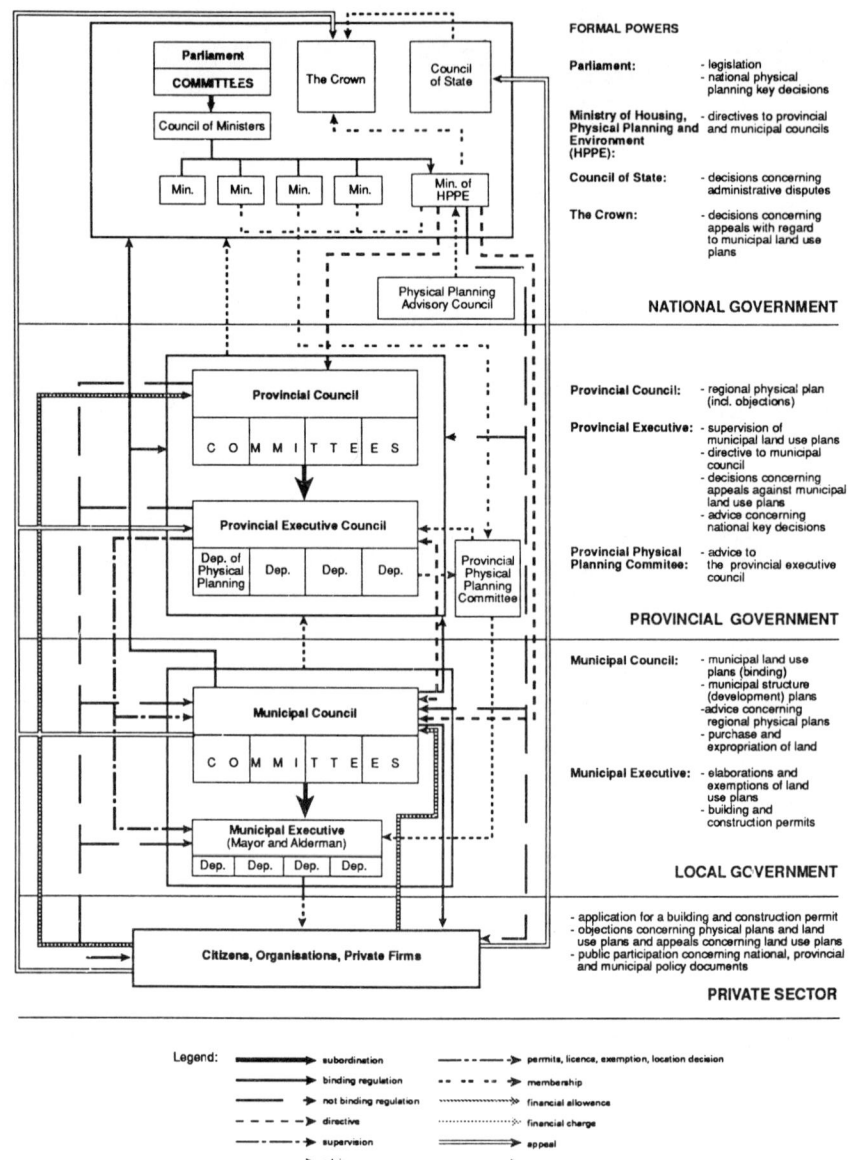

Figure 3.1 General formal network concerning land use and locational questions, the Netherlands

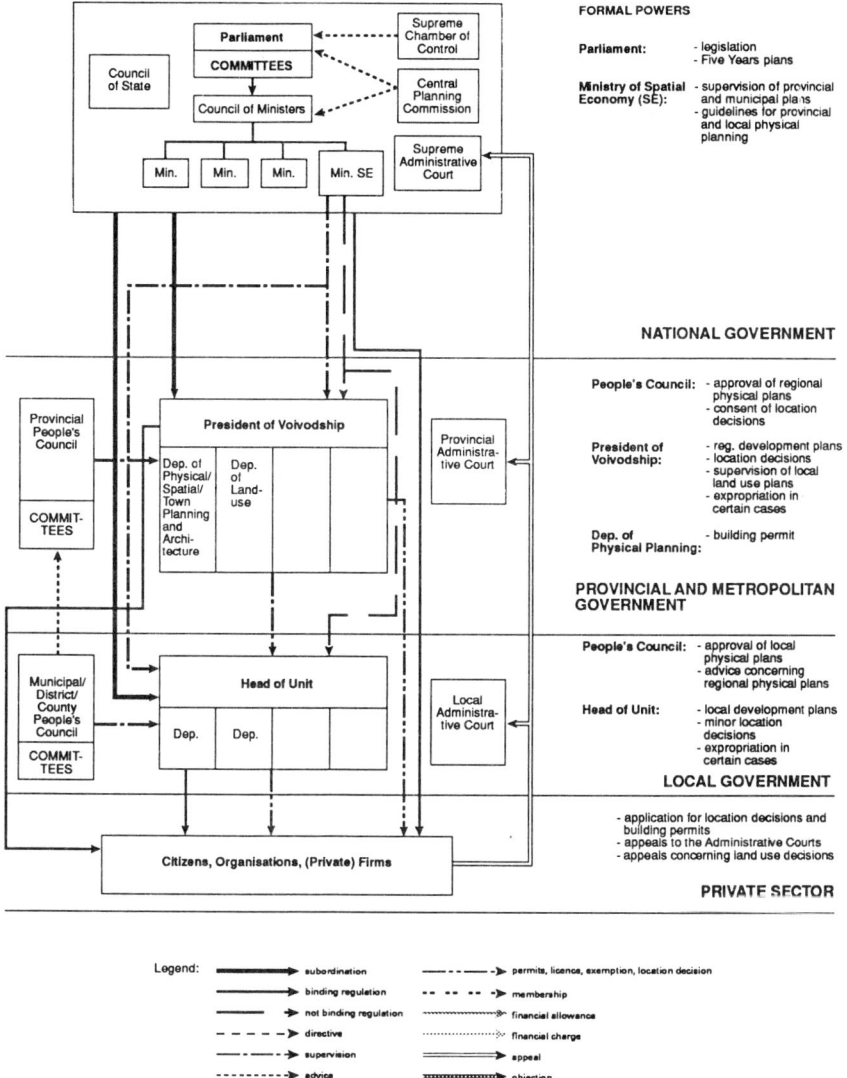

Figure 3.2 General formal network concerning land use and locational questions, Poland

restricted power in such areas. The dual dependency of the voivodship authorities has to be stressed: they serve partly as bodies of central state and partly as executive bodies for the People's Councils. Citizens enjoy general rights of appeal against administrative decisions. Decisions within the framework of strategic planning (regional development plans), local land use plans and location decisions are binding. The Chief Commission for Urbanism and Architecture serves as an advisory body at the level of the central state and is recruited from professional organisations.

In the sections where the cases are described, the general diagram is complemented with specific powers and relations applicable in the case. In the case of the Polonit-plant, the position of the Ministry of Chemical and Light Industry is relevant as well as decisions concerning environmental permits and standards. In the case of the waste disposal site, the powers of the voivodship authorities are relevant as well as specific environmental decisions. In the case of the urban extension Stara Milosna, the responsibility for public works in relation to a newly developed residential area will be mentioned.

Notes

1. It has to be stressed that the cases studied took place before the return to parliamentary democracy.
2. One case deals with that subject.
3. It has to be stressed however, that some national physical planning key decision are related to locational question of public amenities (electric plants and power lines, infrastructure for traffic and transport).
4. The Municipal Council, the Provincial Council and the Second Chamber of Parliament can set up commissions, e.g. concerning physical planning.
5. For two of the cases in this study, the development of legislation concerning the environment played an important role: regional waste disposal sites and environmental zoning around DSM. The Waste Disposal Act and The Noise Abatement Act came into force while the cases were proceeding.
6. The urban and building activity of the Catholic Church is the most recent example of such activity. The number of new churches under construction in Poland, reached the unbelievable figure of 1,500 (fifteen hundred) and the architecture, programmes and functions of those investments are exclusively at the discretion of the local priests. And very often these new projects are not churches, but huge cultural and educational centres, competing with the state's educational and cultural facilities.
7. Co-operation, co-ordination and conflicts which have existed from the very beginning of socialist planning, between physical (urban) planning and economic planning, have been many times described and discussed. The issue is complicated and creates never ending disputes. What is important here is that the total lack of connection between these two types of planning is responsible, to a great extent, for the general failure of urban planning in the seventies and eighties.
8. In the research project (Koningh, Tj. de, 1985) were reported:
   - many global (but influential) decisions are taken (and can legally be taken!) without the possibility of objection and appeal.
   - decision-making within the framework of the Physical Planning Act

follows the decision-making in other fields.
- the diffuseness of responsibility (see the former points) makes it difficult to address the right body at the right moment.

References

Brussaard, W. (1987) *The rules of physical planning 1986*, Ministry of Housing, Physical Planning and Environment, the Hague.
de Koningh, Tj. de (1985): *Ordening van besluitvorming over de ruimte*, Kluwer, Deventer.
Kreukels, A.M.J. (1980), *Planning en planningproces*, VVUA, Den Haag.
Regulski, J., Jensen, G. and Needham, B., (1988), *Decentralisation and Local Government*, Roskilde University Press.
Staniskis, Jadwiga (1984), *Poland, self-limiting revolution*, Princeton University Press.

Chapter 4

The cases

Tadeusz Markowski, Barrie Needham, Aleksandra Jewtuchowicz, Arie Dekker, Maria Ptaszynska-Woloczkowicz and Leo van der Meer

Introduction to the cases

The empirical research took the form of case studies, and in chapter 1 the strengths and weaknesses of "multiple case-study research" are discussed. Here we need only repeat that the case studies are here not being used to test hypotheses empirically, but to illustrate points made in general and in the theoretical statements. However, there has also been a more interactive relationship between the theory and the cases. The theoretical chapters 1 and 2 were written in draft and the framework thus built was used to structure the case-study research. The subsequent experience in practice led to the theoretical part being modified and extended. The result of that interaction has been a consistency between the theoretical part and the description of practice.

Some of the general statements refer to conflicts in urban development; hence the cases were chosen to illustrate different examples of such conflicts. Chapter 1 gives some theoretical observations on such conflicts.

Taking the practical possibilities into account, including the experience of the researchers, their access to information, and the topicality of the issues, three types of conflict were chosen:
- the location of a waste-disposal site
- the environmental nuisance which a large industrial plant causes in its surroundings
- the problems that can arise when developing and implementing plans for a large scale urban expansion.

The location of the cases is given in Figures 4.1 and 4.2.

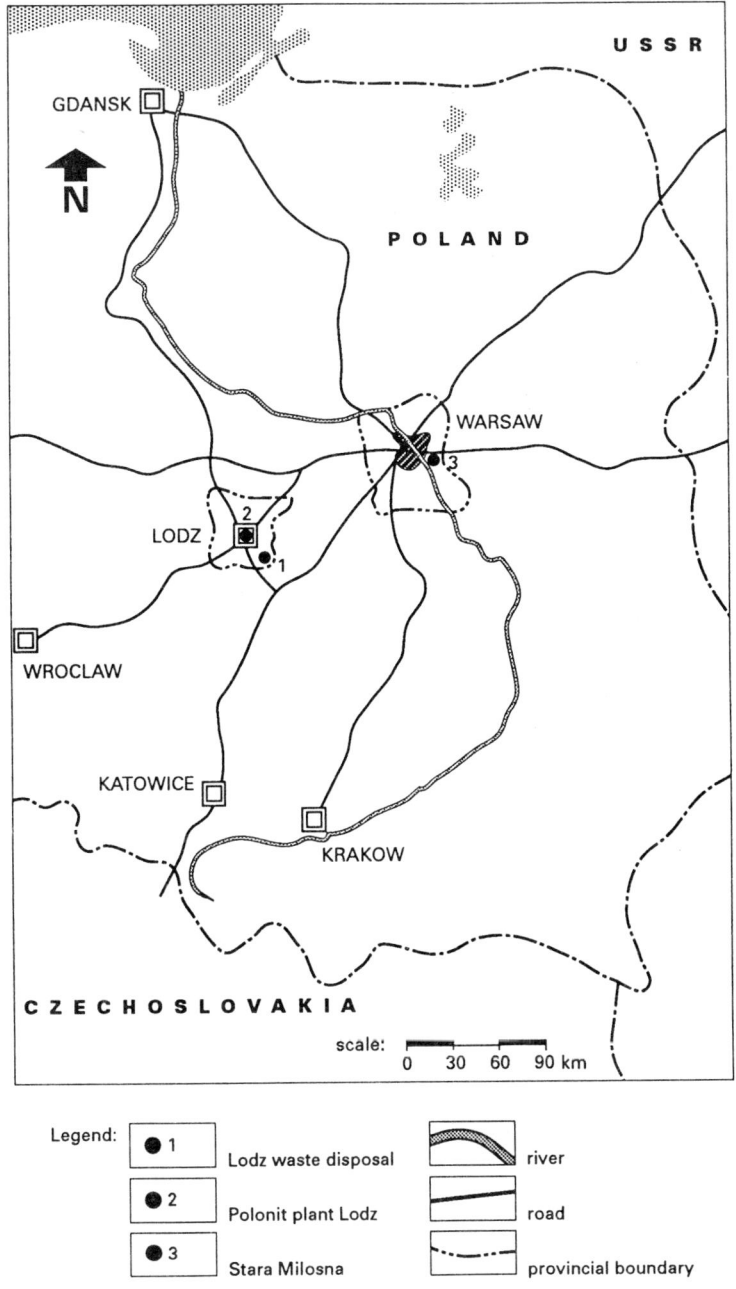

Legend:
- ● 1 Lodz waste disposal
- ● 2 Polonit plant Lodz
- ● 3 Stara Milosna
- river
- road
- provincial boundary

Figure 4.1 The situation of the Polish cases

Figure 4.2 The situation of the Dutch cases

A case was investigated in Poland and in the Netherlands for each type of conflict with, as far as possible, the same type of information being collected in both countries. The reason for carrying out such parallel case studies was as follows. A certain similarity in the technical character of the conflict would give the opportunity of detecting common features, in addition to discrepancies which are caused by the great differences in the policy systems of both countries.

In the event, this research method did not work as satisfactorily as was intended. Before starting the empirical work we could not know what would be discovered and, although the cases of waste-disposal sites had many similarities, the cases of environmental nuisance around an industrial plant showed fewer similarities. The cases of large scale urban expansion turned out to be quite different from each other, each providing useful illustrations but not of the same things.

In chapters 5 and 6 the cases will be analysed in more general terms giving the opportunity to detect the similarities and differences between them.

The cases are all described in the same way using a framework derived from the theoretical chapter 2.
- Firstly the general issue, of which the case is an example, is described briefly, how important the issue is in that country, the relevant legislation, and the general policy;
- Secondly, a short description of the way the data was gathered is given;
- Thirdly, the actors specific to this case are described using the actor-oriented, goals-means approach. For each case, the interests and the powers and resources available for realising these interests are described. The formal system of interaction between the actors is described and illustrated with a network diagram.

Together, these sections provide a picture of the policy system and the formal decision-network for the particular policy field for which the case is an example. As such, these two sections supplement chapter 3 which described the general policy system in each country.
- Fourthly, the course of the conflict is described chronologically;
- Fifthly, the conflict is analysed using the inter-organisational approach, showing the network in operation. The analysis takes the form of indicating which strategies were followed by which actors, how the power balance shifted in the course of the conflict, and which powers were available but not used.

An analysis of the case-studies together is the subject of chapter 5 and more general conclusions about conflicts in urban development are drawn in chapter 6.

The choice of a waste disposal site

Poland: The case of the Province of Lodz

Introduction: the issue

The amount of solid waste produced by Poland is growing rapidly. Of the different ways of treating waste, the most popular way in Poland is simply by dumping. There is no data available concerning the area covered by waste disposal sites. Statistics do show, however, the quantity of industrial solid wastes dumped by enterprises. By the end of 1986 ca 1394 mln tons of industrial wastes had already been dumped and the production of solid waste in 1986 reached 85 mln tons per year (Anonymous, 1988). As far as household waste is concerned, the amount of waste produced per year in Poland is about 9.2-12.0 mln tons [1]. The net demand for areas for disposal sites for household waste is about 950-1150 ha in the next 10 years. If we add the land required for the creation of protection zones, the area required will rise by 8-20 times, depending on the size of sites [2]. For the last 40 years the central totalitarian government and its regional provincial and local governments had not expected nor assumed that any protest from society would be made against the location of this activity.

The problem of household waste grew rapidly in Poland in the seventies when Poland was opened to western credits, technology etc. (see chapter 3). Higher consumption gave rise to more waste. At the end of the seventies the Ministry of Territorial Economy, Housing and Environment prepared some instructive material on the treatment of household and industrial waste in a more orderly and environmentally friendly way.

The quantity of solid household waste produced by the City of Lodz reached 1.5 mln m3 per year in 1984. It was assumed that this quantity would reach 2.6 mln m3 in 1990, and 3.4 mln in 2000. In the 1974-76 programme for solid waste treatment in the province of Lodz, it was assumed that 30-50% of solid waste would be dumped on special sites, 14-20% composted and 30-50% incinerated. From that programme it was calculated that if the dumped waste was between 5 and 15 m. high, the area required for the site would be between 143 and 584 ha for solid waste. Until now, in the province of Lodz there is only one method of treatment and it is dumping. The economic and political crisis in Poland and the resulting fiscal austerity of provincial and local authorities did not allow other more sophisticated technology to be applied. In these circumstances, the area required for controlled dumping is about 600 ha, including protection zones.

The province of Lodz is one of the smallest in Poland, but it is very strongly urbanized and densely populated (754 inhabitants per 1 km^2 in 1988, Poland has 122 inhabitants per 1 km^2) [3]. This makes it impossible to find sites for waste disposal within the Province which neither interfere with other people's activities nor affect the natural environment. A location outside the province cannot be considered. According to the unpublished order of the Prime Minister from 1976 which is still in force, each province is obliged to process its own waste within its own administrative boundary. Such an order "resolved" or postponed the conflicts over waste disposal between provinces, but at the same time provoked conflicts between communes and between the province and its commune(s).

At present the City of Lodz has 3 sites for dumping solid household waste (see Figure 4.3);.
- Jozefow (15 ha), in the South East part of the city where the height of dumped waste is now 26 m,
- Marmurowa street (4 ha) in the North East part,
- Nowosolna (0.6 ha).

All of these sites should have been closed in 1985. The sanitary and working conditions are very dangerous for the people living in the surroundings. The waste heaps are very large. The waste is spread over a wide area by the wind. The hazardous situation is caused by insufficient treatment by the

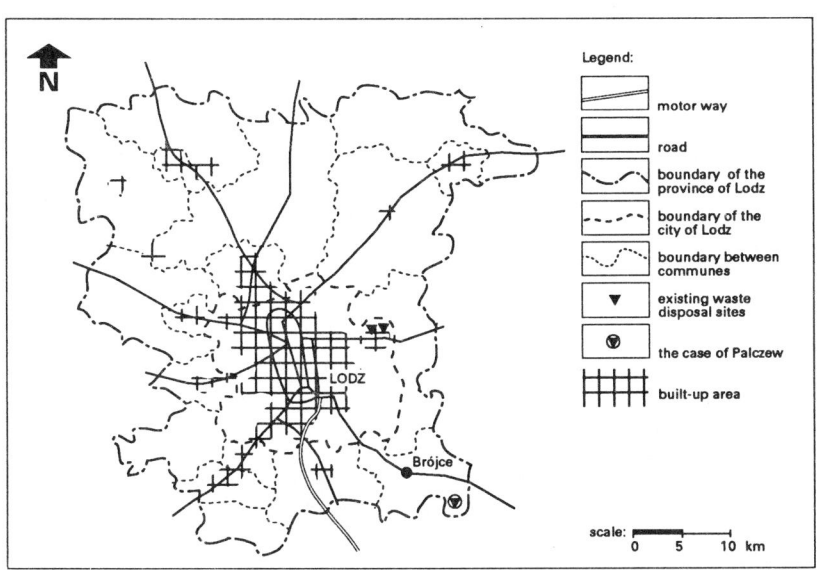

Figure 4.3 Waste disposal sites in the Lodz area

Municipal Cleansing Enterprise and by concentrating waste into these heaps because of the lack of new sites.

The large new waste disposal site for the City of Lodz was supposed to be prepared in 1984. It is located in the village Palczew, Commune Brojce (see Figure 4.3). Since 1980 there has been continuous conflict about the location between the Provincial Administration representing the interest of citizens of Lodz, and the Commune Brojce and its inhabitants and villages.

Formal procedures, actors and the organization of waste disposal sites in Poland

The basic very general legal Act concerning the treatment of all kinds of waste is the Act on the Shaping and Protection of the Environment, passed by Parliament in 1980 (DZ.U.No. 3/1980). The Act states that all units producing waste are obliged to protect the environment and recycling waste (art.53). Waste which cannot be recycled in the process of production or utilized in any other way .... has to be treated in the places designated in spatial plans (art.54). It is also stressed that spatial (physical) plans have to take account of environmental protection (which is consistent with the Act on Spatial Planning, DZ.U.No. 35/1984). According to art. 57, no decision of the territorial administration may violate the principles of environmental protection and they certainly may not violate any rules concerning ways of using the environment which were established in the spatial plans. All producers of hazardous waste have to agree the way it is to be treated with the provincial organ of administration.

In accordance with this basic Act, the Prime Minister issued some further resolutions specifying, among other environmental aspects, the legal and technical methods of waste treatment (location, zoning, fees) in 1980. For instance, in the Resolution of the Prime Minister of 30 September 1980 (DZ.U. No. 24/1980) concerning the protection of the environment against waste, it was written:
- Territorial organs of state administration must guarantee the proper protection of the environment against waste on their territory....;
- They must take account of environmental problems concerning waste treatment in spatial and socio-economic plans....;
- They must protect soil, water and air during transport and dumping and other forms of treating the waste....;
- and ensure the construction of waste disposal sites and other installations for waste treatment.

In the choice of a location for a waste disposal site, all conditions and requirements guaranteeing environmental protection and the interest of owners and users of neighbouring property should be specified.

In 1984 the Minister of Spatial Economy issued a paper to the provinces requiring them to include waste disposal sites in spatial plans having regional significance. This was the beginning of a more integrated approach to waste treatment. In 1988 other instructive materials were prepared by ministerial institutions concerning waste treatment in regional and physical plans. These instructions approach waste treatment only from an organizational and technical point of view. There is nothing in it concerning the implementation of waste disposal sites (Piotrowska, 1988).

There are other Acts which influence the decision making process concerning the location of waste disposal sites. Among the most important are:

- The Agricultural Land and Forest Protection Act of February 1985,
- The Act on the System of People's Councils and Local Self-government of July 1983,
- Act on Spatial Planning of July 1984,
- The Land Use Act of 14 May 1985 and, following this, the practical Resolution of the Council of Minister of 28 October 1985.

In Poland there is no specific Act concerning the planning of waste treatment in the region as there is in the Netherlands. The location of a waste disposal site is included in the traditional way of elaborating the physical plans, approving procedures and implementing them.

Formal possibilities for public participation in the location of waste disposal sites are given by the Act on Spatial Planning (art. 29), which says that physical plans should be presented for public display for at least 21 days. Information about this should be announced in local newspapers. After that, if the remarks and comments of those concerned are not included in the project, the local body of state administration has to inform them in writing. The actors in the formal procedure of regional and physical planning and also in the formal procedure of choosing and designating waste disposal site are described in chapter 3. In Figure 4.4 the interrelationships involved in waste disposal sites are summarized.

Data collection

The course of the conflict has been mostly investigated using written detailed documents collected by several departments of the provincial administration. These departments were directly involved in the conflict because they acted as plenipotentiary bodies to the President of the province.

There were more than 4000 of pages of documents to investigate and the documentation collected was reliable. It included very detailed descriptions of all events and also of the atmosphere of disputes during organized meetings. Even the very rude language used by peasants from the villages have been quoted! All written material was treated by the province as semi-secret. The author of the study had to apply to the President for special permission to review it and had to assure him that it would be used only for academic investigation. The author also managed to interview provincial and local officers, to check if the collected material objectively reflected the course of the conflict. It is worth noting that the material collected also contains all articles published by local and national newspapers on this subject.

The course of the conflict

In the village of Palczew there has been a gravel-pit for several years. The area was bought by the state from a private farmer and given to a provincial (state owned) enterprise to be used for the extraction of gravel. In 1975, the gravel enterprise gave part (4.02 ha) of its excavation to a chemical enterprise for dumping industrial waste. This was formally accepted by both communal and provincial authorities. None of the farmers was against the dumping of industrial waste. One could say that at that time farmers were not so conscious of possible environmental dangers nor that these hazardous activities could affect them directly.

When the household waste problem of the City of Lodz became very

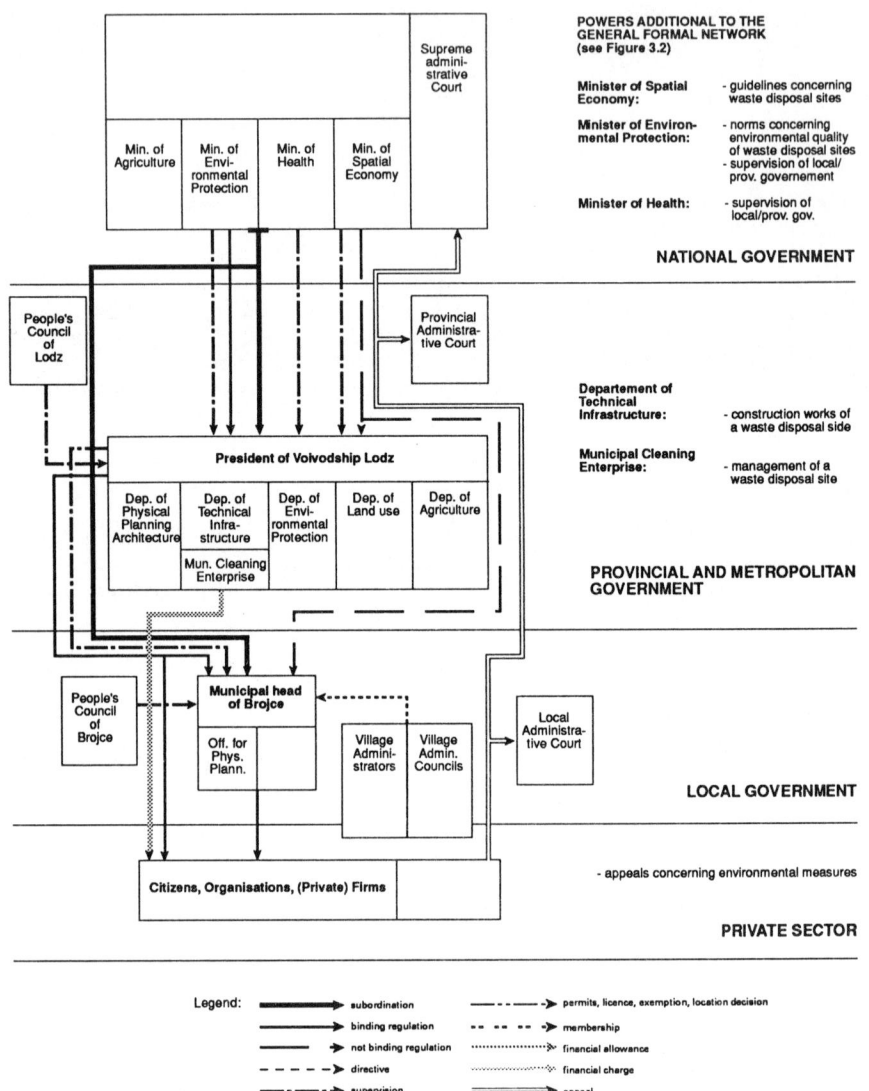

Figure 4.4 Formal network concerning waste disposal sites, Poland, Lodz

acute, the experts found the Palczew site to be the best within the administrative boundaries of the Province for disposing of waste from Lodz. The site at Palczew was included in the Regional Development Plan of the Province and passed by the Provincial Peoples' Council in 1977. This plan was accepted by the Ministry of Administration, Territorial Economy and Environment, which was then responsible for spatial/physical planning.

At that time, the whole of the excavated area (33.7 ha) was designated by the Provincial Administration as being necessary to solve the problem of household waste for the City of Lodz. It is worth noting that, in the beginning of the site location procedures, nowhere was it written how much area was required for waste disposal.

On 29 November 1978 the second phase of the gravel excavation (9.52 ha) was handed over to the Administration of Commune Brojce for the dumping of its household waste.

On 14 December 1978 the Communal Peoples' Council approved the Physical Plan of the Commune (elaborated on the main lines of the provincial plan) and this included the location of the waste disposal site for the City of Lodz. There was no protest, no discussion about the problem during the peoples' council session [4].

On 7 September 1979, in the office of the local administration of the Commune Brojce, the gravel-pit enterprise officially handed over the excavated area (in total 33.7 ha) to the Municipal Cleansing Enterprise (MCE), which was subordinate to the provincial administration [5]. From that moment, all existing and future users of the former gravel-pit area had to get permission from the provincial administration.

In 1979-1981, the Town Civil Engineers Design Office worked out a scheme of waste disposal for the MCE on that location. In Poland in the seventies and the beginning of the eighties, the legal system of land use and the principle of the expropriating of private land ignored individuals' rights. The administration assumed there would be no protest over the location of a public utility project from the "obedient society". This was why a scheme was worked out by the design office assuming the use of 170 ha of the area for the full project and 69 ha for the first stage of its realization. This scheme required from the local commune for the first stage an area was more than twice as large as the area in possession of the MCE (handed over in 1979).

In order to start the construction, some other formal conditions had to be fulfilled. The Provincial Department of Planning and Architecture had to accept it and to check if all the legal formalities had been fulfilled. One of such formal preconditions concerns the ownership of the land. The developer of the site has to own it or the former owner has to legally and explicitly accept the sale of his land. In this case, none of the farmers agreed to sell their farming land. On 2 October 1981, at the meeting organized in the office of local administration with all the actors directly involved (i.e. farmers to be expropriated ca 50 persons), the chief of the local administration, the provincial department of land surveying, MCE and people representing the interest of the Municipal Developer (MD), and the provincial department of technical infrastructure. At that meeting the farmers refused openly for the first time, to accept a waste disposal site for the City of Lodz. It became obvious that the legal procedure of expropriation would be a very long one.

On 13 December 1981 came the introduction of martial law. This situation postponed or suppressed the conflict for the next two years. In the meantime the Provincial Authority made a decision to reduce the area required for the waste site to the former gravel-pit area (ca 30 ha).

On 26 July 1983, the Chief Administration Officer of the Commune Brojce acted on the official record dating from 1979 and confirmed handing over the area to the MCE. In the new scheme, the land to be expropriated from the private owners had been reduced from ca 36 ha to 5.2 ha. The area was required for a service road and the extension of a green belt surrounding the site.

On 18 December 1983 the Municipal Developer (MD) demanded that the local administration expropriate 1.8 ha of farming land in the name of MCE from Palczew village and 3.4 ha from Wardzyn village. Even this relatively modest demand still affected 31 farmers.

On 26 March 1984 the request by the MD was refused both by village farmers and by the Local Peoples' Council. At the same time, the Chief of Local Administration refused to take a decision on changing the use of arable land. This is a legal precondition for starting the procedure of land expropriation [6]. This attitude of the villagers forced the provincial agencies to once more consider reducing the area of private land required. The decision to do this was finally taken one year later (12 August 1985), but only for 2.07 ha. As a result of the farmers' opposition ca 3 ha of arable land was saved.

On 17 September 1984 a resolution was taken by Brojce People's Council that the local community could accept the waste site if:
- a green belt was created around the site before dumping was started,
- the dumping site was restricted to the existing excavation (no expropriation at all) and when the excavations are filled in they would be restored to farming land and recultivated,
- the village of Palczew would have a pavement constructed alongside the road going through the village and a wider public road were made by the province.

The fulfilling of the latter condition could, in the eyes of the villagers, reduce the disadvantages caused by the passing of refuse lorries. The predictions were that 200 lorries per day would use the route.

On 11 February 1985, at the negotiation meeting in Commune Brojce between farmers and the officers representing the departments of the provincial administration, farmers demanded the construction of a new road round the village Palczew in order to avoid the nuisance of the refuse lorries.

On 11 April 1985 a resolution of the Communal Council was passed, repealing the approval for the location of a waste disposal site for the City of Lodz in the village Palczew.

On 16 April 1985 the dangerous situation around the waste treatment in the City of Lodz and the growing consciousness in society of environmental problems, influenced the decision of the local Chapter of PRON (Patriotic Movement of National Rebirth) to visit the villages and hold meetings with those affected by the waste disposal sites in the province. This voluntary body criticized the method of waste treatment in the Province of Lodz very strongly and suggested that the residents of the villages of Palczew and Wardzyn should be compensated, for example by the provision of extra services by the province.

On 25 May 1985 formal objection was made by the Council of Village Administrators of the villages Palczew and Wardzyn to the State Peoples'

Council and the President of Poland about the location of the waste site. In the objection, the Village Administrators Councils complained of the side effects caused by the waste disposal site. For the first time in the conflict, the argument was officially raised that underground water and the source of a small river (Wolborka) would be polluted; this is, indirectly, one of the sources of drinking water for the City of Lodz. According to the farmers, this argument meant that the location was not consistent with the Act of Environmental Protection, which stresses that when locating waste disposal sites drinking water should be protected.

On 1 August 1985 the Minister of Administration and Spatial Economy (Physical Planning) answered the State Peoples' Council and the local communities of Palczew and Wardzyn, saying that this location of a waste site was in order. The Minister supported the idea of constructing a by-pass around the village.

On 12 August 1985 the Chief Administrator Officer of the Commune Brojce finally decided to change the 2.07 ha of arable land into a protective green belt.

On 28 August 1985 and on 5 September 1985, meetings of the residents' association of the commune Brojce with the President of the Province took place. There was an attempt to reconcile both parties involved in the conflict. Residents of both villages directly involved and the local residents' associations presented a list of goods and projects requested as compensation for the disadvantages caused by the waste site location. The wishes of the residents were accepted and the Province treated the problem very seriously, very carefully checking that the wishes were carried out over the next two years. The list contained the following requirements:
- delivering bottled gas for the villagers and assuring a permanent supply;
- constructing two reserve deep water wells for Palczew and Wardzyn;
- reclaiming arable land for both villages;
- supplying an extra 10 tractors and other agricultural machinery such as milk cooling machines, combines etc;
- routing public transport through the Commune, giving good access to the City of Lodz;
- extending the primary school in the Commune with the help and money of the Province;
- subsidizing the construction of "a peasant culture house" and a fire protection station from the provincial budget;
- widening the public road going through the Commune and asphalting some other local roads.

Bargaining about obtaining these requirements enabled the villagers to keep their improved power position for the next 2 years.

On 28 December 1985 the President of the Province created the Commission for Proper Realization of Waste Disposal Sites in Palczew.

On 1 March 1986 the Municipal Developer began to negotiate the acquisition of 2.07 ha of arable land. Farmers responded by refusing to take part in the formal procedures, refusing to sell land voluntarily, refusing to take money for expropriated land, farming illegally expropriated land etc.

In the beginning of 1986, the conflict was concentrated around the new village by-pass. Some farmers disagreed with the proposal to redesignate the farming land required for the new service. In the correspondence, all the relevant provincial departments, the local administration and the Ministry of Agriculture were involved. Farmers did not expect the Minister to accept changing the function of rural land in favour of the road, but he did.

On 9 January 1987 the villagers took legal action against the location of the by-pass. This time they appealed to the Ministry of Spatial Economy and Building Industry.

On 9 May 1987 the Minister of Spatial Economy and Building Industry supported the former presidential decision concerning the location of the by-pass. The Minister explained to the villagers that they could appeal against the Ministry decision to the Supreme Administrative Court (SAC) which had existed in Poland since 1980. The farmers followed this advice several times in the further course of the conflict.

On 6 July 1987 the governing body of the Province decided to start the disposal of waste on the site by using the public road going through Palczew. For the first time in the course of the conflict, the President of the Province gave permission to inform local newspapers about the existing conflict. Information in local newspapers should, according to the President, inform the public every week about the progress of construction works at the disposal site in Palczew and the danger to the health of the residents of the City of Lodz caused by the protesting villagers [7]. The President also ordered that the police be informed and organized for the first day of waste dumping.

On 13 July 1987 the MCE, with the help of the police, attempted to transport the waste to the excavation site in Palczew. Villagers allowed police cars to pass but blocked the path of the refuse lorries with their own bodies. This exciting fight was described in the national journal POLTYKA of 29 August 1987.

On 17 and 24 July 1987 reconciliation meetings between villagers and the Vice President of the Province (responsible for public technical facilities) took place. One of the results of those meetings was the addition of the representative of the Commune to the Commission of Proper Realization of the Waste Disposal Site. Some days later, farmers withdrew their objection from SAC and 23 farmers agreed to have this land voluntarily acquired for the service road.

On 25 August 1987 the Council of Village Administratos again appealed against the decision of the President of the Province concerning the location of a waste disposal site in Palczew. This time the appeal was sent to the President of the Polish Seym. The appeal was signed and supported by:
- the Communal Chapter of the Peasant Party,
- the Communal Chapter of the Farmers and Rural Organization,
- the Organization of Farmers' Wives,
- the Residents and Village Administrators of the two neighbouring communes of the Province of Piotrkow (which could be affected by waste dumping).

On 9 Oktober 1987 the Minister of the Environment, at the request of the President of the Seym, recognized the problem and informed Seym, Local Communities and the Provincial Administration that the location of a waste disposal site had been properly chosen i.e. according to the law. The villagers responded to that ministerial statement very quickly. Some of the farmers concerned appealed against the redesignation of their land for the service road.

On 4 December 1987 the Minister of the Environment, in the official letter to the President of the Province and under the pressure of villagers and another local organizations the Polish Green Peace Party, recommended the protection of the underground water by sealing the bottom of the excavation. This recommendation created a new problem for the province, delayed realization, threatened to raise greatly the construction costs etc., but primarily it was rather helpful to the Palczew Community: the problem remained unresolved and waste dumping was postponed.

In 1988 the conflict had a much more physical character. Villagers took illegal action. They built barricades on the public road and made construction of the service road and other works on the site impossible. Moreover, every possible objection had been made many times over ending in the SAC.

In 1988, the Provincial Authority, through its Technical Department, took serious steps to find other places for waste disposal for the City of Lodz. Fifteen locations within the Province were considered. All of them would affect some farmers. All local societies refused to accept the proposals of the Province. Even the locations which in the beginning of the investigation looked quite promising and were accepted by the local administration were finally rejected.

In 1989 the conflict was still not resolved.

Analysis and conclusions

The case of Palczew has shown that the real network of relationships with respect to the conflict about the location of a waste disposal site is somewhat different from the formal one. The relationships cover more participants than it was formally assumed, for instance villagers administrators and their councils.

Power resources The power resources of the actors involved are considered according to the tiers in the governmental structure. As can be derived from chapter 3, the central level of public administration had available extensive powers:
- a system of centralized planning
- control over the Court System
- finance and its distribution
- the production of consumer goods and their distribution
- the introduction of new laws
- control over public mass-media
- the police force
- influence over the state administration and elected officials through the nomenclature system of the communist party
- administrative orders through the system of territorial government (united and hierarchically controlled by the Central Government)

At the provincial level the power resources are the same, but they are restricted because of the legal competencies and because specific permission for using them is given by Central Bodies of State Administration and the Central Organs of the Communist Party.

The local level of government has very narrow formal access to independent power resources. The growing power of local authorities as an opposing body to the upper level of governments has resulted from the efforts made to transform the Polish political and economical system to a democracy with elements of the market economy. At the local level it was the result of the pressure of local communities on the local tier to represent their local interests.

For local communities and voluntary action groups, the main legal power resource for action was the right given (by the 1983 Act on the System of Peoples' Councils and Local Self government) to local groups to give opinions and to grant acceptance to the location of any new activities on their land. These rights were used very eagerly by local groups to stop any unwanted activity. These rights have been misused very often because they gave local people a feeling of "democracy". Another source of power was a genuine and gradual democratization of the political system: the loss of power by the communist party, the destabilization of the economy, the growing inconsistency of law, etc. have created a new network of relationships between actors on the urban scene. This new network subject to continuous political changes was very difficult to steer and control by the Provincial Authority and the officers employed there, who were loosing their former political power and safe seats. Local groups learned very quickly how to use legal loopholes to keep their power position. The other source of power was the moral support given by other communities, voluntarily organized political groups, new parties, journalists etc. Those outside the conflict used the situation for their own political ends as a mean to fight against the communist regime.

Strategies and interests of involved actors At the central level, Ministries had no interest in intervention. They only responded to the residents' protests and appeals by checking the legality of the decisions taken by the province. Ministries tried to avoid the problem at the top level by doing no more than making recommendations and giving advice to the province and residents, such as about the construction of the by-pass road round the village, the sealing of the bottom of the excavation to protect underground water etc. But they did not want to see either the financial problems of the provincial government or the social aspects of the conflict.

The State Council, the President of Poland and the Seym where interested only in avoiding changing the environmental conflict into a political one. These superior bodies responded to the residents' appeals indirectly i.e. through the proper ministries.

The Provincial government wanted to locate a waste disposal site in the commune in order to solve the growing hazardous situation of the City of Lodz. The Provincial government, being responsible by law for household waste treatment within the province, has formal powers to tackle the problem. However, the unstable political situation and the ongoing democratization caused the province to refuse to use those powers.

Executive bodies of the province, having a double administrative role as they represent the interest of the state and provincial council at the same time, see chapter 3, have a very weak position in conflict management. They have prepared recommendations for the president of the province, but in fact they have no power and no real interest in solving the problem. The Province even refused to go to the civil court to take action against peasants for their illegal action.

The Chief officer and local council, as representatives of local government, took the side of the local community. They acted against the province, using every legal means (and sometimes illegal) to delay the implementation of orders given by the superior organs of the province. Notice that such action before 1980 and during martial law would not have been possible.

The residents and farmers took the position of "not in my backyard" and "do not trust the government". Under the pressure of the provincial government the residents have gradually organized themselves into stronger groups of common interest. They have gained the support of local authorities, which, in this case, acted as a local independent government in opposition to the province. Different local non-governmental organizations have been used by residents in order to strengthen the power of appeals and protests. The strategy of residents to keep their power positions in the conflict was:
- refusal to let the farming land be expropriated voluntarily,
- refusal to take compensation for expropriated land,
- farm the expropriated land illegally,
- from time to time using physical force to prevent refuse lorries from dumping waste on the excavation site,
- appeal and object to all supervising organs of state and administration, and to the Supreme Administrative Court,
- bargain about material and financial compensation for disadvantages caused by disposing of the waste in the village,
- request construction of the projects which would eliminate spatial disadvantages, and, when accepted by the provincial and central level, to bargain again about expropriation of land procedures.

Generally speaking the strategy of the residents was to change the focus of the fight from that where the residents could expect to lose.

Shifts in the power balance In this case the first shift in the power balance between the province and residents occurred in 1980. This happened after the Solidarity "uprising" when the people realized that they could protest against the communist regime without any serious penalty. The course of the conflict showed that every effort by the provincial government and its executive bodies to regain the power position they previously held had been destroyed by the rapid political change and democratization in Poland. This is why the provincial government always delayed action. Until the end of 1989 there were not any important formal shifts in the power balance of the parties involved.

Powers not used The central organs of authority and administration refused to use their power resources at all, in spite of the strong attempt of the province to force the central level to take the final decision concerning the location of the waste disposal site and to support the Province financially in tackling the problem.

The Province did not exercise its power to take the peasants who were breaking the law to the civil court. It also did not use its legal powers to delegate to local government the implementation of the Provincial decisions.

Local government did not use its legal power position or duties to carry out the decisions of the Province, although if this had been done adequately it could have solved the problem.

The Netherlands: the cases of Beuningen, Borne and Nistelrode

Introduction: the issue

The general issue here is: where should waste disposal sites be located and/or expanded? The method of waste disposal - controlled tipping or incineration - is also an important issue and it played a large part in the following cases, but here we concentrate on the site selection.

The subject of waste-disposal sites has been much investigated in the Netherlands in the past few years. It was, therefore, not necessary to carry out new empirical work. Moreover, the volume and quality of the empirical work done by others was such as to allow three case studies to be analysed here. These concern the municipalities (see Figure 4.5 - 4.7):
- Beuningen in Gelderland, the period 1970 - 1986
- Borne in Overijssel, the period 1979 - 1989
- Nistelrode in North Brabant, the period 1973 - 1989.

All the sources are named at the end of this chapter.

It has been calculated that around 16 mln. ton of solid waste is dumped every year. If present trends continue, approx. 200 ha of waste disposal sites have to be added annually. (Note: this refers to household and industrial waste, but excludes chemical and radio-active waste or used oil and silt dredged from harbours etc) (Klaver, 1991). Solid waste can be treated in three ways, by re-cycling, incineration and dumping. Obviously, the problem of finding waste disposal sites refers to that part of the waste which is dumped, at the moment about 3/4 of all waste (again excluding chemical and radio-active waste, used oil and silt, also the slag after incineration). It is official policy to encourage re-cycling and to increase the capacity for incineration. Also, the total volume of solid waste to be disposed of can be reduced by different production methods, using less packaging, etc. Nevertheless, the volume of waste which is dumped is large and will not decrease greatly. Some of the existing disposal sites will continue to be used and new sites will have to be found.

It should be added that chemical wastes are treated separately and much more stringently under the Chemical Waste Materials Act (Wet chemische afvalstoffen). This legislation was passed in 1976, has been in force from 1977 and since then discoveries have been made about in how many places the ground has been seriously contaminated by uncontrolled and illegal dumping of chemical waste in the past. A huge and expensive programme of clearance of the contaminated sites is in progress.

Here we restrict ourselves to the conflicts around finding disposal sites under the Waste Products Act (Wet Afvalstoffen). It will be apparent that although this involves important environmental issues, the threat of heavy chemical pollution is no longer one of them. This Act (1977) ends the practice whereby each municipality had its own dump. Adjacent municipalities must combine because waste disposal and dumping is restricted to regional sites of at least 20 ha. This should have the advantage that the site can be professionally managed, the necessary equipment can be financed, measures to reduce environmental nuisance can be taken, and industrial processing becomes possible. Also, one regional site occupies less space than many local sites. Environmental requirements have been specified which all new sites must meet regarding isolation, management and supervision.

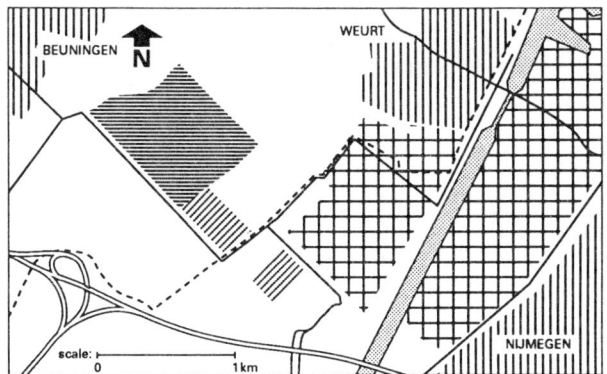

Figure 4.5 Waste disposal site Beuningen

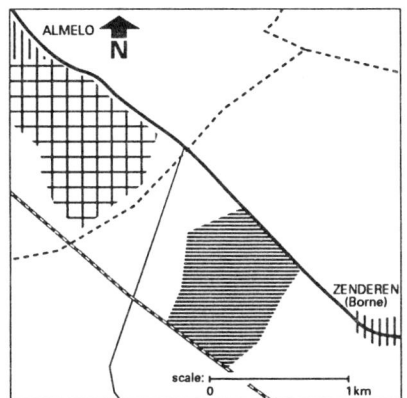

Figure 4.6 Waste disposal site Borne

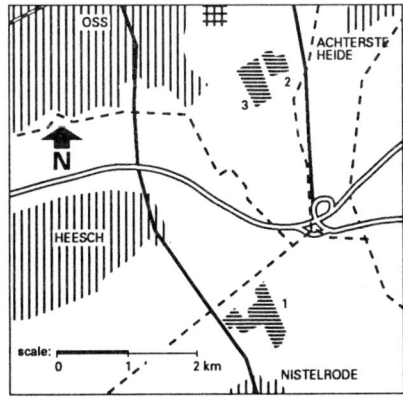

Figure 4.7 Waste disposal site Nistelrode

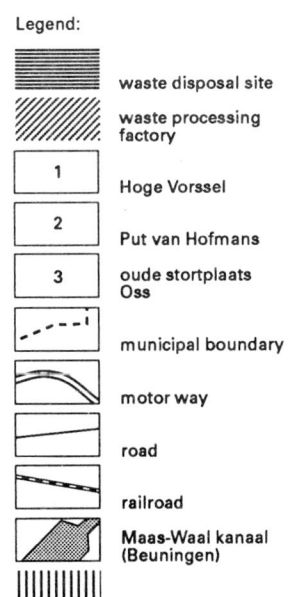

Legend:

- waste disposal site
- waste processing factory
- 1 Hoge Vorssel
- 2 Put van Hofmans
- 3 oude stortplaats Oss
- municipal boundary
- motor way
- road
- railroad
- Maas-Waal kanaal (Beuningen)
- residential area
- industrial area

In two of the cases analysed here, the period studied begins before 1977. The formal "rules of the game" changed, therefore, during the course of the conflict. Previously, each municipality had its own small dump, or entered voluntarily into an agreement with adjacent municipalities in the form of a "stadsgewest", a city region, for the collection and disposal of waste. Under the new law, groups of "collaborating municipalities" are legally established by the province and charged with the processing and dumping of this type of waste.

The formal procedures had therefore been changed in 1977. The procedures prior to 1977 are described here only insofar as they are relevant to the case studies. The Association of Dutch Municipalities (VNG - a very influential societal movement - see chapter 3) set up a committee which reported in 1964, recommending, amongst other things, that municipalities work together when disposing of waste. Central government supported this and in 1969 recommended that the provinces make waste-disposal plans, incorporating co-operation between municipalities. Waste-disposal remained the responsibility of municipalities (singly or in groups) until 1977 and in 1970 there were an estimated 1,000 waste sites. Applications to open and operate a waste site were subject to a "nuisance permit" (hinderwetvergunning). Nevertheless, many sites were causing serious contamination and it was largely concern about this that led to the Waste Products Act of 1977. By 1983 the number of waste sites had been reduced to 384. All the Dutch cases deal with the question of where to locate a regional site for waste disposal. In such cases one or two municipalities were to be appointed as the recipient of such a site, whereas other municipalities were relieved of having to dispose of refuse.

Data gathering

As mentioned before no additional empirical work was necessary. The Dutch cases had been investigated thoroughly in a research project. The cases had then been researched by describing and analysing the process by means of file research and interviews, aimed at the reconstruction of the decision-making process (Knaap van der, 1986).

The actors and the formal network

Before 1977 the main actors were individual or voluntarily collaborating municipalities. The rules laid down in the Waste Products Act 1977 are as follows. Every province has to draw up a waste-disposal plan which shows how, where and by whom waste may be deposited, treated, or re-used. The Ministry of Housing, Physical Planning and Environment (VROM) draws up guidelines for such plans and the provincial plan has to be approved by the Crown. The law creates the powers for taking measures to limit the amount of waste and for encouraging re-cycling.

Each province is divided into a number of "collaborating areas". In principle, all the waste in one such area has to be treated within that area. The establishment and operation of such "collaborating areas" is based upon the Joint Regulations Act (see chapter 3). The province is responsible for issuing permits for dumping. The municipalities in a collaborating area are together responsible for collecting, transporting and handling the waste in conformity with the provincial plan.

The decision-making around the choice of waste-disposal sites can be divided into three stages:
- the province makes and approves the waste-disposal plan. This can include an indication of possible waste sites, but the indication is not binding;
- the municipalities in a collaborating area choose a disposal site (a preliminary selection, followed by a detailed investigation of each site, followed by the final choice);
- the municipality incorporates the chosen site into its land use plan (bestemmingsplan) and the province incorporates the site into its waste-disposal plan and into its regional physical (streek) plan.

With the new Act, the requirement that a waste-site be subject to a nuisance permit had been withdrawn.

In the second stage, the site investigation is crucial (Hooydonk van, 1988). Two sorts of factors have to be taken into consideration:
- environmental health
- suitability.

The first set of factors are specified in centrally produced guidelines and principally concern the effects on soil, on ground water and on land use. The second set of factors concern matters such as transport, continuity in use, disposal methods, capacity, and the location of sites relative to the sources of waste. Usually, a third set of factors is also taken into account - land-use planning - which includes such things as the efficient use of land, the relative location of land uses, the use to which the site can be put when dumping has ceased, etc. The resulting choice of a waste-disposal site is usually a compromise between those three sets of factors.

Since 1987 the collaborating muncipalities have been legally obliged to commission an environmental impact assessment of the site location.

It should also be said that most municipalities have made by-laws (algemene politie-verordeningen) which forbid the dumping of waste and that many municipalities, when they make land-use plans, incorporate general conditions which forbid dumping. Further, under the Waste Products Acts, all dumping is subject to a permit, granted by the province. These rules ensure that dumping takes place only on approved sites. The rules also affect the working out of the procedure for choosing and designating a waste-disposal site. When a site is chosen, the municipality in which it falls has first to ensure that its land use plan allows that use. If necessary, the municipality must modify the existing land use plan, in which case the province has to approve the modification, testing it against its regional physical plan. If that is required, the province will modify its regional plan accordingly.

It has to be stressed that the Waste Products Act has no capacity to force a municipality to accept a site on its territory. If a municipality refuses to co-operate, a directive under the Physical Planning Act (from the province) must be employed (see chapter 3).

The Water Boards (waterschappen) also are involved because of the possible pollution of water draining from the disposal site. A formal application has to be made to the Water Board for a permit to discharge into surface waters. If the site is in or near an extraction area for mains water, then the water supply companies (waterleidingmaatschappijen) have to be consulted. It is, however, the province which gives or witholds permission based on those considerations.

Public participation is formally incorporated in the following ways:
- the provincial waste-disposal plan has to be put on public display for 2 months and has to be examined in public before it is approved;
- both the regional physical plan of the province and the land use plan of the municipality have to be exposed to public comments and reactions before they are approved (or in certain cases) modified.

From the description above of the formal procedures it can be seen that the following actors are important. The situation is described after the passing of the Waste Products Act; where the situation before that was different and where that difference was important for the case studies to be described, this will be indicated. Some of these actors and their roles are described more generally in chapter 3.

The Crown/Central Government In the case of waste disposal, their role is limited and largely passive or reactive. Their main concern is related to deciding appeals against the decisions of the public bodies concerned. The decisions are based upon general and specific legislation concerning objections and appeals. In addition the Crown (in practice the Minister of the Environment) has to approve provincial waste disposal plans.

The Ministry of Housing, Physical Planning and Environment The Ministry also has a mainly passive or reactive role. A part of the role is drawing up guide lines for general waste policies and for waste disposal sites. Through the regional inspectors for the environment and for physical planning, the Ministry is involved in advisory procedures concerning waste disposal and physical planning on the provincial and (inter-) municipal level.

The province The waste disposal plan mentioned previously is the most important task of the province, and the Provincial Council decides upon the plan. The plan provides inter alia guidelines concerning the environmental permit for dumping issued by the Provincial Excutive. It has the power to impose a joint working agreement on the collaborating municipalities concerning waste disposal. By indicating possible waste - disposal sites in the regional physical plan, the Provincial Executive gets the formal power to issue a directive to municipalities concerning a land use plan.

Collaborating municipalities These legally established bodies are responsible for acquiring the site, building the plant and running it. To be able to do this, the finding of a proper site is an important concern of these bodies, which have no legal power to force the municipality on whose territory a site should be established to co-operate. The decision about which kind of waste-processing is chosen is largely the concern of these bodies. Since 1987 they have been obliged to commission an environmental impact assessment of the site location and the operation of the site.

Municipalities Municipalities are generally responsible for waste collection. They take part in the agreement and the board and executive of the collaborating municipalities, and in that way influence the decisions of these bodies. The legal power of deciding upon land use plans is a crucial one in choosing the location of a site. In relation to the land use plan, the Municipal Executive has the power to issue the necessary building and construction permits.

Other public bodies and agencies Other agencies involved are:
- the Water Boards, issuing a discharge permit for the purified percolating water from the site;
- the Water Supply Companies, in charge of areas from where drinking water is extracted and where specific standards for the quality of the water are to be reflected in the permits which are necessary for certain activities;
- national agencies, which are represented in advisory bodies of the provincial government concerning physical planning and the environment.

Residents and the private sector Active participation in decision-making processes and using the right of objection and appeal are the main sources of the power of the private sector.

Some of these actors interact with each other in ways described below.

In the PPC (provincial physical planning committee) many representatives sit who come from central government departments (physical planning, environment, roads and water management, labour, agriculture, nature conservation, recreation, economic affairs). The task of the PPC is to advise the Provincial Executive.

The links between a municipality and the relevant provincial administration are many and varied, formal and informal. Formally, the province is a "higher" authority, with powers of supervision (which mainly involve withholding approval rather than enforcing obligations) over the municipality. But the preferred style is that of co-operation and negotiation. This is partly due to the great number of interrelationships between provinces and municipalities. A second reason is the political party links between the municipal and provincial level.

Obviously, municipalities interact with each other under the "collaborating agreement" for waste disposal, in which case there is a formal "joint working agreement" or joint regulation.

The main relations between actors are given in Figure 4.8.

What can be expected of this formal network? In particular, are the powers of an actor congruent with his goals?

The powers of the receiving municipality and its residents are mainly negative - to obstruct a proposal for a waste disposal site, including taking the case to appeal, with the concomitant costs and delays. This is also their main aim. Insofar as the receiving municipality wishes to deflect the site to another municipality it can use the means of supplying (selective) information about conditions within its own boundaries.

The exporting municipalities and their residents are in a very weak position. They want the site to be located in the proposed municipality. For this, the only means they have is to supply (selective) information, possibly also to threaten to obstruct alternative proposals should the first proposal be rejected. But they also want a decision to be made in good time (they must be able to dispose of their own waste) unless they have spare capacity in an existing waste site, in which case they might want to delay action. Their only means of speeding up a decision is to sacrifice a location within their boundaries. But each exporting municipality will delay doing that in the hope that another exporting municipality will do it first.

The collaborating municipalities, as a separate body, is also in a weak position, for it is powerless if the municipality which should accept the

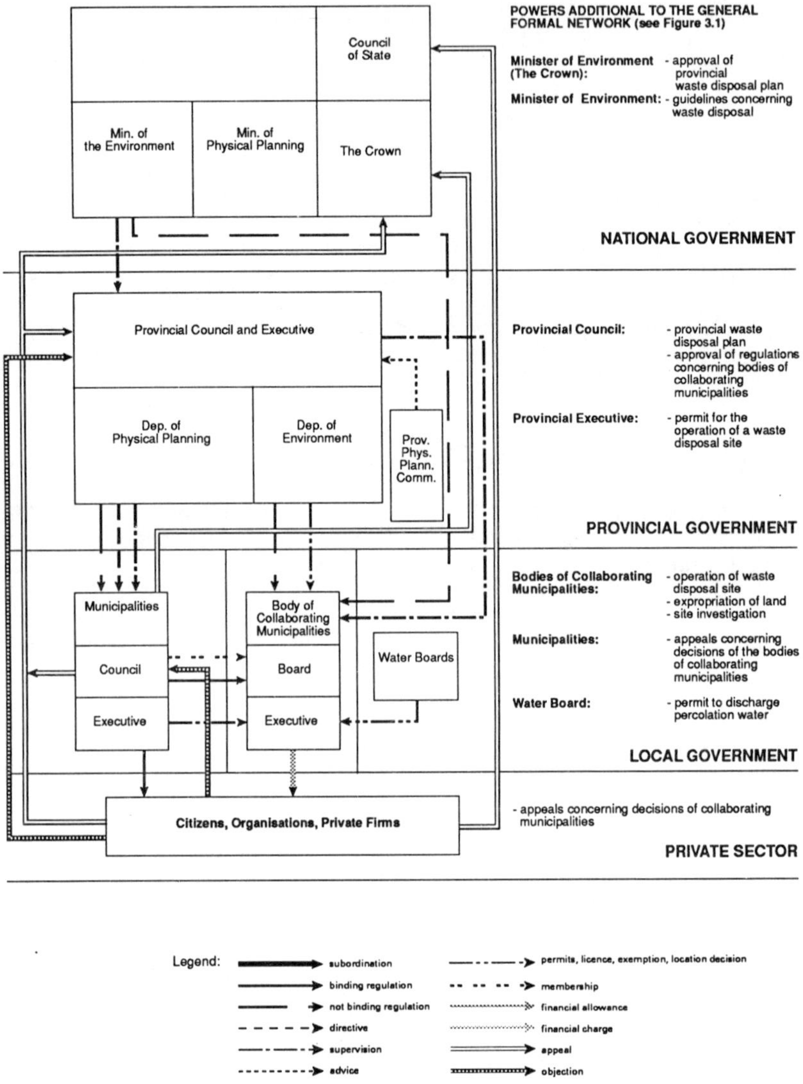

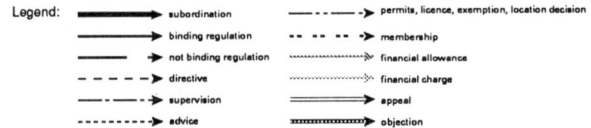

Figure 4.8 Formal network concerning waste disposal sites, the Netherlands

chosen location refuses to do so.

The province has no formal powers within the Waste Products Act to determine the location of a waste disposal site, only to indicate the possibilities. However, the power to designate a site using a directive which was created under the Act on physical planning, was given to provinces precisely so as to be applicable to all land uses.

The picture that emerges is one of inadequate powers of the body of collaborating municipalities to implement policy. Central and provincial governments draw up a general policy for waste disposal, but have few active powers for implementing it. Implementing that policy is delegated to a group of collaborating municipalities. However, although a group can choose a site, it cannot enforce that choice. The powers for building and running a site are for the body of collaborating municipalities. If, however, one municipality where the site is chosen refuses to collaborate - and it is usually not in the interests of that municipality to collaborate - then the body of collaborating municipalities has no powers to implement the policy.

However, the policy must be implemented as the refuse will not just "go away". We can expect therefore that:
- if implementation is by using formal powers, these powers will have to be found elsewhere (i.e. not in the Waste Products Act);
- or implementation will be by using informal powers;
- or there will be a combination of both.

The course of the conflicts

Beuningen   As early as 1970, the mayor (burgemeester) of Beuningen suggested using the Weurtse Polder for waste disposal. This location separates the built-up areas of the two municipalities Beuningen and Nijmegen and the mayor, wanting to keep these apart, thought that a waste-disposal tip would be an effective buffer.

The municipalities in the Nijmegen region had been working together voluntarily since 1973 (a "stadsgewest") on certain topics, including waste disposal, and in 1976 they recommended, with the full co-operation of Beuningen, that the Weurtse Polder be the best location for dumping waste. However, as soon as this became known to the local residents there was strong protest and in 1977 the municipal executive of Beuningen asked the other members of the "stadsgewest" to look for other locations. The Council of Beuningen even went so far as to reject the idea of waste disposal in the Weurtse Polder in March 1978. A few weeks later, the province, in its regional physical plan "Midden Gelderland", mentioned this site as the possible location for waste disposal in the region. As a result of the protest this caused, the province promised to have further research carried out within two years. The conclusion drawn from this in 1980 was that the Weurtse Polder was, indeed, the best location. The province tried to persuade the municipality to make a land use plan to incorporate the site, but the municipaliity refused to consider it. In May 1981, the provincial executive served a directive on the municipality, requiring it to modify its existing land use plan accordingly, but the municipality appealed against this to the Crown.

In the meantime, the province published its waste-disposal plan, drawing up collaborating regions (the Nijmegen region, including Beuningen, was no.V) and indicating for region V the location Weurtse Polder.

The municipal executive of Beuningen saw its opposition as being hopeless, and without prior consultation with local protest groups offered to withdraw its appeal in return for promises that strict environmental norms and other conditions would be imposed. Accordingly, in 1982 the municipality withdrew its appeal and in 1983 published a draft land use plan showing the Weurtse Polder as a waste-disposal site. Three thousand three hundred objections were submitted to the municipality against this. Nevertheless, the Council adopted the plan in 1983, whereupon 5,000 objections were sent to the provincial executive for environmental health. The province allowed a short version of the planning procedure to be followed, which provoked 10,800 objections. In 1985, however, the Council of State declared all objections baseless, and measures for dumping waste and constructing the incinerator began immediately.

Borne The "gewest Twente" was an organisation of 21 municipalities co-operating for certain tasks, one of which was waste disposal. In 1978 research was commissioned to find new waste-disposal sites. In the meantime, the Waste Products Act had come into force, and this placed certain requirements on the site-selection procedure.

The municipalities involved were suspicious and demanded that they be kept informed of the progress of the investigation. It had also been decided to divide the region into two, North and South Twente, each with its waste-disposal site.

The first interim report named 21 possible locations, including Vloedbelt in the municipality of Borne as a site for North Twente. A motion rejecting this was passed by the Council of Borne in May 1980.

In the second interim report of the research group, two preferred locations were named. The one for North Twente was still in Borne but, in response to the objections against Vloedbelt, to the north of this, at Elhorst. However, this also was unacceptable to Borne, which refused to co-operate in further studies.

The municipality of Borne now split into two camps. The Council, some of the aldermen and most of the residents (at least the vocal ones) opposed both Vloedbelt and Elhorst. On the other hand, the mayor, one alderman, and several important officers wanted to avoid being excluded from the decision-making and possibly having a site imposed upon the municipality on unfavourable terms.

The final report came out in June 1981. Elhorst remained the preferred location for North Twente, but the possibility of moving it southwards in the direction of Vloedbelt was mentioned. For South Twente, the location Sluitersveld was recommended.

A few months later the "gewest" took its decision - for North Twente Elhorst was chosen, but for South Twente, Kwinkelerweg. (The location Sluitersveld had in the meantime been strongly criticised by farming interests, which proposed Kwinkelerweg instead.) The "gewest" requested the province to incorporate Elhorst in its regional physical plan as a possible waste-disposal site. The "gewest" also requested Borne to revise its land use plan accordingly. The municipal council, however, instead went ahead with an appeal against the decision of the "gewest", in spite of a plea by the mayor to refrain and to co-operate. Borne proposed an alternative location, Hemmelhorst, but this was unacceptable to the province because of its high landscape value. The province gave Borne until January 1983 to come up with an alternative. However, Borne proposed alternatives outside its own boundaries. Borne also refused to consider formulating the conditions to which possible waste disposal at Elhorst should be subjected.

The province then said that it would have to exercise its own responsibilities in respect to physical planning and the provincial waste-disposal plan. As good as its word, it revised its regional physical plan accordingly. Borne protested against this and 400 private objections were also submitted.

Just before the formal debate in the Provincial Council, an action group presented a report which argued that one site was sufficient (at Kwinkelerweg) for both North and South Twente. Although a decision was postponed for a few months so that this could be studied, the original motion was accepted unchanged by the Provincial Council.

The delaying tactics of Borne provoked the municipalities of Hengelo and Enschede - which were to provide the waste-disposal site at Kwinkelerweg together - to threaten to withdraw their co-operation from the collaborating municipalities and from the province. This was done to put pressure on both bodies to take decisive action. The decision by the province late in 1984 to serve a directive on Borne was sufficient to persuade Hengelo and Enschede to go ahead with the site for South Twente. But Borne appealed against the directive. This appeal was lost and Borne had to revise its land-use plan to accommodate the site. This revision was approved by the provincial executive, but members of the public objected formally to that approval. The Crown had still not decided by October 1989.

Nistelrode The nine municipalities in the "stadsgewest" Oss and the "co-operating municipalities" Uden/Veghel (five municipalities altogether) had decided in 1973 to work together on dealing with their waste disposal. The first task was an investigation of the best location for a joint waste-disposal site. This resulted in a number of sites being selected for further study, some of them in the municipality of Nistelrode (a member of the "stadsgewest"). This local authority objected that Hoge Vorssel, one of the possible sites within its boundaries, although then in use for dumping, was designated in the land-use plan for a different future use.

The researchers were asked to do a further study and came up with a clear preference for Hoge Vorssel. The reaction from the province was that the site in Berghem, which was a private tip, would be better but in November 1976 the "stadsgewest" chose for Hoge Vorssel. The province declared that it had no insuperable objection to that choice.

Nistelrode, although unhappy with the preference, agreed to co-operate if a number of conditions were met. These were accepted by the "stadsgewest". The "co-operating municipalities" Uden/Veghel had in the meantime withdrawn from co-operating with the "stadsgewest" on waste disposal and the "stadsgewest" Oss submitted an application to Nistelrode for the necessary nuisance permit. This was granted in 1979 in spite of many local objections.

It was then necessary to revise the land use plan accordingly. But just before the revised plan was to be adopted by the Municipal Council, some council members claimed that the decision-making had been severely faulty.

The Municipal Executive of Nistelrode withdrew the formal motion to adopt the land use plan. Urgent consultations were arranged by the province and by the "stadsgewest", but to no avail.

The "stadsgewest" asked the province to impose a directive on Nistelrode, but the province said it first needed to incorporate waste disposal into its regional physical plan and that that had to wait until the provincial waste-disposal plan had been approved. In connection with the latter, the province then constituted the necessary "collaborating regions", but it asked those regions to choose the locations themselves. A complication was that the "stadsgewest" Oss and the "co-operating municipalities" Uden/Veghel, which two had come together for waste disposal and then split up, were put into the same collaborating region.

Nistelrode asked the central government to pronounce on the choice of site, promising to abide by their edict, but central government refused and claimed it was a matter for the Provincial Council. The physical planning committee of the province (PPC) gave Hoge Vorssel as its preferred site. Nistelrode responded by setting impossibly high conditions. The "stadsgewest" had to look for an interim solution while existing sites in Berghem, Oss and Uden would continue in use.

It was in May 1982 that the provincial waste-disposal plan was adopted including the necessary elaboration of the regional physical plan. The legal basis for serving a directive was now laid. Moreover, the waste-disposal plan specified the location Hoge Vorssel. One year later, this plan was formally approved and the "stadsgewest" requested Nistelrode to complete the revision of its land use plan, so that Hoge Vorssel could become the regional waste site. Again the answer was negative.

In September 1984, the province served a directive on Nistelrode. A directive was also served on the municipality of Berghem so that a site there could be used for a possibly interim solution.

After the approval of the provincial waste-disposal plan, the province was in a position to oblige the "stadsgewest" Oss and the "co-operating municipalities" Uden/Veghel, formally together in a collaborating region, to set up a joint working agreement. But in the meantime Nistelrode had appealed against the provincial waste-disposal plan and the Crown had decided in favour of Nistelrode. Their judgement was that the choice of Hoge Vorssel had been made on inadequate grounds. So the province asked the "collaborating municipalities" of North East Brabant to start to choose a location once again and include Hoge Vorssel in the alternatives! The interim solution of 1982 i.e. sites in Berghem, Oss, and Uden, are still in operation.

Analysis

Strategies: Beuningen In the seventies, after the proposals had become known, the province and the officials of the "stadsgewest" followed a strategy of presenting information and organising public meetings. However, most of the local actors involved were affected by the knowledge that the contract by which the firm VAM processed refuse in Nijmegen was to expire in 1985. The province reacted to this by switching the strategy to putting Beuningen under pressure so that a solution could be found while there was still time. Beuningen, on the other hand, reacted with delaying tactics, hoping that the urgency would lead to another site being chosen, where there was less opposition. Incidentally, two of the collaborating municipalities, Wychen and Groesbeek, were in no hurry as they still had their own spare capacity, which they wanted to use before having to contribute to the costs of the collaborating region. Both tried to delay decisions in the final stages.

There was a final modification to the strategy when Beuningen tried to bargain with the province - we will permit the location be used if you promise to impose strict norms, to build a new service road, etc. The province decided to use its informal power to offer compensation, which had always been at its disposal and thereby a solution was reacted.

Shifts: Beuningen The first important shift in the power balance was when the Council in Beuningen changed from being in favour to opposing a site in the Weurtse Polder for waste disposal. The reason for this is clear: the Council had favoured the location as long as the local population knew nothing about it and as soon as the proposal became known a petition of signatures was conected from 97% of the local electorate, and one of the action groups threatened to stand against the established parties in the forthcoming local elections. Even so, it is arguable that this shift came too late. The municipality of Beuningen had proposed a site within its own boundaries, other municipalities had accepted this gladly and thereafter this site attracted all the attention.

The second shift came with the disbanding of the "stadsgewest Nijmegen" from 1 January 1978. This organisation of municipalities in the region co-operating voluntarily, had tried to co-ordinate waste-disposal policy, and had done the influential research about site selection and had recommended the Weurtse Polder. The co-operating municipalities disagreed on a number of issues - of which waste disposal was only one - but that, in turn, shifted the initative to the province.

In fact, the involvement of the province in this matter grew throughout the process. The third significant shift came when the province decided to use the only positive power open to it - imposing a directive under the Physical Planning Act. It was probably that which caused the municipality to shift its position from opposition to conditional co-operation.

Powers not used: Beuningen It is not known whether the other collaborating municipalities put pressure on Beuningen to accept the waste-disposal site after the disbanding of the "stadsgewest". It would have been in the interests of these other municipalities to do this, even to pay more than their "fair share" of the costs within the collaborating region, in order to get a solution accepted in time and outside their own boundaries.

Also, after the disbanding of the "stadsgewest", the province could possibly have played the collaborating muncipalities off against one another. This seems to have happended just once when in the site selection report published in 1980 by the province, it said that the Weurtse Polder was politically a good choice as only two muncipalities, Groesbeek and Beuningen (of course), were against it.

Strategies: Borne Most noteworthy was the consistent strategy followed by the "gewest" and the province, who had one approach and supported each other thoughout the whole process. Also noteworthy is the fact that, although the municipality of Borne was internally severely divided, the majority of the Council and the residents also followed one consistent line, that of obstruction.

Shifts: Borne There was no tipping of the power balance, more a gradual increase in the involvement of the province and an accumulation of advantage to this authority. By doggedly following the formal procedures, the province acquired for itself the legal basis from which it could impose a directive on the municipality, although this took many years.

Powers not used: Borne The council of Borne refused to use its power to bargain with the province. That strategy has been urged by the mayor and municipal secretary but explicitly rejected by the Council. Now that the outcome is known, we can see that the municipality would have been better off if it had, indeed, used this power, for it has forgone the opportunity to negotiate compensation.

Strategies: Nistelrode The province followed a formalistic strategy, perhaps because it knew that there was no great haste to find a solution, there being spare capacity at existing sites. That was also certainly one of the reasons why the exporting municipalities could not form a united front and thus exert greater pressure on Nistelrode. The "co-operating municipalities" of Uden/Vehghel had spare capacity to be used.

After first co-operating, Nistelrode adopted the strategy of "stone-walling" - continually obstructing. It had acquired an additional power which strengthened its position, having bought the land for the Hoge Vorssel site, and could thus refuse to supply it to the collaborating municipalities without a compulsory purchase procedure!

Shifts: Nistelrode The first shift came when Nistelrode reversed its stance, from that of co-operation to that of refusal. This came in part for political reasons, as a new political party had won seats on the council and wanted to win further electoral support. The means it used was to gain inside information from the province about earlier decision making, information which was exploited to argue that that decision-making process had been at fault.

There was a gradual shift throughout the process, whereby the involvement of the province increased. The second big shift could have come with the formal approval of the provincial waste-disposal plan, which should have given the province powers to designate sites and to encourage joint working agreements, but part of that plan is now invalid after the decision by the Crown in favour of Nistelrode.

Powers not used: Nistelrode Both the province and the exporting municipalities reacted weakly to Nistelrode's obstructionism. Perhaps (see above) there was no great need to do otherwise in the short term. Now, however, the need is becoming urgent and there is still no solution.

Environmental nuisance of a large industrial plant

Poland: The case of the location of a housing estate close to the Asbestos Ware Plant "Polonit" in Lodz

Introduction: the issue

This contribution presents an analysis of the conflict that arose between the residents of a neighbourhood in Lodz on the one hand and the Packing and

Asbestos Ware Plant "Polonit" together with the local authorities on the other. The cause of the conflict was the location and construction of a housing estate close to a noxious production works.

The present state of industries in Lodz, the location of the particular plants, the town development and spatial form, are the consequences of the spontaneous processes of the founding and development of the town in the economic conditions of the nineteenth and twentieth century, and also of the changes which have occurred in this field in the last forty years. Lodz is an industrial town and, up to now, industry has had a key function.

The whole policy for the development of Lodz in the period after the second world war was dominated by the extension and modernization of the enterprises that are located there. The programme of adaptating and modernizing industry called for the closing down of the outdated and hazardous complexes, the relocation of some of them to new sites, and the construction of new plants, first of all on the outskirts of the town. Both the industrial complexes which were to be relocated and the works to be built anew were expected to be located solely in the area of specially designated industrial zones. The programme also anticipated the closing down of industrial works from the (widely defined) central district of the town. In spite of the plans, many old factories have been left standing and operate from the old premises. One of them is The Packing and Asbestos Ware Plant "Polonit".

The branches of the plant are in three parts of the town viz. Branch A in the east (Widzew), Branch B in the north (Baluty), close to the urban centre, and Branch C in the centre (see Figure 4.9). The plant was founded at the end of the nineteenth century (in 1891). Branch B is the most noxious and troublesome. It produces over 80% of the goods of the plant. The research presented refers to this branch. The staple products are asbestos yarn, asbestos cords and fabrics, gaskets of all kinds, frictional asbestos and rubber pressed goods, and asbestos boards. The plant holds the country's monopoly on the production of metal-asbestos packing. Of the other goods it produces 20-30% of the domestic production.

The basic nuisance which the plant caused the neighbourhood, is air pollution and noise. It emitted asbestos dust, formaldehyde, phenol, petrol and sulfur dioxide to the atmosphere. Because of that the plant had, exceptionally for Lodz, a protection zone of 300 meters determined in 1967. Since 1985 this zone has been extended to 500 meters. However, protection zones in town centres are not observed nowadays. There is not enough space for them. Here, however, due to the harmful emissions, the zone was necessary. Moreover, the location was regarded as temporary, plans being anticipated to relocate Branch B to another place. According to the town development plan, worked out in 1972, the site was to be developed for housing after the removal of the plant.

Data collection

The case study was elaborated mostly on the basis of written material i.e. correspondence exchanged between the parties involved. These documents have been collected from the departments of the Provincial Authority (such as the Department of Health and Environment and The Department of Architecture and Physical Planning) the "Polonit" Factory, and the Housing Co-operative "Lokator". Additional sources of information were articles

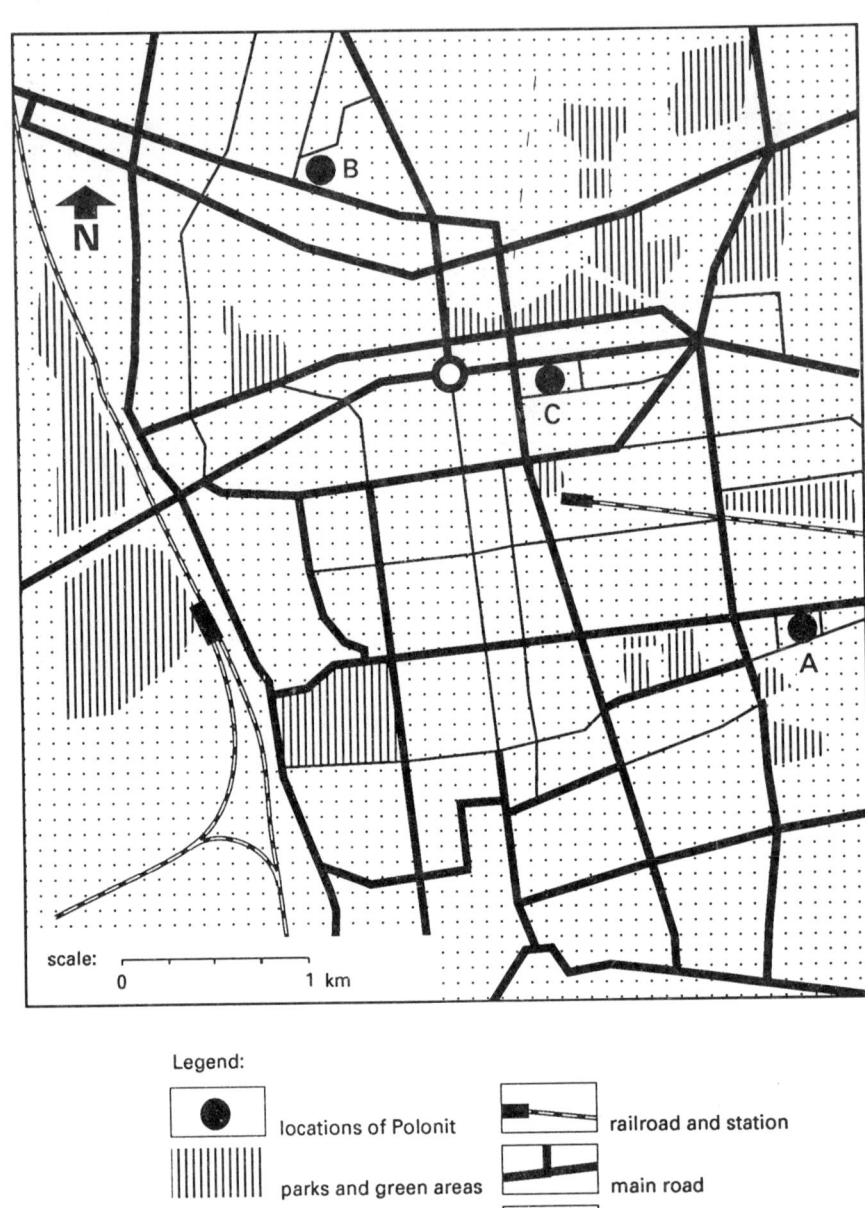

Figure 4.9 locations of Polonit in the city centre of Lodz

published by local newspapers and national journals. These investigations were carried out in March and April 1989. The analysis covers the period of 1978-1988.

The actors and the formal network

The main actors in this case were:
- the management of the Packing and Asbestos Ware Plant "Polonit", which comes under the jurisdiction of the Ministry of Chemical and Light Industry; in that way the latter is an important actor as well;
- the town authorities of Lodz, both the administrative authority and its representative bodies;
- the Housing Co-operative "Lokator";
- the residents, particularly those of the housing estate situated close to the plant.

In addition to the main actors other parties played a role, such as judicial bodies, both at the district and the national level. With reference to the general picture of legislation and actors concerning locational and land use questions (see chapter 3), in the "Polonit" case the formal positions can be listed as follows.

On the level of the central state, the Ministry of Chemical and Light Industry is powerful. This Ministry decides upon the production, location and finance concerning "Polonit". The management of the plant is subordinated to the Ministry in many respects. The General Arbitration Committee in Warsaw acted as a body of appeal concerning some questions which arose.

On the level of the province, several bodies are relevant. Some of them act as an extension of central state agencies. It has to be stressed that in Lodz, the provincial authorities also act as the town authority. In terms of general policies the President of the town and the People's Council are responsible. For particular tasks, the Department of Physical Planning and Architecture, the Department of Health and Environment, and the Sanitary Inspection have powers concerning the location of a housing estate.

The Department of Physical Planning and Architecture is responsible for the preparation of spatial plans and for location decisions. So this department is important for housing location as well as for the relocation of the Polonit plant. The State Sanitary Inspection has advisory powers concerning location decisions and discretionary powers concerning emission permits of industrial plants. The latter power is shared in some respects by the Department of Health and Environment. The District Arbitration Committee serves as an instrument of justice concerning decisions of public administration on the provincial level.

The Housing Co-operative is responsible for the construction and management of housing estates, within the limits put forward by the state and local authorities. The relations between actors are summarized in Figure 4.10.

How the conflict arose

At the beginning of the seventies Poland received large loans from western countries, which finance was used to modernize and develop industry. There were widescale and very ambitious plans for the reconstruction of the

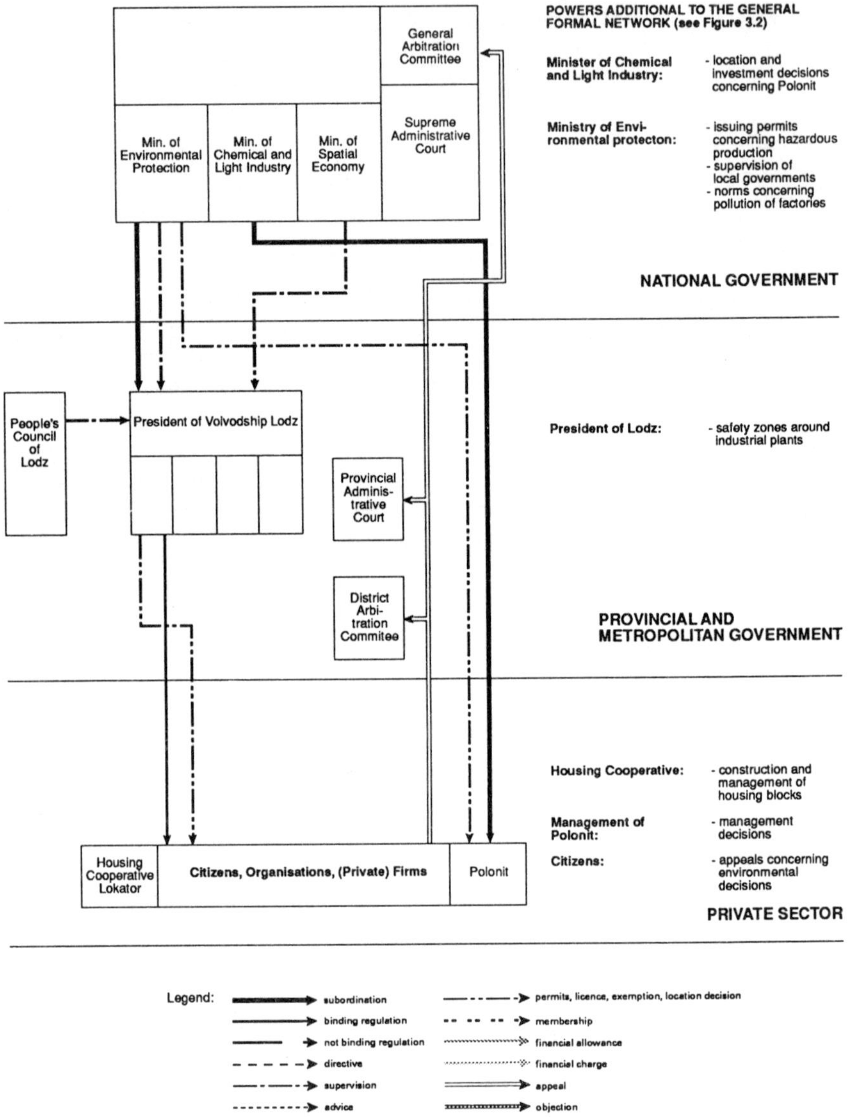

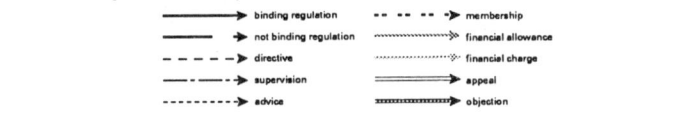

Figure 4.10 Formal network concerning environmental zoning around the Polonit plant, Lodz, Poland

particular government departments, among them the Ministry of Chemical Industry and Light Industry which included "Polonit". The plan to develop this branch included the intention to close down the plant in Lodz and to construct it at Szadek which is now in Sieradz province. On this basis, in 1976 the Department of Physical Planning and Architecture of the Province Administration gave a location decision for the Workers' Housing Co-operative "Lokator" to have a housing estate built in the neighbourhood of Branch B (see Figure 4.9). However, as early as 1975 the first visible symptoms of the economic crisis began to occur. The means to make new investments were limited.

In 1977 The Association of Technical and Fancy Goods informed the town President that the erection of the plant at Szadek had not yet been decided. This was confirmed by the letter from the Ministry in December of that year. In the letter the Minister officially informed the President that, due to the lack of adequate funds, building the plant at Szadek had had to be cancelled. The branch in Lodz could be closed down only after a new complex had been built. The time and location of the construction were not stated. The town authorities failed to see the significance of this.

In 1978 the office designing the housing estate applied to the State Sanitary Inspection of the Province to express their opinion on the plan particularly on the location of the housing estate. The health officer gave a negative recommendation but in spite of that, the plan was approved. Then the construction of the estate began. The town authorities had thought that setting up the housing estate would be effective in accelerating the relocation of the plant. The reality turned out different.

In December 1978 the management of the plant applied to the President with the request to cease the construction of the estate. The Sanitary Inspection sent a similar appeal, in which the harmfulness of the substances emitted by the plant were stressed, and a reminder was given of the previous negative recommendation. The town authorities again ignored these warnings.

In the Spring of 1979 two blocks of flats were already completed. In April there was a meeting of the political authorities of the province with representatives of the Ministry. The representatives of the town authorities were informed about the definite withdrawal of the plan to construct the plant at Szadek. It was decided that the closing down of the plant could occur at the earliest in 1982-1983, after a new location had been found.

In October 1979 two of the newly built blocks were in use. The wall of one of them was 3 metres away from the plant railing. The new flats were inhabited by 128 families who had not been informed about the detrimental effects of the plant.

In the years 1978-1980 the town authorities carried on negotiations with the Ministry. Debates, conferences and the exchange of correspondence followed. These actions brought no results. The Ministry did not have the funds to have the plant relocated, and closing the plant was unthinkable. The plant was the only producer of metal-asbestos packing in the country and provided all the other factories with this product.

In May 1980 the plant appealed to the Sanitary Inspection to receive permission to exceed the standard of emitted gases and dust. Their petition was rejected.

In 1981 the residents of the estate realized the position they were in. At that time a public debate on the harmfulness of asbestos in Poland began. It was in connection with asbestos boards, which had been used to insulate the flats. At last the residents became aware of the nature of the production of the neighbouring plant and how it could affect their health. Then an outright conflict broke out and the residents struggled for a change of the location of the plant or for a change in their accommodation.

At first the people living in the nearest two blocks lodged a complaint to the President of the town. Further letters were sent to the co-operative Managing Board, the Department of Environmental Protection, the People's Council, the Committee of the Polish United Workers' Party, the Lodz Group of Deputies, and finally to the Founders' Committee of the trade unions. The results of these complaints were insignificant. However, the case got more and more publicity. Press notices appeared in local and nationwide newspapers, and television and radio broadcast special programmes devoted to this problem. Opinions varied considerably. Neither the Ministry nor the Town Authorities gave any definite reports on the impact of the asbestos dust emitted by the plant. The Ministry stated that they had not had sufficient means, either in 1981 or 1982, to have had the plant built in a new location. The date of the relocation was settled for 1985.

The residents carried on their struggle and continued to protest. They informed the Ministry, the Town Authorities, and social and political institutions, that their living conditions were deteriorating. The plant was not only operating 24 hours a day from Monday to Friday but also on Saturdays. On Sundays noisy repair work was carried out.

In 1982, as a result of these protests, the plant presented a programme of activities aiming at limiting the hazards of the plant to the environment. The section producing frictional goods, which emitted mainly phenol and formladehydes, was closed down. The plant installed new ventilation systems, limiting the emission of asbestos dust and petrol vapour burners. The information about reducing detrimental effects did not convince the residents. After all, they had to put up with having the chimneys of the plant only a few metres away from their windows. Besides, the ventilation devices made extra noise because they work day and night. The protests of the residents went on. Also the Housing Co-operative began to protest, demanding the closing down of its anti-social neighbour.

Meanwhile, the negotiations of the town authorities with the Ministry continued. The relocation of the plant outside Lodz was out of the question and the case became a local issue. The town authorities were expected to suggest a new location that would suit the Ministry. Further suggestions were rejected, mainly on economic grounds. There was no development of a building site, nor the necessary utilities. The plant applied to the Sanitary Inspection again for permission for Branch B to exceed the allowable emission of pollutants in the atmosphere. The argument was the activity undertaken to limit the emission and a new date for the closing down of the plant. This time, both the Sanitary Inspection and the Health and Environment Department of the Town Authorities gave permission, which was valid until the end of 1985. In this way, the plant did not pay the fines for excessive air pollution. The residents' protests carried on. Meanwhile a new location has not been found and the plant did close down at the time appointed.

After having tried all possible actions, the residents tried another form of protest and stopped paying a certain amount of their rent. The rent was increased by the Housing Co-operative as compensation for rising administrative costs. Legal action was taken against the tenants and each was sued individually. They lost their cases.

Next, the Co-operative itself appealed to the District Arbitration Committee in Lodz to have the production in the plant stopped. The complaint was turned down. Even an appeal to the General Arbitration Committee in Warsaw did not help.

Finally, in 1985 the Town President signed an agreement with the Minister of Chemical and Light Industry about the relocation of the plant to the "Dabrowa" industrial zone to the south of Lodz. Unused buildings of the Felt Works were to be adapted for the plant. The zone has all the other necessary utilities.

The inhabitants of Lodz, including those living in the "Gorna" district where the industrial zone is, learned about the decision from the local press. The members of the People's District Council also learned about it in the same way. The conflict arose anew, this time in another district. Violent protests followed by the residents of the district. Factory employees from the industrial zone joined them. The exchange of correspondence continued for over two years. It was only when the assurance was made that new technology would be applied which would practically eliminate asbestos dust and when experts gave their opinions, that the question of starting adaptation works was finally settled. The whole plant was to be relocated. The three old plants would definitely be closed down. The date set for this is 1992. But the question is: will it be kept to?

Analysis

The situation described above can be defined as:
1. The conflict between the Ministry and the town authorities, resulting from the location of the plant "Polonit" in the neighbourhood of a housing estate;
2. The conflict between the town authorities and the residents resulting from the fact that the local authorities which represent the residents interests, did not perform their declared functions;
3. The conflict between the Housing Co-operative and its members.

The example chosen and presented here can be characterized as being a clash between individual interests, the interests of the local community, the interests and objectives of the state policy represented by industry and, in part, by the interests of the town administration. The conflict was caused by erroneous decisions made by the local authorities. Some of their activities were even in discord with the legal regulations e.g. concerning the protection of the environment. It is, however, understandable that they undertook illegal activities. Thus the fundamental question emerges of how such situations were possible and such decisions made.

To understand the behaviour of the particular participants in the conflict, the causes, and the ways of solving it, it is necessary to place it in the wider context of state organization and the process of making decisions in Poland. The characteristics of mutual interactions explain the conflict:
1. The authoritative position of some of the actors which influenced their behaviour;
2. The discrepancies between the official functions which individuals are designated to perform and their actual activities;
3. The different values followed by the different actors;

4. The real goals and the declared goals, and the way they could be realised.

Strategies In the conflict between the ministry (and the management of Polonit) and the Lodz authorities, the ministry used its powerful position so as to continue the operation of the Branch B plant and to exceed the emission standards. The management tried to prevent the construction of the housing estate. As far as the relocation of the plant was concerned, the ministry avoided binding decisions and agreements and appeared not to be capable of realising the intention to relocate. Later on, the management took various measures to reduce pollution and nuisance.

The Lodz authorities used the construction of the housing estate as a means of pressure. The authorities purposely neglected the protection zone around the plant and accepted that environmental norms be exceeded, notwithstanding the advice of sanitary and environmental agencies. In this way, the spatial development plan was implemented before the necessary conditions for the relocation of the industrial plant had been met. The town authorities pursued a continuous policy of negotiations with the ministry with the aim of getting a relocation of the plant. The Housing Co-operative promoted the construction of the housing estate actively and accepted the plan for closing down the industrial plant later on. In this way it formed a coalition with the town authorities. The co-operative finally appealed to the District and General Arbitration Committee.

The residents appeared to be poorly informed, but they deployed active opposition in several ways against the town authorities and the housing co-operative. They addressed many organisations including the communist party and trade unions and tried to mobilize public opinion by gaining publicity. The refusal to pay the full rent was a landmark in the opposition of the residents.

Shifts The main shift to be seen is the postponement of the relocation of the plant for financial reasons. This postponement is also the main source of the conflict. Nearly every attempt to influence other parties failed to achieve a significant shift.

Powers not used Though the formal and real power of the town authorities concerning land use is restricted, due to the powers of central state agencies and the subordination of local government to central government, the Lodz authorities did not use their power to refuse a location decision for a housing estate before the industrial plant had been relocated. At the central state level, the agencies responsible for environmental protection and health care failed to use their powers to affect the decision of the ministry of chemical industry and light industry.

The Netherlands: The case of environmental zoning around the Dutch State Mines (DSM) plant

Introduction: the issue

The chemical industry of DSM is the most prominent industrial plant of the province of Limburg. The chemical industry is the residual of the State

Mines of which the last was closed around 1970. The closing down of the mines in southern Limburg (both state owned and private) caused an economic decline in the region. In time, DSM developed into a large many-sided chemical industry with plants all over the world. The corporation's headquarters are in Geleen and in Heerlen. The plant in South Limburg covers 700 ha. Approximately 10,000 people are employed at the plant, which includes the DSM headquarters. Until 1989 National Government was the only shareholder of the company. Since 1989 the shares have gradually been sold to the private sector.

The plant is situated in an area with a complex urban structure (see Figure 4.11). The built-up area of the city of Geleen (34,000 inhabitants) and the municipalities of Beek (16,500) and Stein (26,500) are very close to the factories, refineries and other installations of DSM.

The case deals with environmental zoning around the DSM-plant. Although the problem has been defined or perceived in different ways over time and by different actors, the issue can be described as follows:
- how to define a zone with land use restrictions between the chemical plant of DSM and the areas already built-up or to be developed for mainly residential purposes, taking pollution into account;
- how to apply the zoning system to the parties involved in individual policy cases.

The three main polluting factors in relation to zoning are: noise, risk of accident and stench. Three forms of zoning can be seen in the DSM case: zoning concerning risk of accident, zoning concerning noise, and comprehensive zoning, which takes into account all three and even other factors. The definition of the problem implies that the main topic of concern is the establishment of a "transfer zone" between sources and receivers of pollution or risks. Measures such as at source abatement, technical measures at the receiving object, or removal of undesirable situations either in the plant-area or in the residential area are not the focus of the study, but are only considered in relation to the pollution related spatial problem. Environmental zoning is in fact a kind of strategic measure with far-reaching consequences: it can restrict several kinds of land use (especially housing) by the establishment of rules in terms of public law, which are binding on public bodies and citizens. The number of dwellings involved in the area is several hundred. Zoning systems often cause a redistribution of development opportunities. In such a situation the question of who pays for the resulting damage is an important one.

The problem contains different conflicts. Generally speaking, the main conflict is between broad economic interests and the provision of housing on the one hand, and the quality of the urban environment on the other. In this conflict, different parties take different stands. As it proceeded, the number of conflicts between the parties involved was influenced by the fact that an increasing number of environmental legal measures came into force, through which different parties acquired various new legal obligations. Fulfilling these legal obligations brought them into contact with other parties involved in co-ordinating and supervising procedures.

Methodology and data gathering

This contribution is based upon sources using the theoretical-analytical framework as a guideline:

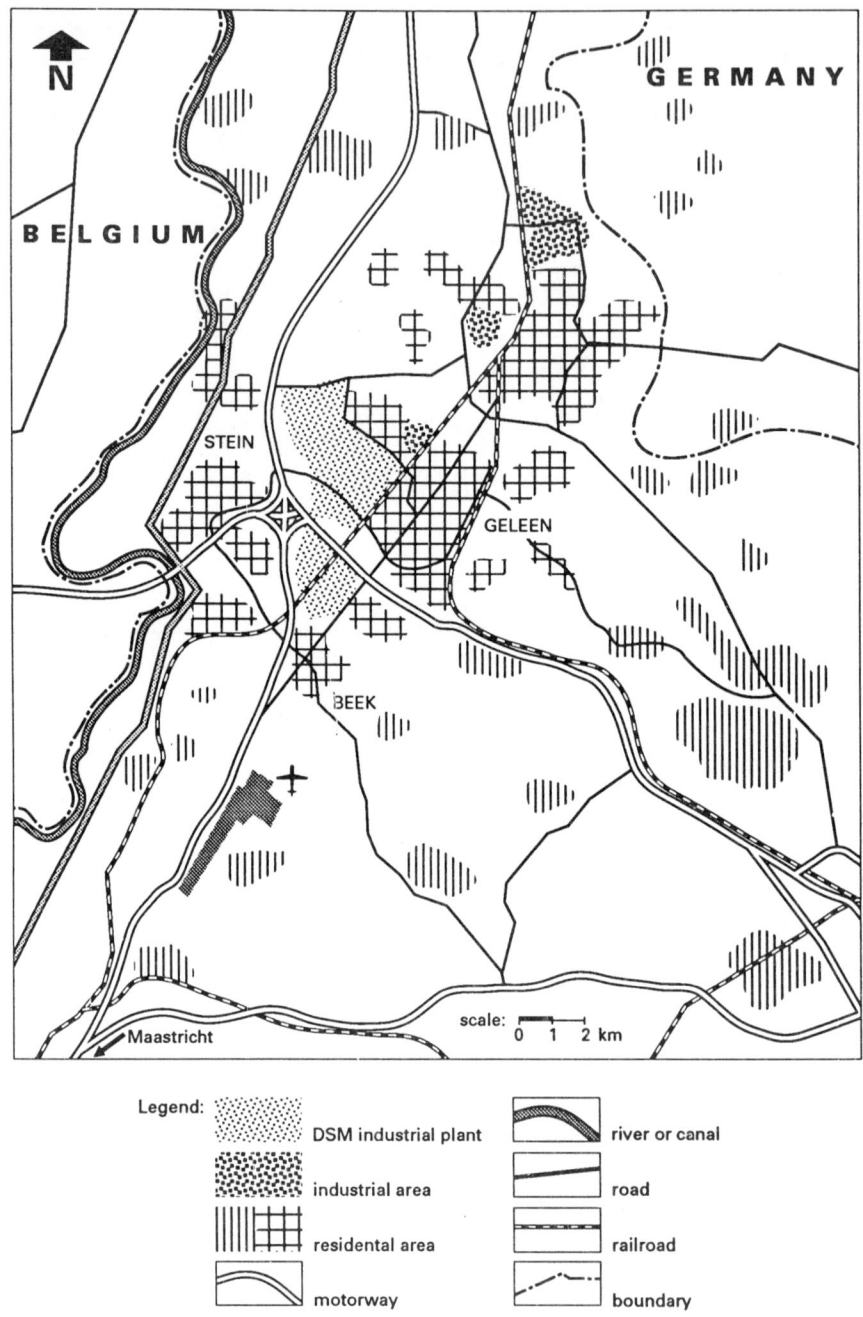

Figure 4.11 Geographical situation of the DSM plant

- published policy documents and reports and articles in professional journals;
- the files of the Province of Limburg;
- interviews with persons involved in the processes of decision-preparation and decision-making.

The information was compiled in a historic account as consistently as possible. Nevertheless, in a complex situation like this, no guarantee can be given that all the relevant matter has been found. The research concerning this case is reported separately (Gribling, 1989).

The actors and the formal network

In the field of environmental zoning, the formal powers are divided between the three main policy fields at stake: environmental policy, physical planning, and public housing.

The most important regulation applicable to the environmental zoning of the study area is the section "Zoning around industrial areas" of the Noise Abatement Act. This section came into force in September 1982. It is the Provincial Executive which should designate zones around industrial areas if such zones are situated on the territory of different municipalities. In such a zone the construction of new dwellings and other buildings is hardly possible. If the province is not able to designate such an area, the Minister of the Environment is obliged to take the final decision. This is a kind of supervisory power. Further, the province can draw up environmental plans and is responsible for issuing several environmental permits.

For zoning in relation to stench, risk of accident and for comprehensive environmental zoning, no legal arrangement is in force.

National government grants subsidies concerning environmental protection (soil cleansing, acoustic measures) to municipalities. For DSM, several permit procedures are applicable, such as environmental and construction permits. The Physical Planning Act (see chapter 3) provides the Provincial Government and the Municipal Government with legal powers concerning land use.

The zoning, which results from the application of the Noise Abatement Act, should be part of the municipal land use plan. The provincial government has the power to make environmental zoning systems part of the regional physical plan and in that way to develop explicit policies for such areas. Directives to municipalities can be based upon a regional physical plan (see chapter 3).

The Physical Planning Act provides both the regional physical plan and the municipal plan with exemptions and the possibility of elaborating global regulations. National government is involved in the application of the Physical Planning Act on the local and provincial level by means of advisory and appeal procedures in which the inspectorates of housing, physical planning and the environment take part. The Executive of the Province has to approve the municipal land use plans and exemptions. The regional physical plan is the basis for the approval.

With regard to public housing, substantial national allowances are yearly distributed to municipalities. The province plays an advisory role in this. Subsidized houses are mainly built under the auspices of housing corporations.

The resulting network of formal relations is summarized in Figure 4.12.

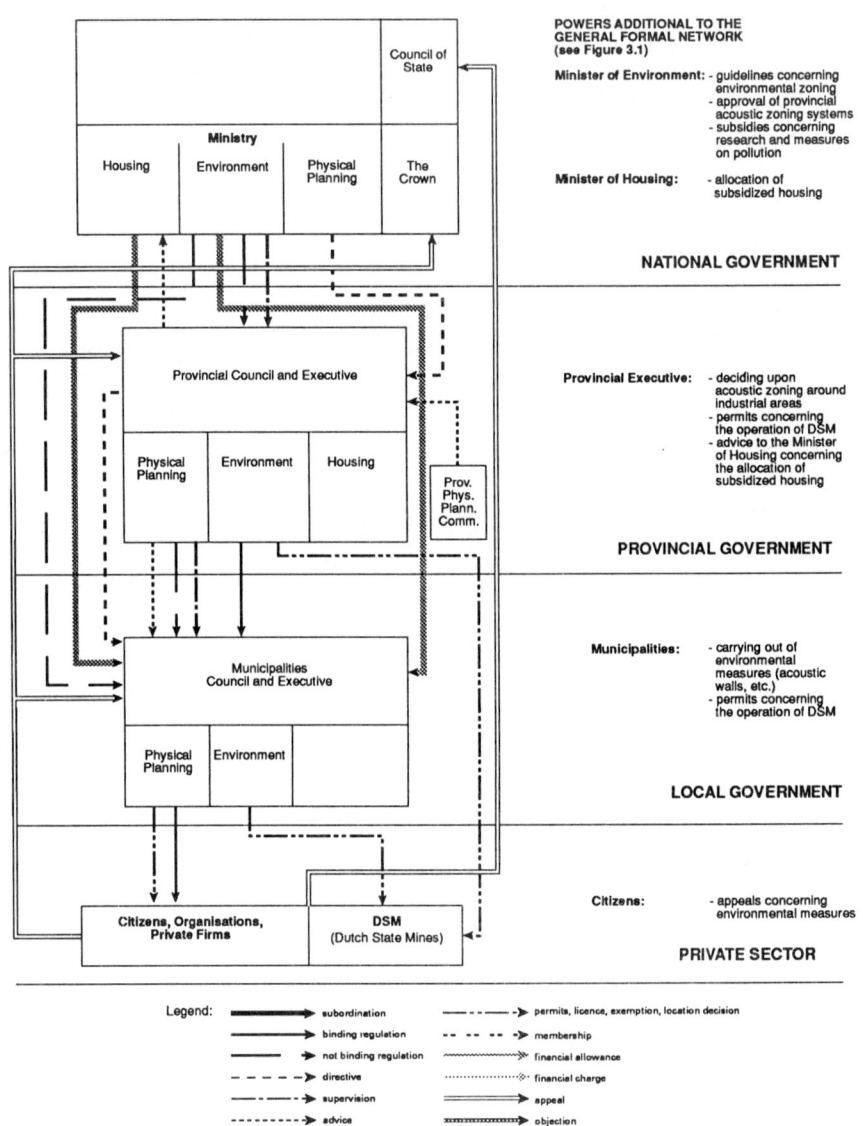

Figure 4.12 Formal network concerning environmental zoning around DSM, the Netherlands

As mentioned before, two legal arrangements are applicable in the case of DSM: the Noise Abatement Act and the Physical Planning Act. These Acts define the role of some of the actors. Additional roles are related to housing construction, risk zoning, and comprehensive environmental zoning policy. Putting together the various roles of actors the following picture emerges.

The Crown and the Administrative Disputes Department of the Council of State
The role of the Crown is passive; only in the case of objections and appeals against a land use plan does the Crown function as a body of justice. Other decisions of public bodies can be brought to the Administrative Disputes Department of the Council of State, which checks the decision against the general principles of public administration.

The Minister of Housing, Physical Planning and Environment (HPPE) The role of the minister is performed by three agencies:
- The Agency for Housing, which is responsible for the allocation of subsidised housing to municipalities and for the inspection of housing standards;
- The Agency for Physical Planning, which is responsible for the implementation of national policies by provinces and municipalities;
- The Agency for the Environment which is responsible for many tasks concerning the environment, for preparing legislation and provisional policies concerning environmental zoning, and for the allocation of environmental subsidies.

All three Agencies have a regional Inspectorate.

The Provincial Council The Provincial Council decides upon a regional physical plan and a plan for the environment.

The Provincial Executive The role of the Provincial Executive is multi-purpose:
- to approve municipal land use plans and exemptions;
- to decide upon zones around industrial areas in accordance with the Noise Abatement Act;
- to give advice upon the annual allocation of subsidised housing;
- to issue a directive to a municipality concerning a land use plan, when the municipality refuses to implement a regional physical plan.

The Provincial Physical Planning Committee This Committee (see chapter 3) advises the Provincial Executive concerning physical planning topics such as the regional physical plan and the approval of municipal land use plans. The three Inspectorates of the Ministry of Housing, Physical Planning and Environment are members of the Committee.

The Municipal Council The Municipal Council decides upon land use plans. In general the Municipal Council is the highest authority in the municipal administration, and the Executive is answerable to it.

The Municipal Executive The Municipal Executive issues building permits and construction permits and negotiates with Housing Corporations about the construction of subsidized housing. The Executive prepares land use plans and discusses these with representatives of the province, of national agencies, and other bodies.

The private sector including DSM Although DSM was a state owned company during the course of the case, in terms of public law the firm acts as a private firm. The private sector has the right to submit an application and to issue objections and appeals against land use plans and exemptions.

The representation of the formal arrangements and the actors (see Figure 4.12) shows many interdependencies between actors in this case.

For achieving their goals and interests, the parties involved are dependent as follows:

a. The Ministry of HPPE re: comprehensive zoning. Since there is no legislation with regard to comprehensive environmental zoning, the Ministry is dependent on the co-operation of the other parties involved. If other parties (the province and the municipalities) agree with a policy, it is highly probable that they will behave in accord with that in their strategic and operational policy-making. Consensus with the provincial government could be enough, and an explicit provincial policy in the form of a regional physical plan can be made compulsory for the municipalities by means of a directive or by the approval of land use plans and exemptions: also it can provide the conditions for issuing environmental permits.
b. The Ministry of HPPE re: noise zones. The establishment of a noise zone is in this case the legal obligation of the province, and because of this the ministry is dependent on the province. This also works in the opposite direction, the province being dependent on the Ministry if the province is not able or willing to establish such a zone in due time. It is then that the minister takes over the legal obligation. In all cases a provincial zoning policy needs the approval of the Crown (i.e. the Minister).
c. The municipalities re: urban extension and housing. The municipalities need the co-operation of the Provincial Executive for extensions to existing urban areas, in the form of the approval procedures of the Physical Planning Act. As 70-80% of newly built houses are subsidised in one way or the other by the Minister of HPPE, the municipalities (and housing corporations which are responsible for the construction and management of subsidised dwellings) are financially dependent on the Minister. In several ways Geleen is dependent on DSM e.g. for anti-pollution measures and the interior zoning of the DSM plant.
d. Environmental Interest Groups are completely dependent on all governmental bodies. The only formal power that they have is to lodge objections and appeals against the decisions of public bodies.
e. DSM is dependent on many of the parties involved for permits, land use plans, legislation and informal pressure.
f. The province is by and large a relatively independent party in the network, but has many links to other parties involved.

A historic account of events

As mentioned before, three kinds of pollution play a role in the area studied, viz. noise, bad smell and risk of accident. These different kinds separately and together provide the lines along which the historic account can be told. In part, these lines run parallel to the lines of regional physical planning, municipal physical planning and the assignment of housing subsidies to municipalities by national government.

Risk of accident The perception of the pollution involved as a physical/spatial problem became overt in 1975 when a major explosion at the DSM plant took the lives of 14 people and shattered windows in a large area around the plant. The awareness of the risk caused the necessity to be broadly felt of establishing a safety-zone of 500 m with building restrictions around the DSM plant.

The Regional Physical Plan South Limburg, endorsed by the Provincial Council in January 1977, provided such a zone as part of a provisional agreement which was to be elaborated by the Provincial Executive. This extension should be based upon a risk analysis for which the provincial government took the initiative. Due to the lack of adequate methods and the diminution of risk-awareness, the province stopped the risk-analysis in 1982.

In the meantime national government started to develop a general risk-analysis methodology. This activity was promoted by guidelines from the European Commission put forward after the Seveso-disaster. The method of risk-analysis became available in May 1984.

During the period 1977-1984, the province followed a provisional spatial policy concerning the safety-zone. Decisions about the land use of DSM, housing, and the granting of permits were based upon a flexible interpretation of the limits of the safety-zone.

In 1982 the municipality of Geleen published a report which referred to an emergency situation in the availability of the land for house building. This report asked for the province to take a flexible attitude to granting exemptions in land use plans in the safety-zone.

From 1983 the risk-factor was incorporated into comprehensive zoning (see the section concerned).

Noise abatement The main incentive for dealing with noise was the coming into operation of the regulation concerning noise zoning around industrial areas (September 1982). In this way, the province was legally obliged to decide upon such a zone by September 1986 at the latest.
The following events took place:
1. The Inspector of the Environment made a plea for other polluting factors to be taken into account when designing noise zoning systems (1982, 1983).
2. DSM made an inventory of the noise-situation which was completed in August 1983.
3. As a reaction to the signals of the municipalities that spatial problems were worsening, the province established a task-group (December 1982) which had to make an inventory of the spatial problems of the municipalities of Geleen and Stein in relation to the DSM plant. A provincial official took the chair and an official of Geleen was appointed secretary. The other municipalities participated.
4. Since the middle of 1983, the Inspectorate of the Environment became increasingly critical of the provisional policy concerning newly built areas by means of exemptions. The Inspectorates of Housing and Physical Planning later shared this opinion.
5. The province approached the Minister of Housing, Physical Planning and Environment so as to promote a more flexible attitude.
6. It contrast, the Minister decided to freeze housing subsidies until the

environmental situation had been investigated and the zoning procedure had been launched.
7. The province decided to establish a temporary policy for the area with regard to noise (Sept. 1983).
8. From 1983, the municipality of Geleen put increasing pressure on the province and the Ministry of HPPE. The municipality even pleaded for a change in some parts of the Noise Abatement Act.
9. In February 1984 the Provincial Executive had a meeting with the Minister of HPPE. As a result, one housing area could be built, on the basis of an exemption.
10. The establishment of a noise zone became part of the comprehensive zoning discussion (see the next section).

Environmental problems in general and comprehensive zoning Partly due to the activities of environmental pressure groups, the general environmental situation became a public and political issue. Both DSM and the provincial government were addressed in the early eighties. The Minister of HPPE was questioned by members of Parliament. He decided that a comprehensive plan for DSM should be developed, aimed at improving the environmental situation. The province was asked to develop an environmental policy against which the activities of DSM could be checked.
The following actions took place:

An agreement was made by the Minister, DSM and the provincial government in which was deployed a particular approach. This agreement was sent to Parliament (March 1984). As a result, DSM published "an Inventory of Environmental Problems and a first step to an environmental action programme" (EAP, Dec. 1984). Discussion with the ministry of HPPE and the provincial government led to a package of measures partly for the period 1990-1995. These measures were aimed at DSM but were insufficient to solve early enough environmental problems as perceived by the municipalities in the zone between DSM and the built up area.

The established task group (see the previous section, point 3) made a plea to incorporate physical planning elements in the before-mentioned environmental action programme (February 1984). In the meantime, the municipality of Geleen became dissatisfied with the proceedings of the task group because municipal interests were not adequately taken into account. The construction of houses around DSM had almost come to a stand-still.

The province decided to co-operate with the Ministry of HPPE in the project Comprehensive Environmental Zoning (CEZ), a physical planning strategy which was to be complementary to the EAP. The province took the initiative for activities aimed at such zoning (June 1984). A special task force (TF) was established consisting of a steering committee, a co-ordination committee, and two technical working groups, which were to supervise the necessary surveys and research. The steering committee held prime responsibility and was chaired by a member of the Provincial Executive. In the steering committee and working groups, the municipalities, provincial agencies, national agencies and DSM took part. The aim was to operationalise the 500 m. zone around DSM in relation to building activities and permit procedures, taking into account noise, risk of accident and stench. The risk analysis played an important role.

From the very start of the project CEZ, the municipality of Geleen took a critical position. The municipality feared a reduction of its autonomy by the activities of the provincial and the national government, and it supported the approach to an internal zoning of DSM. If that were done the construction of houses in the 500 m zone would be possible. A large part of the land in the zone was in the hands of the municipality. In the meantime the province had become irritated about the fact that housing subsidies from the ministry of HPPE had almost stopped (see the previous section, point 6). This caused some ambiguity in the attitude of the provincial government towards the project.

Partly to encourage the co-operation of Geleen, the decision was taken that an independent consulting firm (DHV) should carry out the physical planning research (Nov. 1984). An English consulting firm (Technica) was charged with the environmental research (Sept. 1984) lines of equal risk, other nuisances and the integration of all environmental research. Another firm (TEBODIN) investigated the noise situation.

DSM criticised the methodology of noise and risk calculation, which caused delay.

In December 1984, Geleen published a report critical of the project CEZ. The main criticisms were:
- parts of the initial agreement were not taken seriously by other parties;
- one working group failed to keep to the technical task and discussed policies.

The criticism were considered by the task-force and caused further delay.

It appeared to be impossible to take into acount the concept of "stench" and some other kinds of nuisance. These factors were therefore abandoned. The discussion then focussed upon the risk-criterion. Should it be the $10^{(-6)}$ or $10^{(-8)}$ line (i.e. the probability that industrial activity causes a fatal accident in 1 mln or 100 mln years respectively) (see Figure 4.13). The $10^{(-6)}$ line was acceptable to all parties, as this line almost corresponded with the outer limit of the DSM-plant.

The Provincial Executive did not take a clear stand on this question during the period mid 1985 - beginning of 1986. The officials of the national government supported the $10^{(-8)}$ line, based upon a non-binding national policy document 'Indicative mid-term Environmental Programme' (1985). In this situation, officials in a working group developed a "relative objective weighing technique" which could be applied by the authorities to individual cases in the zone between the $10^{(-8)}$ and the $10^{(-6)}$ lines (Nov. 1985).

At the end of 1985 and the beginning of 1986, the municipality of Geleen was active both inside and outside the working group in order to promote its point of view. The Mayor of Geleen, newly appointed in 1985, appeared to play a prominent role. Geleen emphasised the lack of status of the risk-lines and the impossibility of applying the $10^{(-8)}$ line in other comparable situations (Rotterdam-Rijnmond). In addition to the arguments mentioned before, Geleen argued that comprehensive zoning would cause stigmatising and consequently a deterioration of the neighbourhood Lindenheuvel. In this way the consequences of pollution caused by DSM and of the policies promoted by higher authorities would be shifted on to that neighbourhood. On several occasions, Geleen criticized the loss of autonomy of the municipalities if higher authorities were to establish environmental zoning systems and to apply them rigorously.

Increasingly, discussions took place outside the task-force: Municipal Executive with the Provincial Executive, Municipal Executive with the Minister of HPPE and so on. The three national inspectorates of

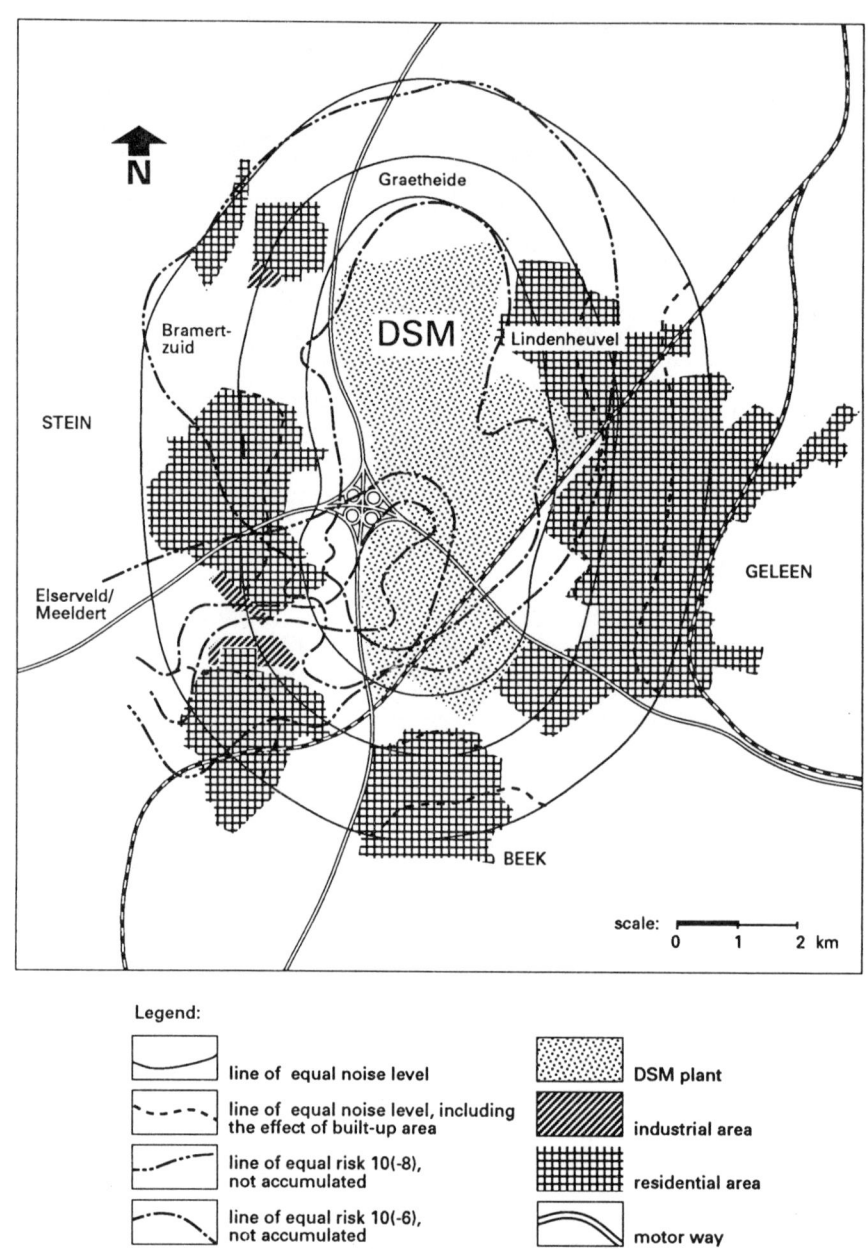

Figure 4.13 Lines of equal environmental influence around DSM

Environment, Housing and Physical Planning graduately disappeared from the picture. The official point of view presented in the province moved in the direction of the opinion of Geleen (Spring 1986).

In the politically rather confused situation of Autumn 1986 the Provincial Physical Planning Agency took the initiative of bringing out a report aimed at maintaining the momentum "Zoning around DSM, Spatial Research and Policy Proposals" (Dec. 1986).

In October 1986 a local Environmental Interest Group (Greatheide committee) addressed the Environmental Committee of Parliament, claiming that the Provincial Executive had stopped the project CEZ. This reaction was late and one of the causes was that there had been a lack of public information about the progress of the project CEZ.

By June 1986, the legally fixed date before which the noise zoning should have been designated by the provincial government had expired (see the previous section).

The information about the lack of progress of the project CEZ induced the minister of HPPE to take action. He asked the Provincial Executive officially to inform him about progress, because the house building activities of Geleen were being delayed (Nov. 1986).

The national Agency for the Environment reacted by establishing a Special Task Force (STF) with mainly officials of the Agency as participants. Officials of the province and of DSM took part. Municipalities were not represented. The task force should report within 10 weeks. This intervention could partly be based upon the fact that the power to designate a noise zone had by then been transferred to national government. The STF used the report mentioned earlier of the Provincial Agency as a base for its activities. These activities were directed at zoning in relation to noise and risks of accident and the reduction of pollution. The physical planning aspects other than zoning were left aside.

The Report of the STF appeared in February 1987. The $10(-8)$ risk line was proposed in the report. The provincial representative was withdrawn shortly before the end. DSM disagreed with some parts of the report.

The appearance of the report launched many activities:
- Geleen organised a hearing for the residents of the neighbourhood Lindenheuvel which is partly situated between the $10(-6)$ and the $10(-8)$ line;
- the Provincial Executive and the Municipal Executive of Geleen had several meetings;
- the Provincial Executive now adopted officially the view of Geleen (April 1987): zoning on the basis of stench and risk of accident needed a legal basis and further research, and the other municipalities involved (Stein and Beek) shared this view.

In April and May 1987, the draft decision concerning the noise zone was laid down for public inspection, together with the Report of the STF and the viewpoint of the Provincial Executive and the Municipal Executives.

Objections were lodged by DSM, the municipality of Geleen, residents of Geleen (4500 objections) and of Stein (less than five). The municipality of Geleen had encouraged the citizens to object. A hearing in Geleen was attended by 500 people, whereas in Stein fewer than 10 people appeared. DSM stipulated that if the $10(-8)$ criterion was adopted and was applied to the plant itself, a large part of the plant would be closed. The Provincial Federation for the Environment (an interest group) supported the proposals of the STF.

In July 1987 the municipality of Stein changed its mind and supported the comprehensive approach of the STF. In the meantime Stein succeeded in getting support from national agencies concerning building activities, research costs with regard to the environmental measures to be taken by the municipality, and the costs of the measures such as the construction of walls or barriers around built-up areas.

In August 1987, Geleen invited the Environmental Committee of Parliament to visit Geleen. This visit to a large extent influenced the opinion of members of parliament. The majority shared the view of Geleen concerning the unacceptibility of the 10(-8) line.

In September a rather unusual technical briefing of the Environmental Committee of Parliament took place.

In the period September-November 1987, many informal talks took place in which political parties, DSM, agencies of the ministry, the province and Geleen took part.

These events caused a change in the position of the Minister of HPPE:
- the 10(-8) line became only indicative and was no longer to be included in the regional physical plan; the three inspectorates should take the 10(-8) line into account when they advised about housing plans and environmental permits;
- an agreement with DSM was made to reduce the stench and to carry out preliminary research; zoning in relation to stench was abandoned for the time being, but could be introduced again if the measures proved to be ineffective.

The provincial government did not agree with the indicative 10(-8) line and gave its views to the Minister.

After consulting the Parliamentary Committee, the Minister took his final decision according to the revised position outlined above (Dec. 1987), see Figure 4.13.

The final decision was the starting point of the elaboration of the regional physical plan of South-Limburg of February 1987 for the area in question. The endorsement of this plan was expected to take place within 3 years. One point worthy of attention is the provision of alternative housing areas north of Geleen. The scope of such an elaboration was limited because the final decision of the Minister had already determined so much.

The building stop for the area was cancelled. In the transitional period, a temporary committee (chaired by a provincial executive and with the national inspectorates, municipial executives and officials of the province as members) [1] was charged with appraising the housing plans of Geleen and Beek. For Stein a provisional policy was no longer necessary. Experience so far shows that the noise factor is the main criterion; the stench and the risk are only marginal factors. The decisions concerning some locations which have been very disputable were postponed.

Analysis

The historical account can now be analyzed in the light of the theoretical-analytical framework.

One preliminary remark has to be made. When taking the environmental zoning around DSM as the focus for the study, many policy processes were touched on to a greater or lesser extent. A very complex decision-system was involved in which it is impossible to trace all the links to the process of environmental zoning in the period 1977-1989. Were we to have done that, the number of actors and relevant events would have multiplied.

Although the definition of the problem seemed to be rather objective, the historical account showed a striking difference in the perception of the problem between the parties involved. For some parties the perception changed over time. In terms of goals/means, the two extreme positions were:

a. the National Agency of the Environment (including the Inspectorate) which promoted an experiment concerning comprehensive environmental zoning based upon an extensive survey of the environmental situation. This was to lead to a consensus about an unambiguous set of policy rules and standards to be applied by all parties involved when taking decisions in this area. The approach was based upon the conviction that the environmental situation in the area required that a variety of measures be taken.
b. the Municipality of Geleen gave different weight to the environmental issue. Solving the housing problem and urban development in general were more important. Environmental zoning should be restricted to the legal obligations and the zoning, once established, should be applied as flexibly as possible.

The position held by other parties was somewhere in between.

Strategies The different parties developed various strategies over time. The main ones were as follows.

The Ministry of HPPE (Minister, Agency for the Environment and Inspectorate) pursued from the late seventies a policy aimed at zoning, later at comprehensive zoning. The Ministry attempted to get the co-operation of the province concerning the Environmental Action Programme and the project Comprehensive Environmental Zoning. The initial success of this approach was that the province took the initiative and primary responsibility for this project. The province established a task force aimed at gaining the co-operation of all the parties involved. This initiative was in line with the earlier one to establish a task group to make an inventory of spatial problems. By means of such task groups, new lines of communication between the parties were added to those already in existence. For reasons of impartiality firms of consultants were asked to carry out the research.

The municipality of Geleen used participation in task groups as a means to influence other parties. This strategy was in addition to those such as preparing reports, publicity, addressing the Provincial Executive, speaking to members of Parliament and officials of several ministries and so on. Geleen even tried to change the rules of the game as laid down in the Noise Abatement Act.

In this situation the province was placed between two fires. One was represented by the national officials who took several advisory positions with regard to the Provincial Executive and who had several powerful instruments, housing subsidies for instance, the other was the very active municipality of Geleen. The province published a report about zoning around DSM.

The task-forces were not very successful, which caused delay and much discussion and which allowed communication to carry on outside them with little substantial result. The main success of Geleen was that, in part due to the pressure it applied, it kept the province from an agreement with the Minister of HPPE concerning comprehensive zoning. As a result, the province escaped the situation of being forced to use the powerful policy instrument of the regional physical plan, and the approval procedures of land use plans or directive procedures for comprehensive zoning purposes.

The municipality of Stein chose the approach of direct negotiation with the national agencies of the environment and housing, so as to safeguard building sites and to obtain money for research and pollution abatement measures.

In the meantime DSM followed a mixed approach, involving co-operation and attempts to exert influence by participating in several task groups, carrying out research, criticizing the methods of calculating environmental effects, being a partner in carrying out EAP, and lodging objections and opposition on several occasions.

In the Autumn of 1986, the minister was forced to change the strategy of co-operation between national officials and provincial and local authorities. He took more responsibility than the Noise Abatement Act gave him and launched a Special Task Force with the limited involvement of other public bodies. The withdrawal of the representative of the province from the Special Task Force heralded the definite stand of the Provincial Executive against comprehensive zoning. The Minister became isolated, with no formal instruments other than the Noise Abatement Act. In theory, a National Physical Planning Key Decision (see chapter 3) could have helped, but no such decision had been taken legally upon which he could have based a directive.

One concluding remark has to be made. Political parties played a role behind the scenes and this caused dependencies. The position and the prospects of elected members of public bodies are dependent on their political party. This fact influenced the positions held and strategies developed by a number of the actors.

Shifts The main shifts were caused by the municipality of Geleen. This resulted in the move of the Provincial Executive from co-operation to non co-operation concerning noise zoning and environmental zoning. The attitude of Geleen and the province of Limburg forced the Minister to abandon his ambitions concerning comprehensive environmental zoning. As mentioned before, the municipality of Stein changed its view concerning comprehensive zoning and became the only public body to share the initial view of the Minister.

Powers not used The main power not used was that of the Provincial Council to decide upon a regional physical plan. The Provincial Executive did not want to use its power to designate a noise zone around DSM, which committed the Minister of the Environment to doing so. The municipality of Geleen failed to do what the neighbouring municipality of Stein did, which was to attempt to get compensation in return for co-operation. National Government did not use its representative on the Board of Directors of DSM to promote environmental goals nor did it use the possibility of Parliament endorsing a National Physical Planning Key Decision. The latter would have provided the Minister with the legal power to issue a directive both to the province and to the municipality.

Large scale urban expansion

Poland: a new urban extension in relation to aspects of political-administrative management, the case of Stara Milosna

Introduction: the issue

It has been estimated for the whole of Poland that a total of 3.8 million apartments (including 3,0 million in urban areas) would have to be built by the end of the nineties to meet the needs of families now on the housing list. In the province of Warsaw, a total of 500,000 families are on waiting lists for apartments. In this situation it is understandable that great pressure is being exerted by the housing construction organisations to obtain new locations, preferably in large "empty" areas which are the easiest for construction, although these are areas previously reserved under physical plans for farming or forestry. The deteriorating condition of the natural environment in Poland makes it necessary rigorously to protect the environment from destruction and to restore nature to its original condition. Housing and the protection of the environment are both of paramount importance to Poland.

Both these issues (housing construction, specifically the location of new projects, and environmental protection) are linked and regulated by planning which aims to "...comprehensively model the spatial organization of the country, its regions and urban and rural areas so as to secure the conditions for an improved quality of life and restore the natural balance..., while taking into account and reconciling general and local interests". And further: "...any activity influencing land management and use can only be taken when it is compatible with the provisions of physical plans" (The Act on Spatial Planning). "The decisions of state administrative bodies cannot violate the requirements of environmental protection nor the provisions of physical plans concerning environmental protection. An administrative decision contradictory to this rule is invalid" (The Act on Environmental Protection).

The subject matter of this case study is a conflict created by a housing project (proposed and implemented) in an ecologically sensitive area, which was not designated in spatial plans for intensive building development.

There are two conflicting parties. The first is the future residents of the housing area under construction in Stara Milosna near Warsaw, represented mainly by their spokesmen, the second the residents of two areas in Warsaw which border on Stara Milosna, viz. Anin and Miedzylesie as represented by their Residents' Committees.

Stara Milosna forms a part of Wesola, a small town (several thousand residents) one kilometer away from the administrative border of the city of Warsaw. Anin and Miedzylesie, two areas of Warsaw inhabited by several thousand residents, are typical residential quarters. Both Stara Milosna and Anin and Miedzylesie are separated by a 3 km belt of forest which surrounds the eastern part of Warsaw. As the conflict developed, a resolution was made to turn those forests into the Mazovian Landscape Park, that is into an area under special protection (see Figure 4.14).

There were two actions which led to the conflict:
- assigning the area for housing construction followed by the start of construction work in an area not meant for intensive building development under the Regional Development Plans (in the immediate

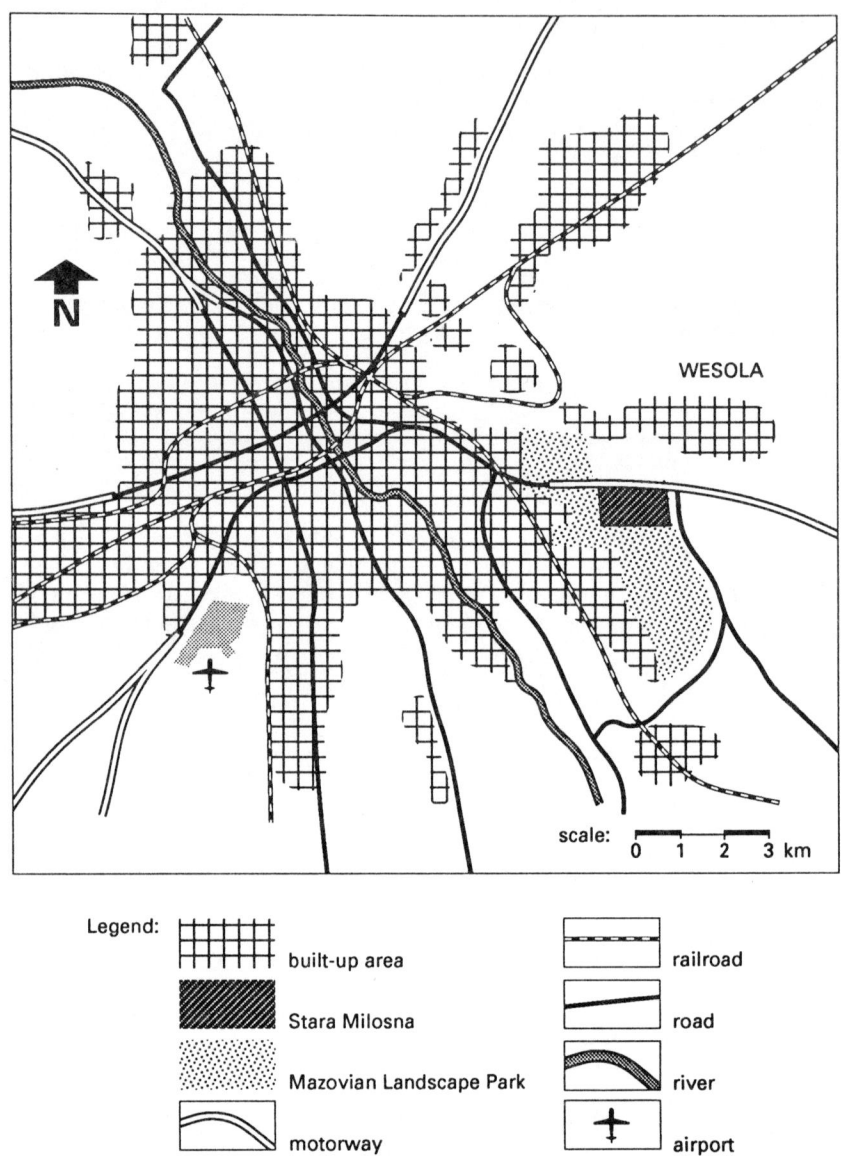

Figure 4.14 Warsaw, Stara Milosna and Mazovian Landscape Park

vicinity of the Mazovian Landscape Park).
- proceeding with the construction of the housing quarter without having solved the problem of the technical infrastructure (heating, water intake, sewage disposal).

The effects of this location decision and the unfavorable infrastructural solutions threatened the immediate neighbours of the housing quarter under construction, i.e. the residents of Anin and Miedzylesie. Therefore, they initiated actions aimed to counteract these threats.

The actors and the formal network

In this case study many actors are involved. The main reason for the complexity is the involvement of provincial authorities as well as municipal and district authorities and their respective People's Councils. Moreover, the area in which the conflict developed is part of two provincial (voivod) territories viz. Warsaw and Siedlce. The main powers have already been described in chapter 3. They are summarised briefly. The main power is in the hands of the voivodship authorities namely:
- the designation of a new residential area in the regional development plan,
- the location decision concerning an application of a developer, which should be in accordance with the regional development plan.

Moreover the designation of a landscape park is the responsibility of the voivodship administration. The municipal and district administrations involved have the power to take more detailed land use and location decisions. They act under the supervision of the voivodship authorities. On the other hand, they have the right to give opinions on matters which are for the discretion of the voivodship authorities.

Both voivodship and municipal or district administrations have to follow the guidelines and norms put forward by bodies of the Central State (e.g. the Minister of Spatial Economy and the Minister of Environment) and they are subordinate to them.

In this case the problem to provide the new infrastructure is important: a sewage treatment plant, water supply, a heat-generation plant. The provision of such facilities, also their environmental and sanitary effects have to be considered by state and provincial (voivod) bodies in relation to standards and norms.

The formal network of powers along four lines (physical/spatial planning, environmental policy, health, and technical infrastructure) can be seen in Figure 4.15.

Data collection

The analysis presented below is based on the following sources of information:
- material collected in the institutions concerned with the problem,
- documents and interviews regarding the causes of the conflict,
- reports and articles in professional journals.

Out of necessity, this report leaves out many events and details and is largely restricted to indicating the mechanisms responsible for the origins and progress of the conflict. It should also be realized that in a complex situation such as this, not all relevant matter has been - or could be - found.

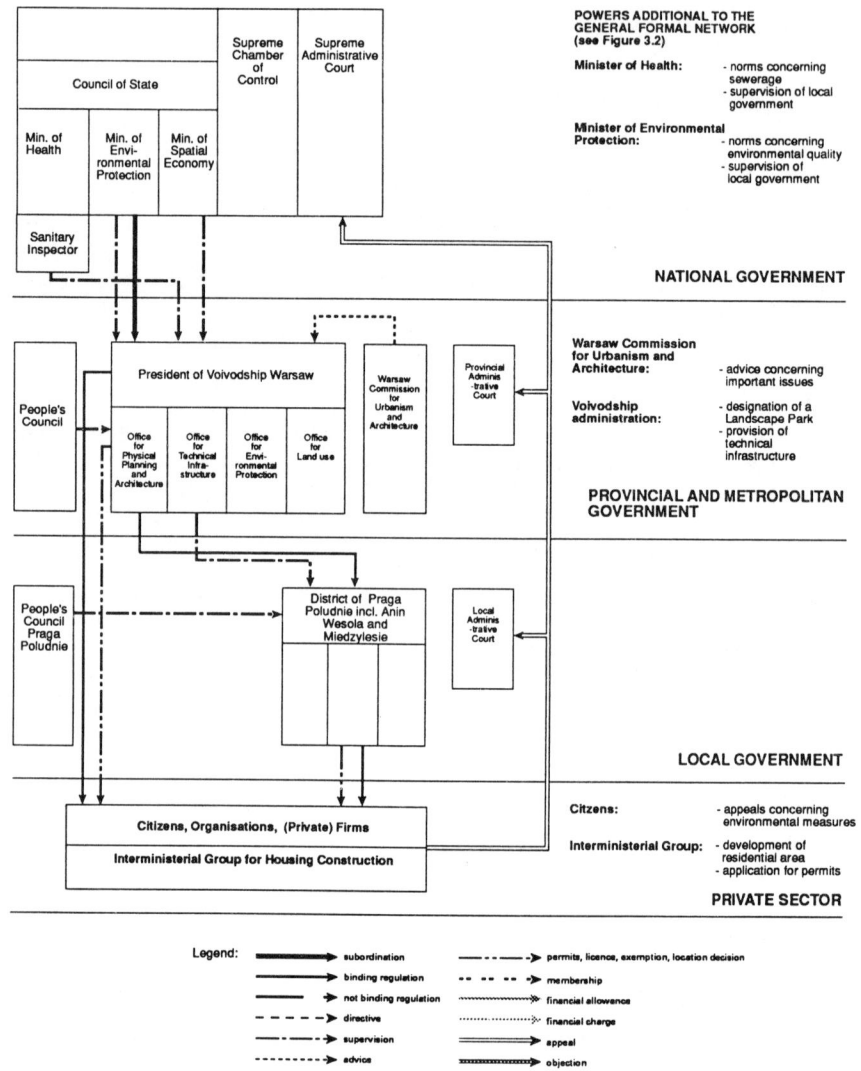

Figure 4.15 Formal network concerning urban expansion Poland, Stara Milosna

The course of the conflict

The year 1987 can be considered to be the beginning of the conflict, but irritations and controversies predate this and were related to the procedure for determining and approving the housing location. The events can be traced back to 1983 when the Inter-ministerial Youth Team for Housing Construction was appointed at the Ministry of Labour, Wages and Social Affairs on the initiative of the Polish Socialist Youth Unions, an organization operating within the Ministry. The Team planned to construct a housing quarter of several hundred single-family houses. The initiative was joined by seven other ministries and later by the representatives of other institutions (their number amounting to about one hundred). The Team changed its name to the Inter-ministerial Employees' Group for the Construction of Detached Houses and Flats (in short "Interministerial Group"). It is worthwhile mentioning that a limited liability company of an identical name started to operate in 1985. The initiative was supported by a deputy prime minister, eight ministers, and secretaries of factory committees of the Polish United Workers' Party.

In February 1984 the Inter-ministerial Group which was the developer was offered two locations by the Chief Architect of Warsaw, who was acting on behalf of the President of Warsaw. The Group chose Stara Milosna. Neither location proposed by the Chief Architect was included in the binding Regional Development Plan for Warsaw Province, but came as a result of research carried out by the Chief Architect of Warsaw. In Warsaw Province, no area was available for the concentrated development of detached houses. The physical plan for Warsaw Province which was valid at that time, and is still valid today, was approved in 1978. It had been prepared and accepted in a totally different socio-economic climate than the one in the period when the construction was implemented. The new trend of developing concentrated detached houses for several thousand residents was not reflected in regional plans. For several thousand residents, the selection of the area in Stara Milosna for a housing quarter meant that the provisions of the physical plan for Warsaw Province were infringed with regard to:
- management of natural resources,
- settlement structure,
- technical infrastructure.

In October 1984, the Municipal People's Council in Wesola passed a resolution on changing the local physical plan (the master plan) for Wesola. The adoption of the resolution was limited by the following:
- the Municipal People's Council in Wesola, while passing the resolution, was not authorized to decide about changes in the local physical plan; it acquired such powers only after 1 January 1985;
- the resolution was not published according to the formal procedure, and, therefore it was not binding;
- the resolution significantly changed the general concept for management of the given area and was therefore in conflict with the Regional Development Plan for Warsaw Province. This meant that it should not have been passed without a prior change to the entire general concept of management in that area.

In return for allowing the construction of a housing quarter within its area, the town of Wesola was to receive the right to allocate 20 per cent of the appartments to be built, also facilities making it possible to connect the entire town to the sewage and water supply systems, as well as providing sewage disposal, water and heat for the current residents of the Stara Milosna quarter.

In November 1984, the Advisory Team on Locations reacted positively to the location of the housing quarter in Stara Milosna, despite reservations voiced by individual participants.

On 11 January 1985 the Chief Architect of Warsaw gave a decision on the location, fixing the place and the conditions for the construction of the housing quarter in Stara Milosna. This decision, however, was invalid because:
- it was based on a building regulation which had been abrogated at the time the decision was made;
- it was in clear conflict with the legally binding physical plan for that area. The decision on the location given by the Chief Architect of Warsaw provided a basis for proposing an "adjustment" plan for the residential quarter in Stara Milosna. The "adjustment" plan was given approval by the People's Council in Wesola in May 1985 and was examined by the Warsaw Development Physical Planning Office. The Warsaw Development Planning Office made a number of critical comments and pointed to the invalidity of the resolution of October 1984.

In April 1986, the Municipal People's Council in Wesola passed a resolution on approving a detailed physical plan for Stara Milosna. This resolution, however, was also invalid because it was a consequence of the invalid resolution passed in 1984.

On 27 February 1987 a resolution of the Municipal People's Council in Wesola approved changes to the local physical plan of the town of Wesola. The fact that work had started in 1986 on elaborating the local physical plan and that in 1987 these additions were under consideration was obvious to those involved. Why should a new plan be made if work based on previously agreed principles, allegedly correct, was underway?

The absorption of changes into the local physical plan and the detailed physical plan approved by the resolutions of the People's Council in Wesola provided the basis for the Municipal Office of the Capital City of Warsaw to approve an action plan for the housing quarter on 28 January, 1987. This action plan ignores several vital matters such as the delimitation of the border line of the Mazovian Landscape Park and the forest area under legal protection.

In 1985, the owners of the areas where the Stara Milosna housing quarter was being constructed received letters sent in envelopes stamped by the Ministry of Labour, Wages and Social Affairs. The letters, briefly quoting the decision on fixing the site and the conditions for developing the project, presented a "final offer" for the sale of the building plots. If an owner failed to present his position, the Interministerial Group would take moves aimed at expropriation. The expropriation price would be lower and paid in instalments. The "final offers" proved to be effective as 90 per cent of the required land was purchased. The resolution of the People's Council in Wesola obliged the Interministerial Group to adhere to the principle that the land be acquired voluntarily. Besides, instituting expropriation proceedings was illegal in two senses because:
- housing in Stara Milosna was not developed in the form of concentrated detached houses, something which could be the only basis for expropriation at the time;

- the Inter-ministerial Group did not operate as a co-operative but as a limited liability company.

Efforts to turn the forests which separate Stara Milosna from Anin and Miedzylesie into the Mazovian Landscape Park have been in progress for many years. A Landscape Park is an area under special protection, and the land incorporated into the Park should be used in the original way (farming and forestry) and no plans provided for a change in this use. It took two and half years for the Warsaw People's Council to pass the resolution, starting from the time the Council was provided with full documentation of the plan for the park. The resolution was passed in 1987 i.e. two years after it had been adopted by the Provincial People's Council in Siedlce (the Mazovian Landscape Park is situated in two provinces, and the decision on its establishment was to be taken simultaneously by both Councils). Also, some hasty corrections introduced into the draft resolution distorted the original concept of the authors. The draft resolution included a provision banning housing construction, the construction of economic objects, and summer houses in the area covered by the Mazovian Landscape Park. However, the corrections introduced into the draft allow, for instance, "housing developments provided for by physical plans of town and rural areas" to be built within the Park. This sanctioned the Inter-ministerial Group constructing the housing quarter and the decision on the location made by the administration.

The conflict actually manifested itself on May 1987 when the residents of Anin and Miedzylesie learned about the planned housing quarter. Their protest and anxiety were caused by the proposed technical infrastructure for the housing quarter under construction, namely:
- the fact that sewage from the sewage treatment plant in the housing quarter was to be carried by a drainage ditch which flows for a dozen kilometers among residential quarters (Anin and Miedzylesie) and falls into the Vistula river just above the water intake for the part of Warsaw situated on the right hand bank of the river;
- the location of the housing quarter, and especially of the sewage treatment plant, was to be in the border zone of the planned Mazovian Landscape Park;
- the expansion of the heat-generating plant in Miedzylesie (mainly to meet the housing quarter's demand) from 60 Gcal/h to 140 Gcal/h. This would result in an increased emission of dust and chemicals and the necessity to store more ash. This problem has, as yet, not been satisfactory solved;
- the supply of water from deep-water intakes would effect groundwater within a radius of 2-4 kilometers i.e. in the area of the Mazovian Landscape Park.

The first letters of protest were sent by the residents of Anin on 11 May, 1987 to:
- the Department of Complaints and Motions of the Central Committee of Polish United Workers' Party,
- the President of Warsaw,
- the Head of the Praga Poludnie District of Warsaw,
- the Department of Health and Environment of the Municipal Office in Warsaw,
- the Health Ministry.

Two weeks later the residents of Anin and Miedzylesie sent a joint letter to the Chief Sanitary Inspector in Poland. The writers protested against the technical infrastructure and demanded that an inspection be carried out and the construction of the sewage treatment plant be stopped until the legality of the decision was established and responsibility taken for it. They also stressed that there had been no consultations with local residents' committees on the planned housing quarter. Next, the residents sent letters to offices, institutions and organizations at the municipal and central level, re-iterating their arguments and pointing to the criticisms already made.

In July 1987 the Residents' Committee in Miedzylesie appealed to the Seym (Parliament) and sent copies to:
- the Society of Polish Town Planners,
- the Society of Polish Architects,
- the Polish Ecological Club,
- the League for the Preservation of Nature,
- the Warsaw Development Planning Office,
- the President of the Polish Academy of Sciences,
- the Warsaw Economic Planning Commission,
- the Provincial Nature Conservator,
- the Department of Health and Environment of the Municipal Office of the Capital City of Warsaw,
- the Residents' Committee in Anin,
- the opposition, i.e. the Interministerial Employees' Group for the Construction of Detached Houses and Blocks of Flats.

The residents received three significant, though negative, replies to these letters:
- The State Provincial Sanitary Inspectorate stated that both the design of the housing quarter and the design of the sewage treatment plant had been approved by the National Chief Sanitary Inspector and his consent had been dependent on so many requirements being fulfilled that the "fears of residents' committees should be considered groundless";
- The State Inspectorate of Environmental Protection wrote about a field inspection carried out on 18-22 May, 1987. The inspection saw no hazards, everything was in order with earlier arrangements and the Inspectorate saw no chance of taking action aimed at changing the location;
- The Ministry of Health replied (July 1987) that the "location of the sewage treatment plant and the planned disposal of water posed no threats to the environment".

In October 1987, the Interministerial Group published a paper on the progress of work at the housing quarter in Stara Milosna, refuting the charges in two ways:
- the work on the investment project was being carried out according to the law as it has been approved by appropriate offices;
- the existing land use in Stara Milosna posed a threat to the environment. Both in the forest area and in its border zone there had been an avalanche development of recreational buildings, greenhouses and workshops. The construction of the housing quarter put an end to this unplanned process and the introduction of the general sewage system would improve the environment.

The residents' protests were supported by two ecological organizations. In a letter sent to the Minister of Spatial Economy in July 1987, the Polish Ecological Club demanded that the design should be approved by the Chief Commission for Urbanism and Architecture. This Commission is an independent body grouping Poland's most outstanding specialists and its quality should guarantee the objective character of its assessment. Acting under the binding regulations, the Minister proposed in his letter to the President of Warsaw of August 1987 that he "consider the possibility of examining the issue by the Warsaw Commission for Urbanism and Architecture", and if the Warsaw Commission failed to solve the problems, to send the case to the Chief Commission for Urbanism and Architecture, which, in turn, required a motion from the President of Warsaw.

In June 1988 the League for the Preservation of Nature sent a complaint to the Government Committee for Law-Abidingness, concerning the infringement and irregularities connected with the design and construction of the housing quarter in Stara Milosna. It asked further for a halt to the construction work in the area until the matter had been examined and a decision taken by the Chief Commission for Urbanism and Architecture. It also appealed for a decision to be made by an appropriate state administrative body to reduce the scale of the housing quarter, to control the activities carried out by the developer and to make those who had permitted this situation responsible for it.

The Patriotic Movement for National Rebirth (PRON) also took a stand on the housing quarter in Stara Milosna on two occasions. In July 1987 PRON produced a report which gave a negative assessment to the project in Stara Milosna and its implementation. It also demanded that the issue be taken before the Chief Commission for Urbanism and Architecture. In May 1988 it re-iterated its proposal to take the issue before the Commission.

The Child's Health Centre Memorial Hospital had taken a particular position on the issue in December 1987, but now considered it necessary "to counteract the degradation of the environment with the full strength of the law". Similarly, a letter from Institutions located in Anin and Miedzylesie addressed to the Residents' Committee in Miedzylesie (April 1988) rejected the proposed technical infrastructure.

The residents' complaints which were repeated many times in mid-1987 proved ineffective.

In February 1988, a meeting of Anin residents approved the activities pursued by the Residents' Committee until then and obliged it to institute legal proceedings in connection with the breach of the law by the developers and by those licensing the investment project.

The first trial of the complaint from both Residents' Committees was held before the District Court of the Praga Poludnie District of Warsaw on 12 May 1988. Another two trials produced no solution. The information on the course of the fourth trial is based on press reports. On 7 September 1988, at a closed-door session, the District Court ruled that the Residents' Committees could not appear as a party before the court because they lacked the "legal capacity" of being an organization of the working people of towns and the countryside". The claim was therefore dismissed.

The position taken by the general Prosecutor's Office has also become public from the press reports. Having examined the complaints of the Residents' Committees, the Prosecutor's Office found that no breaches of the law had taken place that could justify the questioning of the implementation of the investment project. On the other hand, irregularities were found in the administrative proceedings carried out by the Department of Spatial Planning, Architecture, Town-Planning and Building Supervision of the Municipal Office of the City of Warsaw, and formal moves were taken against those responsible for these offences.

Representatives of the Warsaw authorities (President, Chairman of the People's Council, First Secretary of Warsaw PZPR Committee) argued in a letter sent to the President of the Council of State, General Jaruzelski, that the decisions taken with regard to the housing quarter in Stara Milosna were justified and correct. They also stressed that concerned and critical comments were being analyzed and then acted upon.

In the first half of 1988, the residents of Anin and Miedzylesie wrote to the District People's Council of the Praga Poludnie District of Warsaw with a vote of no confidence in the Chairman of the District People's Council, saying that he had failed to defend the interests of local residents in a dispute against a community from outside. In reply, the District People's Council appointed a three-man Team to examine the issue in Stara Milosna. The Team found it necessary to have another experts' report on the degree of degradation of the natural environment. The Chairman, however, presented a different opinion at a Council session. While recalling that the decision to build the housing quarter was made at the level of the Warsaw authorities several years ago, he proposed that the Council accept the Team's position and pass on the whole issue to "competent authorities at a higher level" without taking a formal, unequivocal position on it. The motion was formally approved.

The session of the Consultative Council (an advisory body to the President of the Council of State) scheduled for July 1988 was to deal with environmental protection. Among the members of the Consultative Council were also representatives of the national opposition. The residents of Anin and Miedzylesie managed to get their problem to General Jaruzelski, thanks to their informal contacts. This time it was effective and the Council of State commissioned the entire matter to go the Supreme Chamber of Control (NIK).

In July and August 1988, the Board inspected the progress of work on the housing quarter and produced a 23-page report which said that "the findings of the inspection proved that the concern of the local population was justified". It also confirmed specific charges previously made by residents, namely that:
- the location of the housing quarter would be unfavorable to several residential quarters in Warsaw;
- the area of the housing quarter infiltrated the Mazovian Landscape Park and took up a belt meant for a future 400 kv-power line;
- the chosen type of treatment plant had not been tested in practice;
- the heat generating plant lacked the required protection zone, while the emission of dust to the atmosphere after the expansion would increase elevenfold and that of gas by three-and-a half to eleven times.

In the opinion of the Supreme Chamber of Control it was necessary to:
- stop the construction of the sewage treatment plant and re-examine the method of sewage disposal from the housing quarter;
- consider the expansion of the heat-generating plant;
- unequivocally determine the number of residents in the housing quarter and the density of houses (documents speak of 12,000 to 23,000);
- ban further development in a zone where development is prohibited or remove the prohibitions.

In the board's opinion, meeting these conditions would require expert advice and reports. These should be financed from the provincial budget as the necessity to prepare them was the consequence of hasty administrative decisions. Since several central offices had been involved in the issue, this advice and reports should be prepared by units outside those institutions, preferably from outside Warsaw province, but with the help of specialists and information from the Warsaw Development Planning Office.

The report prepared by the Supreme Chamber of Control reached the body that had commissioned it, the Council of State, and on 24 October 1988 the Board ordered the Municipal Office of the city of Warsaw to put the its recommendations into effect. The decision to stop the construction of the sewage treatment plant and to stop development in the protected zones was given by the Head of the town of Wesola, who quoted a written order by the Chief Architect of Warsaw. The work was to be stopped on the day the instruction was given, i.e. on 28 October 1988.

The decision, however, was deemed invalid by the Interministerial Group, because the Head of the town of Wesola failed to make it immediately enforceable. So, the developer continued the construction work, intensifying it primarily at the sewage treatment plant and in the immediate vicinity of the forest. After the Interministerial Group had appealed against the decision on 5 November 1988, the decision to stop the construction was cancelled by the Chief Architect of Warsaw on 20 December 1988.

The Residents' Committees from Anin and Miedzylesie decided to stage a protest march in October 1988. Having made the necessary applications, they were given administrative consent to stage a demonstration. It turned out, however, that on the same day, the developer, i.e. the Inter-ministerial Group, had staged a picnic nearby!

An inspection carried out by the Chief Board of Supervision prompted the reaction from the Warsaw authorities. At a session of the Warsaw People's Council held in October, the Vice-President of Warsaw promised that "the municipal authorities would appoint an independent team of experts to examine the characteristics of the solutions from the point of view of environmental protection. If sufficient grounds were found, action would be taken with a view to cancelling the decision mentioned". In November 1988, Warsaw's municipal authorities appointed an independent commission, which was changed with finding out within a month whether or nor the construction of the housing quarter in Stara Milosna threatened Warsaw.

A session of the Warsaw's People's Council, held in December 1988, passed another resolution to appoint a Special Commission of the Council to deal with the issue in Stara Milosna day by day. Previously on 11 January 1989 the First Secretary of Warsaw's PZPR Committee stated that additional experts' reports which had been made (only one of them has been made public so far) had not confirmed the doubts. After temporary setbacks to the progress of the project, the housing quarter would certainly come into existence.

The conflict caused by the housing quarter in Stara Milosna was finally subjected to critical assessment and discussion during the "round table" talks in March 1989. It was decided that the Chief Commission for Urbanism and Architecture would be appointed to examine the case.

One of the weekly papers (April 1989) published an open letter from the residents of ten Warsaw residential quarters located in the Praga Poludnie district of Warsaw concerning ecological threats. The residents demanded:
- strict and immediate execution of all post-inspection measures recommended by the Supreme Chamber of Control.
- the immediate appointment of the Chief Commission for Urbanism and

Architecture.
- punishment for all those responsible for ecological vandalism and disregard for the law.

The Chief Commission for Urbanism and Architecture had not yet met, though fragmentary advisory work was being carried out with a view to providing grounds for the Chief Commission to adopt a formal position.

Up to 15 September 1989, the Special Commission appointed by the People's Council of Warsaw had visited the construction site of the housing quarter several times, making a number of comments, frequently contradictory.

On 29 June 1989, the People's Council of Warsaw voted to stop the construction of the housing quarter in Stara Milosna in part, while the entire report by the Special Commission was to be the subject of the Council's further work. The work on the construction site continues nevertheless, as does the conflict.

Analysis

The problem of the housing quarter in Stara Milosna has been discussed in about one hundred publications and also a dozen radio and television broadcasts. The initial information spoke in superlatives about the construction of the housing quarter, giving no mention of the conflict with local residents. The Residents' Committees tried to inform the public about the conflict but the reaction of different papers to their position was minimal. It has transpired since that many journalists in Warsaw were waiting for their houses to be built in Stara Milosna. Nevertheless, the conflict was coming into the open. There proved to be a few independent journalists and liberal papers, and some reports appeared later. The first report on the negative side of the construction of the housing quarter was published in late 1987, others quickly followed. In reply, the other party, without entering into a discussion on the substance, formulated an uncompromising definition of the conflict and the parties in the following way: this is a social conflict between the millionaires from Anin and homeless workers from Warsaw factories, also a political conflict - the protesters are underground, anti-socialist and radical forces supported by Radio Free Europe and the CIA. The tone of press reports changed after the inspection made by the Supreme Chamber of Control and the decision on stopping the construction work. No more mention was made of anti-socialist forces and enemies of homeless workers. Economic arguments were gaining more ground and some 10 billion zlotys had been invested in the project. Many people had put their life savings into it. The conflict was now defined as a clash between Poland's two priorities, housing and ecology.

This account of the dispute shows, however, that saying that it is a local conflict typical of a clash between housing construction and the requirements of environmental protection is oversimplifying. The public protest is not aimed against housing but against:
- faulty town-planning decisions,
- a disregard for ecological criteria,
- the arrogance and incompetence of the administration.

The actors in this conflict can be grouped into two, the opponents - residents, Social Ecological Movement, Patriotic Movement for National Rebirth (PRON) - and the remaining actors:

- the Inter-ministerial Employees' Group for the Construction of Detached Houses and Blocks of Flats,
- Warsaw's municipal authorities,
- the institutions and offices dealing with environmental protection and health care,
- the remaining legislative, executive and advisory bodies.

These groups used different sources of power and chose different strategies. In their official statements, the residents, represented by the Residents' Committees, protested against ecological threats and later, also against disregard for the law by the state administration. It cannot be ruled out, however (and this opinion is based on private talks with the residents) that, in the initial stage of the conflict, public action was prompted by private interest such as people's fear of losing the "exclusive" character of the quarters of Anin and Miedzylesie (which would undoubtedly lower the price of land and apartments in the area) fear of the social composition of the new housing quarter, and, finally, prejudice against and envy of some social groups such as the Party, the Ministry of National Defence, and Ministry of the Interior expected to reside in the housing quarter. However, considering private motives to be too weak and personal, the residents put forward a number of ecological arguments which, though initially treated in an instrumental way, later turned into genuinely held opinions. The activities taken by the residents of Anin and Miedzylesie were supported by various other groups. These were, first, institutions which did not directly register as a protesting party, but supported the actions of local Residents' Committees (expressed either in oral or written form). These were; the Church, the local party organization, and some of the few establishments operating in that area. Secondly, independent private people had links with the residents privately and informally. These people enjoyed high esteem within their professional groups, being academics or journalists. Thanks to them, the conflict in Stara Milosna and the residents' arguments could become the subject of consideration for such bodies as the Constitutive Council or the "round table", both bodies virtually inaccessible to those without personal "connections" to them.

Strategies The residents pursued their actions by employing the following actions:
- petitions/complaints,
- demonstrations,
- press campaigns,
- legal proceedings,
- mobilizing influential people and organizations to support their view.

The pressure the residents exerted steadily mounted. However, these actions failed to produce legal negotiations in which the conflicting interests could be expressed.

In this conflict, the ecological movement is represented by two independent organizations of a national character, both coming out in favour of environmental protection on behalf of and for the benefit of interests broader than local ones. Under the Law on Environmental Protection, the state administration is obliged to support social organizations in pursuing their statutory activities. In fact, this support is dependent on the "good will" of the state administration. The efforts made by ecological organizations can make their point if they can influence public opinion. In this case, ecological organizations tried to do this, but in Poland, with the mass media at that time being in the hands of the political and administrative authority, the role played by ecological organizations was very limited.

The Patriotic Movement for National Rebirth (PRON) is a semi-social body organized and controlled by the Party and, theoretically, it has some areas of power. PRON intervened by producing a report favouring the stance of the residents, but PRON's position was restricted and ignored. The Warsaw authorities explained in a letter to General Jaruzelski that PRON had joined in the conflict under the influence of people opposing the project.

The Inter-ministerial Group was the originator of the conflict. It was also the main target of charges of unlawful activities. However, the Group operated on the basis of administrative decisions and provisions made by appropriate state bodies. But it did not restrict itself to following official roads in gaining the necessary documents, meeting the dates and stages of the project's development etc. This strategy of "fait accompli" - action first, documentation next - is not totally alien to the Polish reality. Sometimes it is taken on the basis of promises (sometimes oral sometimes telephoned) to give an appropriate decision, sometimes it gets "news" of the possession of the required document which still remains in the appropriate office. The force deployed by the Interministerial Group is impressive. Its power was based upon being strongly embedded in the governmental system and can be illustrated as follows.

An inter-ministerial agreement supported the initiative and declared its assistance as soon as the Inter-ministerial Group was established. By assistance it meant not only financial but also technical, assistence also which, directly or indirectly, could overcome many obstacles. The Group succeeded in taking advantage of the priority given to housing construction in the national economy and of the political willingness to create the best possible "exemplary" conditions to support and encourage "social initiatives".

Municipal authorities appeared to be co-operating with the Inter-ministerial Group in land use planning, location decisions, infrastructure and so on. What is understood here to be municipal authorities are, the People's Council (elected body) and an executive body, the Voivod President along with the office subordinate to him (a body appointed by the state administration). During the conflict, the People's Council showed a willingness to examine the objections of the residents by establishing a team of experts. This action ended in deadlock.

Institutions and agencies for environmental protection and health care and involved in this conflict are state units under the appropriate ministers or municipal authorities. In this conflict it was precisely these units that broke loose from a homogenous front of people and institutions indiscriminately supporting the construction of the housing quarter and that gave the decision to stop the development. These decision were based on laws and basic regulations laid down by the state. But, apart from the basic regulations concerning norms, standards etc., there are also special regulations providing for the possibility of deviating from these norms in certain cases. It is not unusual for a case to be deemed "special". The state (i.e. political and administrative authorities) which made the law, is also allowed to deviate from it.

Of the remaining institutions and organizations involved in the conflict, clear positions in favour of the residents were taken by:
- the Consultative Council,

- the Ombudsman,
- the Round Table,
- the Supreme Chamber of Control.

The first three of these included members of the opposition. These bodies did not follow explicit strategies during the conflict, but played a role as mediating bodies.

Shifts The main shift to be seen is in the increasing support for the residents's views given by many private organizations and public bodies. Individual parties did not change their positions radically. The municipal/voivod authorities changed from being explicit supporters of the Interministerial Group towards holding a more critical position, but without substantial results.

Powers unused The pattern in this case was the following. Powers used in favour of the Inter-ministerial Group, mainly the powers of the Warsaw authorities, were not used to meet the demands of the residents of the area and their increasing circle of supporters.

The present conflict shows the position of individual actors and the relationships existing between them, it also indicates the opportunities which they have to express their interests and ways of solving conflicting situations.

Conflicting interests are normal, and behaviour in situations should be regulated by the law. Polish law does not meet such requirements as no specific ways of solving conflict are given and no guarantees of legal protection have been created to make it possible for those involved to claim their rights. Under these circumstances, the alignment of the individual actors and their ensuing behaviour are of basic significance in the settling of conflicts.

The Netherlands: the case of the expansion of Duiven-Westervoort

Introduction; the issue

The municipalities Duiven and Westervoort are in the metropolitan area of Arnhem. The city of Arnhem, which is the provincial capital of the Province of Gelderland, has about 130,000 inhabitants. The whole city region (see Figure 4.16) has about 300,000 inhabitants at the present day. The city and the region have experienced steady growth since World War II.

In the beginning of the sixties, the city boundaries were considered too tight for the long-term housing needs and new locations had to be found. The villages of Duiven and Westervoort, each with fewer than 5,000 inhabitants were designated by the provincial and national governments as areas of future expansion in the Arnhem region.

The designation of "growth cities" is an important part of the physical planning policy of national government, which was initiated in the sixties and further developed and implemented in the seventies and eighties. Starting in the sixties, this project exposed a conflict of interests between the three governmental layers involved and also between the two municipalities as well. Conflicts arose about:
- the merger of two municipalities into one,

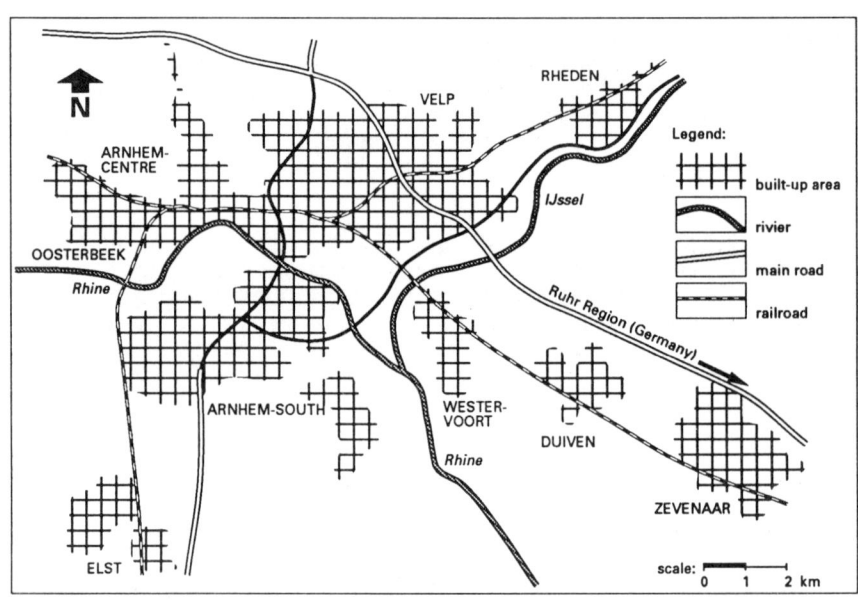

Figure 4.16 The Arnhem region

- the initial target of 70,000 inhabitants for the growth town,
- the allocation of costs and damages which arose from changes in policy over time.

In the seventies, the idea of 70,000 inhabitants was abandoned as was the idea of making one municipality. Many negotiations and financial deals took place between all the parties involved, including the Provincial Electricity Company. The latter company had interests in the development as the provider of community heating systems.

The process ended with an "agreement" in which Duiven and Westervoort were to remain separate communities, officially recognised as an expansion area and striving for separate building sites, aiming at a total population of 40,000.

Data gathering and methodology

Using the theoretical-analytical framework as a guideline this analysis is based upon several sources:
- published policy documents
- files from the province of Gelderland
- interviews with people involved in the various processes which took place

The research is reported separately (Winkelhuyzen, 1989).

The actors and the formal network

In the process of plan-making and plan-implementation for concentrated urban growth beyond the boundaries of city centre, Arnhem in this case, many formal relationships are involved. All three governmental layers, national, provincial and municipal, take part in the decision-making processes concerning the overspill from the central city into a growth town such as Duiven-Westervoort.

The national government in the form of the Minister for Housing and Physical Planning, is involved primarily because of the request of the municipalities and the province to designate Duiven-Westervoort as an officially recognised growth town. Official recognition implies subsidies from central government for infrastructure, services and other extraordinary costs as well as priority from the ministry of housing in the allocation of subsidized housing. The province has an advisory role in this allocation process. It has to be stressed however, that, although the designation and implementation of growth towns has been adopted as a corner stone of national physical planning policy for a long period, its formal status has been relatively poor until 1976. In that year growth towns became part of the Physical Planning Key Decision concerning Urban Development discussed in Parliament. Only since 1986 have Physical Planning Key Decisions had a legal status in the Physical Planning Act (see chapter 3).

The province is involved as the authority responsible for regional physical plans which give guidelines for municipal planning. Local plans should comply with the provincial regional plan endorsed by the Provincial Council. The province is also the body which supervises municipal land use plans (see chapter 3).

The municipalities are responsible for land use and structure plans and the implementation of large parts of them. This implies the buying and selling of land and properties and the providing of infrastructure and services. In this case the contract with the Provincial Electricity Company (PGEM), the supplier of central heating for the entire growth town, should be mentioned. The PGEM is an independent yet semi-governmental company. The chairman of the Board and two other board members are members of the provincial executive and the provincial council respectively. The municipalities are furthermore obliged to get provincial approval for all major financial transactions. This means that in this case the province also became involved in the planning and implementation of the growth town including the issue of central heating. As mentioned before, the merger of two municipalities was part of the process. The merger of municipalities needs a special Act prepared by the Minister of the Internal Affairs and endorsed by Parliament. The provincial government has the right to make proposals in this respect.

In addition to the formal part of the network, some important informal parts can be added. The first concerns the role of the municipality of Arnhem. This city was involved in the process of regional plan-making. Arnhem used all its informal influence to convince the Province that the regional physical plan should shift housing provision from Duiven-Westervoort towards Arnhem. The same was done by Arnhem in the Inter-governmental Steering Committee. In order to ease the process of plan-making and plan-implementation, the province took the initiative of creating an official advisory body, the Inter-governmental Steering Committee mentioned above. All important matters and conflicts were discussed in this committee, and it made proposals to the three governmental layers participating.

The population was not directly involved in this case. No public participation took place.

This case can consequently be described in short as an "inter-governmental conflict-solving process".

In Figure 4.17 the main formal relationships are illustrated. For more general information about the formal governmental aspects see chapter 3.

Description of the policy-making process

The whole process leading to the construction of houses, facilities, roads, etc., in Duiven-Westervoort as a growth town near to the donor-city Arnhem, can be divided into three distinct periods. These periods mark the crucial changes of policies for the new town of Duiven-Westervoort.

The period 1965-1974   The first period started in the mid sixties with the concept of a new-city of Duivoort, the combination of Duiven and Westervoort into one new town having 70,000 residents, in accordance with the Second Report on Physical Planning produced by the national government. This period ended with the suspension of the Steering Committee in 1974 as a consequence of a provincial document called "Problems Connected with a too ambitious Development in Duiven-Westervoort". A large (70,000) Duivoort seemed to be unrealistic. The main characteristic of this period was the influence of strategic physical plans made by the national and provincial governments on local policy-making. Special attention was paid to the activities of the Steering Committee, an advisory and consulting body on which local, regional, and national governments were represented, that had the preparation and realisation of

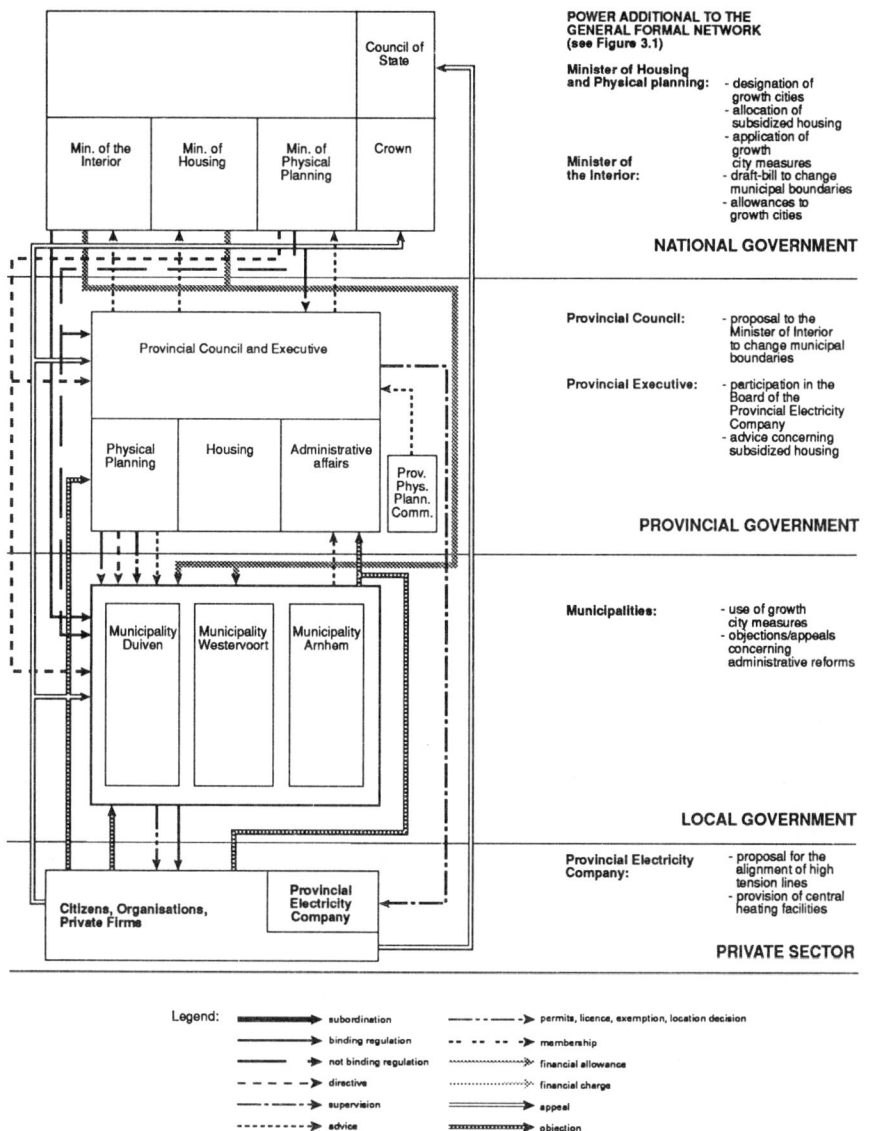

Figure 4.17 Formal network concerning urban expansion / growth cities, the Netherlands

Duivoort as its aim. We will see that a few years later this aim did not coincide with the insights that had been gained during the preparation of a new regional physical plan. The most important events in this period are the following.

1966: Second Report on Physical Planning published by the national government, in which the overflow of population from the main city regions was given ample attention.

1967: Duiven and Westervoort started with the preparation of a structure plan to be finished in 1971. Aim - one large city of 70,000 inhabitants (see Figure 4.18).

1970: The founding of a common physical planning agency for both local authorities. The Province discussed the option of a merger of Duiven and Westervoort.

1971-1972: Duiven and Westervoort very strongly opposed the idea of one local authority. The Provincial Physical Planning Committee (PPC) advised Gedeputeerde Staten (The Executive Council) to create a consultative body to improve co-operation between the three governmental layers. A working group of provincial experts warned of the consequences for traffic if Duivoort were to grow to a population to a 70,000.

1973: In January an inter-governmental steering committee was founded as a consultative body. It was chaired by the member of the provincial executive responsible for physical planning The National Physical Planning Agency, the city of Arnhem, the municipalities of Duiven and Westervoort, and the Provincial Physical Planning Agency were represented on the committee. The tasks of the committee were:
a. to implement a plan for Duivoort with 70,000 inhabitants;
b. to enhance the co-ordination and co-operation between all partners;
c. to solve the problems of fast growth (traffic was specially mentioned);
d. to monitor during the course of the process whether the 70,000 Duivoort concept should be reconsidered. This task could be seen as a sort of "time bomb" in the Committee.

1973-1974: Discussions took place in the Steering Committee about a new provincial report which was under preparation. Forecasts for the period after 1985 seemed to be inconsistant with plans for the 1985-2000 period. The Provincial Planning Agency pushed for a reconsideration of the 70,000 concept. A modern process-planning approach did not seem to co-incide with fixed growth east of Arnhem. The old regional physical plan, including Duivoort, was considered to be unrealistic. The member of the provincial executive responsible for physical planning played the crucial role on the political level. His strong position in the Provincial Council and the provincial committee as well as his influence at national level, made his role and that of the Province in the whole process dominant. He pleaded for a reconsideration of the Duivoort concept within the framework of the provinces regional physical plan-making process. The Steering Committee was temporarily dismissed until the regional physical plan was opened for public inspection. By doing this, that member of the provincial executive took all power into his own hands, since he was responsible for the preparation of the regional physical plan.

The period 1975-1981 The second period started with the presentation of the first official document by the provincial council in the process of making a new regional physical plan for the entire Arnhem-Nijmegen region (Mid

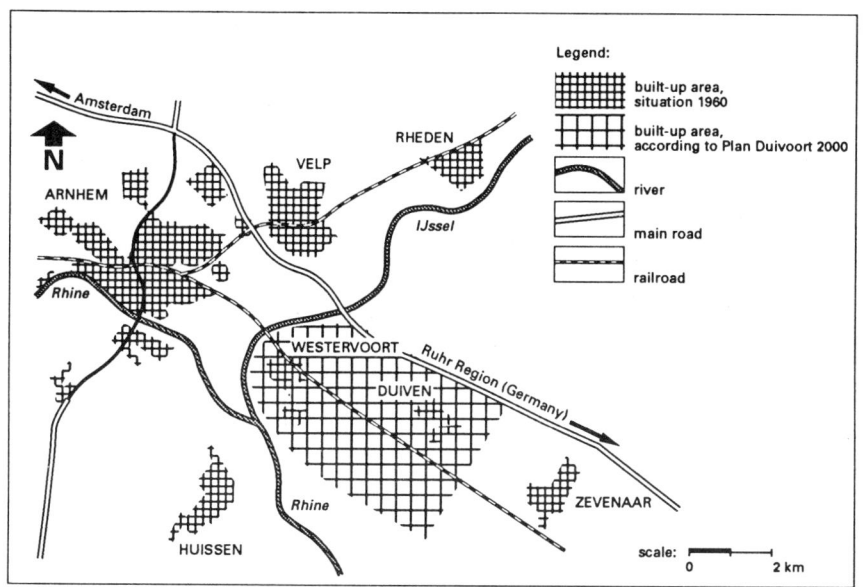

Figure 4.18 Duiven-Westervoort expansion, plan Duivoort

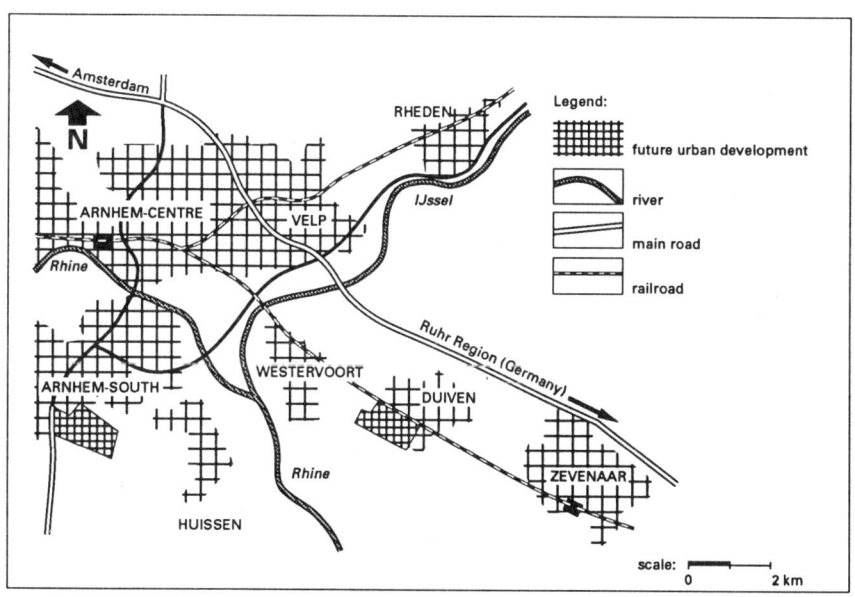

Figure 4.19 Structure plan Duiven-Westervoort 2000

Gelderland). This period ended with an official document signed by the Minister of Housing and Planning in 1981. This document stated that Duiven and Westervoort were to be appointed as an official growth-city of 40-50,000 inhabitants, that they should not integrate but remain separate. The following events took place.

1975: A provincial report on "alternative models for Mid Gelderland" was published in which five alternatives were presented. The positions of the various tiers of government proved to be very different. National government preferred a concentration in Arnhem-South and Duiven-Westervoort. Westervoort wanted a small development and ruled out the creation of one local authority of Duivoort. Duiven appeared to be in favour of growth in accordance with earlier plans. The Province envisaged an expansion in Duiven and Westervoort after 1985: the area between Arnhem and Nijmegen should be a green area, with no further urban development.

1976: The national government Report on Urbanisation offered the possibility for Westervoort to be designated a national growth town. National funds become available, once this status is made official. The Steering Committee Duiven-Westervoort was re-established after much pressure by the provincial executive for physical planning.

1977-1978: The regional physical plan by the provincial executive council was laid open to public inspection:
a. Duiven and Westervoort should develop separately with the emphasis on the period after 1985;
b. the concept of Duivoort, with population of 70,000 was no longer acceptable;
c. the administrative re-organisation in Duiven-Westervoort was necessary.

The reactions of Duiven and Westervoort were that there should be no administrative re-organisation and compensation should be paid for the investment already made for the 70,000 plan. The Provincial Council did not consider that the arguments put forward by the executive council for the reorganisation were decisive. Duiven and Westervoort should remain independent.

1978: The Steering Committee started discussing financial compensation for Duiven and Westervoort. The procedure to obtain official "growth town" status was started. The minister of physical planning also did not wish to change the two separate municipalities into one.

1980-1981: The joint physical planning agency of Duivoort was dissolved and the separate towns themselves became responsible for the necessary rapid growth. Crucial to the result was that a former minister of housing and physical planning, Schut, was hired by the Province to be the project co-ordinator in order to get the finance demanded by the two towns. Two different financial instruments were applied after much negotiating with the ministers of physical planning and internal affairs. Also the appointment of a new mayor in Westervoort, a former town-clerk from the growth town of Nieuwegein near Utrecht, contributed to positive decision-making, since previously Westervoort itself had never been too eager to grow greatly.

The period 1982-1988 1982-1988 was a period in which, under pressure from the city of Arnhem and with the support of physical planning experts from all over the Netherlands who wished to enhance and strengthen the position of cities (the compact city movement), a further reduction of the Duiven-Westervoort target took place. This period ended with a new agreement between the partners plus the city of Arnhem. Westervoort, and Duiven especially, were confronted again with changing policies due to changes in economic, demographic, and housing demand (see Figure 4.19).

The following events are relevant.

1982-1983: The structure-plan of Arnhem proposed that more houses should be built in Arnhem-South. An alderman from Duiven pointed out that if this happened, housing in Westervoort and Duiven would no longer be necessary and this would not be in accordance with the recent agreement. Demographic forecasts and a study of the options to increase the density of housing per hectare led to three possibilities:
- to reduce Arnhem Rijkerswoerd - costs: Dfl. 70 - 80 mln,
- to reduce Duiven-South - costs: Dfl. 60 - 75 mln,
- to reduce Westervoort - costs: Dfl. 12 - 16 mln.

Westervoort, which was already implementing the plan, saw no opportunity to cut down its target. Duiven wanted to continue and had no desire to solve Arnhem's problems. Arnhem stated that it as the donor-city should be given priority. National government representatives in the province held that growth town status should not be endangered, and those who wanted it should pay for it. The province, at that moment, did not see enough reasons for breaking the agreement and moreover they wanted to have more long term information about demographic and housing developments.

In the early eighties, government planning goals changed. The concept of compact-cities (concentrations within cities themselves) replaced that of concentrated suburbanisation. This new doctrine became very important in the Duiven-Westervoort case.

1983: An analysis of housing demands showed a remarkable over-capacity in all the schemes put forward so far. The provincial physical planning agency argued that it was not possible to absorb the over-capacity by unrealistically high figures for net immigration. National government representatives asked the province to take time to decide and to negotiate with all three towns. The province was convinced that priority should be given to Arnhem. The province was no longer interested in the Steering Committee in which Arnhem did not participate. The national Report on Urbanisation was published, which stated that the growth town status should continue, but that discussions were necessary about future housing problems in the region.

1984: Who was to break the agreement and who was to pay compensation to Duiven and Westervoort? That was the central issue to be negotiated at this stage. The new minister of housing and physical planning made clear that the policies of national government were not changing, claiming that it was therefore not possible to involve national government nor could it be pressed to pay. Westervoort was not much interested because, by then, it had almost completed its share. Duiven was of course very reluctant to embark on anything that might endanger its position. A new working group made new proposals after revised calculations had been made. The role of the provincial physical planning agency was very important initially, but later the role of the financial departments of all partners became the most important one. It was pointed out to national government that its policy had indeed changed, by cutting down migration from the Randstad area to the provinces of Brabant and Gelderland. The province stated that it had not caused the change in the situation and had no money to help Arnhem, therefore Arnhem and national government had to pay. Finally, the minister proposed the "final offer": Arnhem and Gelderland were to pay and national government was to preserve the growth town status. This proposition was not accepted by either the province or Arnhem. A new initiative from Arnhem in which it was to pay a lump-sum to Duiven was accepted by Duiven and by the province. Discussions went on for months between the partners, the minister, and the Parliamentary Committee on Housing and Physical Planning. A formal request from the parliament led to a proposal that had to be discussed and approved within three months. In fact it took much longer and the minister was again obliged to join the negotiating table.

1985-1987: Arnhem's position was getting stronger. The province and national urbanization policy were helpful. Westervoort was indifferent, Duiven could not cope with the situation and put itself into the position of being a trouble-maker. It claimed too much compensation (16 mln guilders instead of 11 mln) and did not agree to losing its growth town status. A new provincial executive entered the scene. Finally, the Queen's Commissioner for the province was asked to find an agreement based upon the Arnhem/Province proposal, which was now primarily a financial one, based on housing forecasts. In the end it proved that one of the major problems was the claim of the Provincial Electricity Company (PGEM), which had to give up its plans for the Duiven central heating system. The solutions of the Queen's Commissioner were not agreed to by Duiven. The minister then threatened to return to his "final offer" of the previous year unless all regional partners agreed on the slightly amended proposal of the Queen's Commissioner. After a whole series of negotiations between the minister, the province, cities, towns and PGEM, a solution was reached.

In December 1985 a proposal in the national government Physical Planning Key Decision on Urbanisation was accepted by all parties. The claim of the PGEM would be compensated by giving them comparable options in Arnhem-city, as calculations had shown. Duiven lost its growth-status by lowering housing targets but got substantial compensation from Arnhem and the ministry (total ca. Dfl. 5 mln). Westervoort got Dfl. 3.5 mln and was very satisfied with the result. Negotiations with the PGEM lasted until 1987, ending with the agreement by Arnhem and the province that the PGEM was to be given permission to develop a new heating system but, as it was controlled by the Province via the Board, it was not allowed to sue the local authorities to compensate for its losses.

1987: The agreement was signed and sealed with a celebration dinner.

1988: The Steering Committee Duiven-Westervoort was disbanded. The only money paid by the province during all the negotiations was the cost of a boat-trip with all the former members of the Steering Committee!

Analysis

Like the historical account iself, the Duiven-Westervoort case will be analysed in general terms. It is not possible to cover all the sub- and side strategies and subtle changes in power that took place during the long and complicated process. The process will be analysed mainly using the positions of individual governmental partners.

Strategies and powers used The province of Gelderland chose a composite strategy:

- using formal powers to prepare and endorse Regional Physical Plans in order to realise provincial planning policies; initially aiming at a large twin city, Duivoort, and later at smaller separate developments at Duiven and Westervoort;
- consistently aiming at acquiring and maintaining growth town status for Duiven and Westervoort, to be granted by the minister of housing and physical planning;
- using the expertise concentrated in the physical planning agency at several stages of the proces;
- bringing the partners together into organisational frameworks and negotiating procedures;
- initially aiming at the merger of Duiven and Westervoort into one municipality;
- appointing or promoting the appointments of people who were expected to carry out provincial policies.

By doing so, the province used, or tried to use, a series of formal and informal powers. The legal power of the regional physical plan was used several times to force the municipalities of Duiven and Westervoort to change their policies and the ministry of housing and planning to change its policy. This instrument played an important role. We should, however, emphasise the importance of the fact that a particularly influential member of the executive council and subsequently a former minister had been appointed project manager. These two were in the position to contact the minister directly on formal and informal occasions. The member of the executive council also used his power and influence to create the intergovernmental steering committee. He questioned the necessity of a large scale concept for Duivoort and temporarily dismissed the Steering Committee.

The minister of housing and physical planning pursued a policy of concentrating overspill from Arnhem initially into Duivoort, later in Duiven and Westervoort separately, and of granting official growth town status only if absolutely necessary. The minister tried to reject claims for compensation caused by changes in goals and targets that he had initiated.

Important policy instruments concerning growth towns are in the hands of higher authorities, and the power of municipalities is limited. Their real power is in making local structure and land-use plans and reacting to provincial physical planning proposals. The municipalities had frequently to deal with moves and changes in policy by the province.

The municipality of Duiven initially adopted a policy of creating one Duivoort and acquiring growth town status. It tried then to avoid a merger with Westervoort and tried in the end to acquire a large share of the subsidised housing and financial compensation for the changing policies of the higher authorities. Duiven was, however, in no position to realize the opportunities given by the provincial plans in the time available, so the municipality could not reach its targets.

The municipality of Westervoort initially wanted to keep Westervoort small and autonomous, but later it showed aspirations to grow autonomously. Westervoort claimed compensation just as Duiven had. Initially, the two municipalities co-operated by establishing a joint physical planning agency. Later, both municipalities prefered to go their own way in many respects. The appointment of a Mayor who supported growth changed the position of Westervoort. This municipality started to effect the proposals that were part of the new provincial regional physical plan (1978). The municipality of Westervoort was also effective in negotiations concerning financial compensation. It got a fair share of the compensation paid by Arnhem. The fact that Westervoort became a very co-operative municipality made its position stronger than before.

The influence of Arnhem on the province proved to be strong because of the change towards the compact city ideal. Arnhem was successful and powerful enough to convince the provincial council and executive council to move housing from Duiven towards Arnhem. Arnhem however had to pay Dfl. 6 million bill for compensation to Duiven and Westervoort.

Shifts In the preceding sections some shifts and movements were to be seen. These shifts were in policy goals and targets as well as in positions taken or strategies chosen with regard to other parties involved. As a result of massive pressure from all lower authorities, the minister was forced to become involved and could no longer refuse to pay compensation for changing policies. The province had to give up the proposed policy of a merger of the two municipalities and shifted to a position of mediator between parties. The municipalities of Duiven and Westervoort shifted from co-operation to a more competitive position. The municipality of Arnhem, which was out of the picture in the initial stage of the process, pursued new housing targets actively, but had to pay compensation, which it refused to do initially, and in that way bought co-operation from other parties. The provincial electricity company had to give up its claim for compensation when forced by the provincial government.

Instruments not used Whereas organisational measures and negotiations played an important role, formal and legally binding instruments for carrying out or enforcing policies were hardly used. The province used the power to make a (non-binding) physical plan several times, but did not use the power of the directive nor the legal power to approve municipal land use plans. The municipalities did not use the power of making legally binding land use plans to oppose the policies of higher authorities. Formal objection and appeal procedures by citizens were not reported, although the municipality of Duiven and Westervoort formally objected to proposals concerning administrative reform (the merger of the two municipalities) and the draft regional physical plan.

Notes

1. Our calculation on the basis of a coefficient recommended by the Institute of Environmental Protection (H. Piotrowska, J. Bluhm-Kwiatkowski, 1988, p. 34).
2. In Poland the zone for household waste disposal site is 500 m.
3. The population of the province of Lodz in 1988 was 1,148,000, City of Lodz in 1988 was 857,000.
4. Note that the year 1978 was the last year of Polish prosperity in terms of the level of consumption (financed by the West) and at the same time, the year of the strongest centralization of economic and political power by the central administration and the communist party.
5. Note that, at that time, state owned enterprises were not allowed in law

to sell the land and other fixed assets to each other.
6. Act on the Protection of Arable and Forestry Land, 27.02.1985. (DZ.U.No.11.poz.79).
7. This decision was taken at the time when the Commission for the Proper Realization of the Waste Disposal Site created by President, assured him by official record that all actions taken since that moment were consistent with the law.
8. DSM takes part on an advisory basis.

References

Anonymous (1988), *Statistical Year Book 1988* (Maly Rocznik Statystyczny 1988), Warszawa, p. 16.
Gribling, C.C.M. (1989), *Milieuzonering rondom DSM*, PIN, Nijmegen.
Hooydonk, N. van (1988), Regionale afvalverwerking: een meerkeuze-vraagstuk, Methodisch referaat, Sociale Geografie, University of Nijmegen.
Klaver, J. (1991), Waste pollution, in *European Environmental Yearbook 1990*, Milan.
Knaap, J.W.M. van der, Heiden, C.N. van der, Bremen, W.M. van den (1986) *Lessen van eigen bodem*, Kluwer, Deventer.
Piotrowska, H., J. Bluhm-Kwiatkowski (1988), *Materials for designing the regional and physical plans - treatment of waste* (Materialy do projektowania regionalnych i miejscowych planow zagospodarowania przestrzennego, Gospodarka odpadami,) Institute of Spatial and Communal Economy (IGPiK), Warszawa.
Winkelhuyzen, R. (1989) *Beschrijving van het beleidsproces Duiven-Westervoort*, PIN, Nijmegen.

Chapter 5

Analysis of the cases

Arie Dekker

Introduction, synopsis and quantitative analysis of the cases

In this chapter the cases will be analysed further. The descriptions of all the cases included the following:
- the question or issue at stake,
- a description of the formal network of relationships between the parties involved,
- a chronological account of the relevant events,
- a brief analysis concerning the strategies and the powers used, the shifts and the powers not implemented.

For this chapter we will use a synopsis of the chronological account of the cases as a starting point. This synopsis is given in the Appendix. The most important actions and events are characterised in terms of powers used by actors and of interactions between actors. In this way the relationship with the theoretical framework is achieved.

The alphabetical list of powers and interactions is to be found in Table 5.1 together with the abbreviations used in the chronological synopsis. In the alphabetical list the counter-actions are coupled with the primary action, e.g. a claim for compensation is listed next to "compensation".

It has to be stressed that the categorisation of actions and events was not always unambigious. The categorisation of actions and events, however, gives us the opportunity to make a global, quantitative picture of the cases.

In the next sections the result of the analysis is given by:
- giving an overview of the frequency of interactions per case;

Table 5.1 List of powers and interactions and frequency of them in the cases

abbreviation		power (P) or interaction (I)	LW	NW Be	N	Bo	LP	DSM	SM	DW
adv.pow.:	P	advisory power (A)		1	4	2	2	4	5	3
agr.:	I	agreement between initially opposing parties (C)					1	2		2
arbitr.:	I	arbitration (C)								
cl. arbitr.:	P	claim for arbitration (A,B)								
block.:	P	blockade (B)	2							
civ. dis.:	P	civil disobedience (B)					1			
coal.:	I	coalition of different parties (B)						2		
co-op.:	I	co-operation (C)	1	3	1			2		1
comp.:	I,P	compensation (A)	1	1			2	1	1	1
cl. comp.:	P	claim for compensation (B)	1	1	1				1	4
dem.:	P	demonstration (B)						1		
dir.:	P	directive (A)		1	1	1		1		
cl.dir.:	P	claim to issue a directive (A,B)			1	1				
exp. adv.:	P	expert advice (C)		1				1	3	
cl. exp. adv.:	P	claim for expert advice (B)						1		
inf.:	I,P	information (A)	2			2		9	1	
cl. inf.:	P	claim for information (B)						1		
i.o. t.force:	P,I	interorganisational task force (A)	2					3	1	2
investig.:	P	investigation or research (A)	1	1	2	2		5	1	1
cl. investig.:	P	claim for investigation (B)			1	1		3		
inst. arr.:	P	institutional arrangement (organisation, rules, procedures) (A)		1	2	1				2
meet.:	I	meeting between opposing parties (C)	3	1			1	4		4
med.:	I	mediation (C)								1
cl.:	P	claim for mediation (A,B)								
neg.:	I	negotiation (C)			1		3			
mob.:	P	mobilisation of public opinion or opinion leaders (B)	1				1	2	2	
obj. and app.:	P	formal objection and appeal (B)	4	5	1	4		2	2	2
obstr.:	P	obstruction (B)	2	1	2	2				
prot. & compl.:	P	protest and complaint (B)			1	2	4	5	5	
publ.:	P	publicity (B)			1	1	1	4	4	
stat. pow.:	P	statutory power (A, B) (bind.: binding; ind.: indicative; strat.: strategic; op: operational; jur.: jurisdiction; sup.: supervision)	6	8	3	7	8	6	12	8
cl. stat. pow.:	P	claim to use statutory power (A,B)	2		1	2	3			

LW: Lodz Waste Disposal
NW: Neth. Waste Disposal
Be: Beuningen
N: Nistelrode
Bo: Borne
LP: Lodz Polonit
DSM: Dutch State Mines
SM: Stara Milosna
DW: Duiven-Westervoort

A: forcing power   B: mitigating power   C: mediating power

- giving a brief comparative analysis of the Dutch cases, the Polish cases, the pairs of cases and all cases together in the light of the policy systems, using the formal network of relationships;
- comparing the cases in terms of formal networks of relationships, the character of the conflict, the course of the conflict and the powers and interaction used;
- evaluating the cases.

The last section leads on to chapter 6.

Quantitative analysis

In the synopsis of the cases the events and actions of the relevant parties are listed (see Appendix). These events and actions are characterised in terms of (inter)actions between the parties. The powers and strategies can be subdivided as follows:
- in all cases, parties can be distinguished which initiate policy; these parties meet a greater or a lesser degree of opposition to their initiated policy and they possess the instruments to cope with the opposition (category A); we call these powers "forcing powers";
- on the other hand, when opposing parties possess instruments to articulate opposition (category B); we call these powers "mitigating powers".
- various instruments can be used to bring together opposing parties, either at the initiative of the actor who pursues a policy, or at the initiative of the party in opposition (category C); we call these "mediating powers".

It has to be stressed that third parties play a role in several cases. Some of them cannot be said to be either initiating or opposing party. These parties were sometimes "outside players" (e.g. the ministry of chemical industry in the Polonit case), although they can be very influential. In other cases they were at the heart of the game but in a position somewhere between initiator and the opposition (e.g. the province in the case of DSM). And of course there are parties which changed position during the course of events.

An observation has to be made concerning the importance of actions and events. The influence of the actions and events on the outcome of the cases varies very much. This makes a quantitative approach difficult to interpret. A more qualitative comment on each case will be given in the subsequent section, where the importance of actions will be taken into account and related to the outcome. At the present moment we restrict ourselves to the observation that the arsenal of actions to be seen in the cases is great, and that the use of mostly informal means of orientation and organisation is strikingly frequent.

To finish this quantitative analysis a table (Table 5.2) is given which summarises the results of Table 5.1. In the first part of the table the number of times that powers were used and interactions took place are calculated per case. In the second part the categories of instruments (forcing, mitigating and mediating) are added per case.

Table 5.2 shows a striking similarity in the frequency distribution of the various categories. The main significant differences are:
- the higher frequency of interactions (especially forcing and mediating) in the Polish waste disposal case as compared with the Dutch ones;
- the higher frequency of interactions in the Dutch cases concerning environmental zoning and urban extension as compared with the comparable Polish cases.

Table 5.2 Frequency of use of power, interactions and type of instruments

	Lodz waste		Netherlands waste						Lodz Polonit		DSM		Stara Mil.		Duiven West.		Poland average	Neth. average
		%	Be	%	N	%	Bo	%		%		%		%		%	%	%
Power	19	68	23	85	22	92	26	100	22	81	41	73	40	98	22	71	84	82
Interaction	9	32	4	15	2	8	0	0	5	19	15	27	1	2	9	29	16	18
forcing instruments (A)	13	47	11	41	11	46	18	69	11	41	27	48	22	54	17	55	48	51
mitigating instruments (B)	11	39	11	41	11	46	8	31	11	41	20	36	16	39	6	19	40	34
mediating instruments (C)	4	14	5	18	2	8	0	0	5	18	9	16	3	7	8	26	12	15

Qualitative analysis of the cases

When looking at all cases at a glance it is striking that for two of the pairs of cases, the expectation that the problem was the same in both countries turned out to be false. This fact causes the necessity of defining the conflicts in more generalised terms. We start now with a short description of Dutch and of the Polish cases separately.

The Dutch cases

The similarity in all the Dutch cases is the conflict between a higher authority, which tries to pursue a policy or to change a policy, and a lower authority, which perceives its interests and autonomy to be threatened. In two cases the national government was one of the important parties. In all cases provincial government played a crucial role. The main differences are to be seen in the degree of application of legal powers and in the strategies of both higher and lower authorities. The role of citizens, societal organisations and ad hoc interest groups differs from case to case. In two cases the municipality came to share the view of opposing groups or even promoted opposition against higher authorities (DSM). In all cases the period in which parties were involved in a conflict situation was long, even in the situation where the law provided the opportunity to take a final decision. Within the exception of one subcase, all cases arrived at a solution. In two cases legislation changed during the process (waste disposal and environmental zoning).

The Polish cases

The similarity in the Polish cases is the conflict between the local community and/or interest groups on the one hand and public administration in the person of the State on the other. In Stara Milosna the local residents and an interministerial group were in opposition. The differences were: the duration of the conflicts and the instruments and strategies used by the local community and interest groups. Because all the Polish cases were located in an area where the Voivodship authorities are also the Town authorities, the voivodship authorities play an important role. In all cases agencies of different State departments played a role. In one case the position of an inter-ministerial interest group was paramount. In no case was a final solution reached. In all cases the relevant legislation changed during the process. A striking similarity in all the Polish cases is the lack of opposition during the decision-making process and the increase of opposition during the stage of implementation. In all cases the opposition broadened in the eighties, when citizen committees, environmental groups and such like became active parties, in alliance with those people whose interests were touched directly.

The Polish and Dutch cases in the light of the policy systems

Part of the differences between the Dutch cases and the Polish cases can be explained by looking at them from the viewpoint of the policy systems. Conflicts between citizens and public administration in the Polish situation would often have been conflicts between civic parties in the Dutch situation. This makes the comparison complicated. As mentioned before, legislation has changed in both countries. In Poland we can add the many changes in opinion about the principles of state and of state administration. The shift in ideology caused a considerable shift in the public attitudes of citizens towards public administation.
Altogether, four cases concern predominantly citizens opposing an aspect of public administration. Two Dutch cases in which the national government took part were intra-governmental in character. The Dutch waste disposal case brought a relatively new party onto the scene, the body of collaborating municipalities. The role of the voivodships in the Polish urban areas is considerable. The interesting question of whether the course of events can be explained by factors related to the policy systems will be dealt with in chapter 6.

The pairs of cases

As mentioned before the cases in Poland and the Netherlands were less comparable than wasexpected. Nevertheless a brief comparison can be made. In the case of the location of a regional waste disposal site, a large degree of similarity between the Polish and Dutch case in terms of the character of the conflict was shown. However, the distribution of legal powers differs. In Lodz there is a concentration of land use and waste management powers in the hands of the voivodship administration, whereas, in the Dutch case, land use decisions are the primary task of municipalities, and waste management decisions are a responsibility of bodies of co-operating municipalities. The course of the two cases differed, also the role of public administration as compared with the private sector. Although massive opposition was reported in the Dutch case, the character of the opposition is different: it was mainly a question of using the formal mechanisms of objection and appeal during the process of decision-making. In the Polish case the opposition took more extra-legal and even illegal steps to avoid the implementation of the decision for a waste disposal site. Both in the Netherlands and in Poland, unexpected events took place inside and outside public administration. New legislation and a relatively new approach to waste management (large regional sites instead of small local facilities) caused adaptation by several parties in the Netherlands. In Poland the circle of people involved in opposition widened from land owners to broader organisations. The use of the instruments to mobilise public opinion and influence people became more and more important. In both countries the processes took a lot of time. In Lodz, no solution was reached for a problem which was broadly acknowledged and urgent. Of the Dutch cases one came to an end, one was near to an end and the third has still to be resolved (the latter being not very urgent).

The cases concerning environmental zoning around a polluting industry appeared to be quite different. In the Polish case the relocation of a large asbestos-factory was part of the issue, environmental norms were mainly a device of a temporary character. Housing construction was completed before a binding decision about the relocation was taken and environmental zoning and norms were violated as a consequence. In the Dutch case an experiment by national government to apply comprehensive zoning with rather strict environmental norms, but without a legal arrangement as a base, appeared to be the main source of conflicts. Autonomy of the municipality and housing needs in the area were goals which contradicted the goals of the comprehensive environmenal zoning. The mainly informal powers of one municipality appeared to be rather effective, although national government with its housing subsidies and provincial government with its regional physical plan have inherently strong powers. The powers of the municipality of Lodz appeared to be dominated by the interests of the ministry of chemical industry. The municipality (which also has voivodship-status) was not able to enforce an established environmental protection zone. Quite the reverse, as the municipality approved a housing location within the zone. From 1980, pressure from residents increased by means of complaints and publicity, support later on by the housing co-operative. The conflict led to a refusal to pay the rent. At the end of the process, the pollution continued with only the hope of a solution in the future.

The cases which deal with large scale urban expansion appeared to differ in almost every aspect. The conflict in the Polish case arose from an unplanned initiative to build a new area by a private group which had strong connections with central government agencies. This initiative was approached with goodwill by the authorities responsible for land use and locational decisions in the area. Their decisions were attacked severely by the local community. In the Netherlands the implementation of the urbanisation policy of higher authorities and the allocation of costs caused by changing housing construction targets were the focal points of the conflict. The consequences of national and provincial urbanisation policy and changes in this were far-reaching for the two municipalities involved. The formal powers were comparable in that the voivodship administration and the provincial administration respectively held important powers concerning larger urban extensions. In the Netherlands the formal and informal powers of local government (i.e. the municipalities) are far more developed than in the Polish situation. In the Dutch case national goals and instruments were important factors. The course of the Dutch case was characterised by the mixture of legal and extra-legal powers used and the negotiations in connection with the processes of formal decision-making. Divergences of opinion between the parties involved at several stages of the process were converted to agreements. In the Polish case a kind of escalation took place. The circle of opposition enlarged as the number of public or semi-public bodies addressed and involved increased. Mobilisation of public opinion and of influential politicians became the most important weapon of the opposition. The result is a confusing picture of the situation.

Comparative analysis of the cases

The formal network of relationships between actors

In chapter 4 the cases are described. Part of the description is the formal network applicable in each case. The formal network is to be seen as a link between the policy system as given in chapter 3 and the way the cases developed. A comparison of the formal networks enables us to perform cross-analysis.

The cases are similar in the sense that a composite set of formal decisions made by different public bodies at different levels is necessary to solve the problem. In five cases a locational or land use decision was the core decision and was accompanied by advisory, consultative, public participation, approval, implementation and permit procedures. In one case (Duiven-Westervoort) long term housing targets for two municipalities were in dispute, and this had two important issues. The first was the merger of the two municipalities concerned, which would have required the passing of a special law: the second was the financial conseqences of a change in policy of the higher authorities. In most cases the distribution of legal powers is clear in principle. This means that although the process was cumbersome in all cases, this has to be seen in the light of the way the authorities used their legal powers and were able to deploy informal influence or to legitimize decisions. The differences between the cases can be seen at government level and in the character of the public body which had decisive power in the case. In the Polish cases the voivodship level of public administration and, within it, the appointed public officials had the formal power concerning the most important decisions. It has to be stressed that most voivodship powers are held by State bodies rather than by autonomous local bodies. In the case of the Polonit plant the ministry of the chemical industry had to be added as a body with great formal power. The Dutch cases are similar in the sense that elected bodies have the main formal power in their hands. The differences between the Dutch cases are:
- in the DSM-case environmental zoning is a provincial responsibility as far as noise is concerned. In terms of comprehensive zoning there is no formal responsibility but the municipality and the province could have used their powers as mentioned in the Physical Planning Act so as to establish such a zone;
- in the case of waste disposal the bodies of co-operating municipalities were in principle responsible; in practice the lack of co-operation or of consensus made the excercise of provincial powers under the Physical Planning Act necessary.
- in the development of a growth town, the initial power was with the minister of housing, physical planning and environment, but to a large extent he depends on the co-operation of the province and municipalities in how they use their formal powers.

The mere description of the formal network of participants and powers demonstrates that in all cases, numerous mutually consistent decisions have to be taken by many bodies before a problem is formally resolved.

The character of the conflicts

The conflicts differ in terms of their complexity, the complexity of the solution-package, the stability over time, the perceptions of the parties involved, the degree of clarity in the legislation about the decisive powers of the parties involved, the relevance to other possible conflicts, the way the conflicts occur, and the main interests which are at stake. To begin with the last, all conflicts are about the clash between a general interest - generally supported or declared by a higher authority or a central state body - and a local or private interest. All conflicts contain environmental interests of different kinds. The location of a waste disposal site is, in itself, a question raised by environmental policy. The location criteria, the zoning around disposal sites and the measures to be taken to safeguard the environment from pollution caused by the operation and management of such a site, are additional environmental factors. Such sites cause the loss of area for other purposes, restrict the development potential of adjacent land, and cause noise from the lorries which transport the waste. The very character of the conflict over such a location is called NIMBY, i.e. Not In My Backyard! The environmental zoning system in the two other cases showed the conflict between the interests of enterprises and of housing needs on the one hand and the desire to improve or safeguard environmental quality on the other. The latter appeared to be an important characteristic of the urban extension in the Warsaw area as well. As compared with the zoning around industrial areas, the environmental issue is more acute viz. an area of natural beauty, the Mazovian Landscape Park. Although the cases show similarities in the kind of conflict of interests, they are not similar in the parties representing these interests. In all cases, however, the many parties supported one interest. It is notable that behind the various interests, financial and productive or other interests were hidden. The case of Duiven-Westervoort differs from the other cases in several ways. During the course of this case, the parties involved met with several conflicts. The degree of autonomy and financial interests were the common factors in the different stages.

The course of the conflicts

In all conflicts it was the policy of a higher tier of government which marked the beginning of the conflict. In the case of DSM and Stara Milosna the activity as such was objected to, in other cases it was the way a task was carried out which was the issue. In most cases locational decisions were questioned. In the case of the Polonit plant it was a combination of industrial relocation and housing. In the Duiven-Westervoort case housing targets over a period of time were the important issue. Conflicts tend to take time to resolve. That is the general picture in all the cases. A second common feature is that hardly any initial conflict can be dealt with in isolation. Most conflicts either reflect a complex set of conflicting interests in the initial stage or they show an increasing complexity caused by the parties involved. The cause-effect relationships are complex and ambiguous. The cases show that even a clear-cut set of responsibilities and powers is no guarantee that a process develops smoothly. In no case is the complex of policy processes and decisions explicitly managed in advance. The number of unexpected events is striking. In two cases a shift in external circumstances had great influence. The Polonit-case shows a substantial delay in the relocation of the plant, the Duiven-Westervoort case shows the influence of changing demographic forecasts and of changes in the policy concerning the capacity of the inner city of Arnhem. The latter shift was partly caused by environmental arguments. The increasing significance of environmental arguments played a clear role in all cases, although the parties involved appeared to attach different weight to these arguments and, in that way, contributed to the conflict. The Polish cases show an increasing mobilisation of citizens and pressure groups during the course of the conflict. Public authorities reacted to this in many varied and curious ways.

The instruments and power resources used and the strategies

As mentioned before, in the Dutch cases, intra-governmental conflicts dominate whereas in Poland the conflict is mainly between a governmental body and citizens. For this reason the instruments and power resources used can be expected to differ. The Dutch cases show an extensive use of organisational measures, such as the establishment of task groups and of consultation and negotiation procedures between governmental bodies. Compensation was used several times to promote the co-operation of parties initially in opposition. In several cases the personal influence of a key-actor is apparent. In the Polish cases the mobilisation of the opinion of influential actors was the main power used. The extensive use of letters of protest and complaint is striking as is the establishment of interest and pressure groups. There seems to be a shortage of established methods of objections and appeal. Two cases in Poland, waste disposal and Polonit zoning, showed the use of civil disobedience. In both countries opposing parties use every opportunity to cause delay, partly in the hope that time would make a decision unnecessary, partly to mobilise opinion in their favour.

In the Polish cases attempts to negotiate land prices and facilities in Lodz and technical infrastructure in Warsaw seemed to be relatively unsuccessful.
The DSM-case led the municipality of Geleen to try to change the rules of the game (the Noise Nuisance Act) whereas the other party (the Ministry of the Environment) tried to anticipate future legislation. National government linked housing subsidies to environmental zoning.

In Table 5.3 the instruments and power resources used by the explicitly opposing parties are summarised. In the table, attention is given to parties which had a role but were not explicit about their stand during the whole process. The use of means of organisation (see chapter 2) is striking. Not surprisingly, the use of statutory powers in terms of binding regulations or directives is used in almost every case. It is interesting to compare the frequency of strategic powers used, as compared with other powers.

Evaluative aspects

Standards for evaluating the cases have been mentioned in chapter 2. Some of these have to be applied when looking at the cases as a whole. This holds true for effectiveness and efficiency in particular. In some cases evaluative remarks will be made concerning individual parties. It has to be stressed, that the standards overlap one another.

Table 5.3 The main power resources used

	production	coercion	orientation	organisation guidelines	link	procedures	public opinion
1. Lodz Waste	AB	A	A		A	B	B
2. Neth. waste		A		A	B		
3. Lodz Polonit	A	A				B	B
4. Geleen DSM	B AB		AB	A	AB	B	
5. Warsaw St. Mil.	A	A	A	A	AB	B	B
6. Duiven-West.			A		A		

A   main initiator
B   main opposing party
AB less articulate party

Effectiveness

Taking the cases as a whole, effectiveness could be examined by asking whether the result is satisfying or, at the least, acceptable to the parties involved. This could be the case even if some parties were not able to accomplish their initial policies. None of the Polish cases could be assessed as being effectively resolved. As far as public bodies are concerned, some isolated actions had temporary success (e.g. talks and negotiations in the Lodz-waste disposal case). The opposition was relatively effective in the Lodz-waste disposal case and in the Stara Milosna case. Of the Dutch cases, Duiven-Westervoort was relatively effectively resolved. An assessment of the other cases is less clear out. Taking into account the generally recognised problem of waste disposal, in the sub-cases where a solution was necessary, such a solution was reached definitely in only one case, Beuningen.

When looking at the individual parties involved, some achieved their initial goals quite well: for instance the municipality of Geleen as an opposing party (the DSM-case) and the provinces and the co-operating municipalities in the cases of the waste disposal sites. The municipality of Stein and the municipalities of Duiven and Westervoort negotiated quite effectively and gained advantage from the process.

Efficiency

Conflicts as these, tend to be tremendously time and energy consuming. The question as to whether the time and energy spent is in balance with the interests at stake is difficult to answer. Parties sometimes fight for goals and ideals which lie concealed behind the superficial conflict. This seems to be especially true of the Polish situation in which a long period of oppression seemed to result in an outburst from the very moment that opposition was accepted as a legitimate expression of civil rights. In the Dutch cases, many of the steps taken can be characterised afterwards as having been rather inefficient and/or unthought out. One reason for the length of such conflicts is that the legal opportunities for objections and appeals were used extensively by the opposing parties. The system seems to be too complex.

Taking account of interests

The course of the cases show that many interests were introduced by the parties which became involved. It is highly questionable, however, whether the relevant interests are seriously taken into account. When parties are in an equal bargaining position, their particular interests are dealt with during the negotiations. When parties are in an unequal position, it depends upon the capacity of the parties with the decisive powers and upon the existence and operation of the countervailing powers as to whether the relevant interests are dealt with acceptably. The Dutch cases show better pre-conditions for taking interests into account than the Polish ones. The distribution of power, the system of supervision, the arrangements for co-ordination, the possibilities for objection and appeal are better developed, and used, than in Poland. The cases show many illustration of this.

Autonomous position of different levels of governmental

As mentioned before, in two Dutch cases the autonomy of the municipality was one of the factors. In Duiven-Westervoort the merger of two municipalities was under consideration and in the DSM case the municipality of Geleen feared a loss of autonomy if a higher authority established a comprehensive environmental zone. In general, the Dutch cases illustrate many events in which lower authorities were able to influence the process and the final result. There is an extensive network of interdependencies, even when a higher authority has statutory powers or the formal possibilities for overruling the lower authority. This is embedded in the way public administration is organised. Relationships within political parties were influential in the background.

The situation in Poland during the cases was more complicated. From the description of the policy system it could be expected that the rigid subordination of lower authorities to the central state would be seen in operation and this was so. Central State bodies had many powers concerning decisions over the territory of municipalities. The executive powers of state bodies were rather impressive. It is not only in the top-down direction that influence works: protests and complaints go up to the very top of the state hierarchy. The case of Stara Milosna showed an extensive involvement of central state bodies in the building initiative, as well as a real bombardment of protests and objections in their direction. In the other Polish cases, central state bodies were addressed as well. Nevertheless State bodies were not able to carry out their policies properly. The real influence of the municipalities was hidden behind the special administrative organisation of the areas of Warsaw and Lodz.

Position of elected state organs

As far as the Dutch cases are concerned, the influence of elected bodies differ. In the DSM case the executive bodies at all levels and their agencies played the most prominent role. The same applies to the Duiven-Westervoort case, although the Provincial Council overruled the Provincial Executive with regard to the proposal to merger the of two municipalities. The subcases of the waste disposal sites showed the explicit role of the provincial council in decisions concerning the regional physical plan and the provincial waste-disposal plan; and the subcases showed the explicit role of the municipal council concerning decisions about the land use plan and decisions to co-operate with the policy of the authority of collaborating municipalities. The position of the council and the executive of the latter authority is noteworthy. Members are elected, indirectly, by municipal councils. In both municipal and provincial government, the members of the executive bodies are elected from the respective councils.

Although in formal terms the relative position of elected bodies in Poland vis a vis executive bodies has many similarities with the Dutch system, the cases show that the real power of executives as bodies of the central state exceeds by far the power of the elected bodies.

Position of the individual citizen

The cases show a surprising paradox. Whereas the rights of citizens in terms of public participation, objection and appeal are generally well articulated in Dutch legislation, their reported effective influence is rather limited. In the Polish cases the reverse seems to be the case. In the case of the waste disposal site in Lodz, several attempts to approach the local communities and groups concerning the selling of land, compensation measures and reconciliation were reported. In the Stara Milosna case the important party of the inter-ministerial group was characterised as being a "social initiative" with apparently influential links with state bodies. In the Polish cases the informal or extra-legal activities of citizens are numerous and varied in character.

Chapter 6

Urban conflict-management at work: conclusions and recommendations

Henri Goverde

Introduction

In chapter 1 the main goals of the study were formulated as follows:
a. improving insight into the performance of the two policy-systems, particularly concerning the management of urban conflicts;
b. making a contribution to the theoretical understanding of urban conflicts.
In order to show if and how the first goal has been realized, the conclusions will be presented at two different levels. First, at the level of the case-studies, an attempt will be made to extract some practical lessons from the cases which were studied in Poland and in the Netherlands. The second level concerns the general performance of the Dutch and Polish political-administrative systems, their similarities and differences as well as the roles of the state.

The second goal of the study is the subject of the subsequent section. Although the aim is relatively modest, we believe that we can make some general statements about the spatial aspects of conflict situations in combination with a policy-networks approach.

We want also to present some more general conclusions. These conclusions are strictly limited by the theoretical reference scheme used in the study as well as by the empirical work. Nevertheless, the co-operation between academics from two countries and the comparative perspectives used by them have produced some ideas about the social-cultural context of the issues which were studied here. In so far as these ideas are relevant and can lead to recommendations for managing urban conflicts, they are placed in the Epilogue separately.

The case studies in the light of the theoretical framework

This section will show some of the lessons from the cases studied in this book. The lessons are drawn from the concluding analysis of the power resources, from the strategies used, and from the main shifts (of which two types are distinguished).
The conclusions will be the result of reviewing all the cases together. At the same time, some examples taken from separate cases will illustrate the statements presented.

How representative are the cases?

The research design used in this book was called the 'multiple case study approach' (chapter 1). The cases studied here were not aselectively chosen. Therefore, it is not possible to claim that they are representative for all urban conflicts in Poland and the Netherlands. Nevertheless, multiple case-study research has a better chance of representing some general phenomena than one case-study alone. Although the authors do not claim that the statements can be generalised, at least the use of a common theoretical framework allows some comparisons to be made.

The power resources used in the cases

Table 6.1 Review of statutory powers (n=58)

Case studies: Categories Statutory powers	Poland waste Lodz	Netherlands waste Beu	Nist	Borne	Polonit	DSM	Stara Mil.	Duiven Wester- voort	total	total Poland	total Neth.
- BINDING - / 'MEANS OF COERCION'											
Strategic	2	-	-	3	-	-	3	-	8	5	3
Operational	1	5	1	1	5	2	4	-	19	10	9
Supervisory	2	-	-	-	-	-	-	-	2	2	-
Legal	-	1	1	2	-	-	3	-	7	3	4
Sub-total binding	5	6	2	6	5	2	7	0	36	20	16
- INDICATIVE - / 'MEANS OF ORIENTATION'											
Strategic	1	2	1	-	2	3	1	8	18	4	14
Operational	-	-	-	1	1	1	1	-	4	2	2
Sub-total indicative	1	2	1	1	3	4	2	8	22	6	16
Total observations	6	8	3	7	8	6	12	8	58	26	32

In chapter 5 (Table 5.1.) a list of 'powers and interactions' is presented. The contents were taken from the chronological account of the cases (Appendix). To improve the insight into the performance of the two policy-systems, the list of 'powers and interactions' will be related to the concepts of 'power resources, strategies, games and dimensions of interactions' as used in the 10-steps schedule (chapter 2, section 2). This requires a more precise view of the different types of 'statutory powers'. Table 6.1. reviews the powers used.

Comments on table 6.1 Statutory powers are power resources (chapter 2), which can be divided into binding and indicative. Binding statutory powers are part of the means of coercion, while advisory powers are part of the means of orientation. Statutory powers were observed 26 times in the Polish cases and 32 times in the Dutch cases. Table 6.1 indicates that almost two-thirds of the statutory powers observed in the cases can be characterised as binding, 50% in the Dutch cases and 77% in the Polish cases. These figures are surprising as far as they seem not to support the opinion of almost every Polish author: these advised looking more closely at a strengthening of the juridicial system as a productive way of managing urban conflicts. Concerning the Dutch cases, the table makes clear that conflicts or dead-locks are often solved by using coercive power resources and not by the means of orientation and organisation.

Table 6.2 reviews the power resources used in relation to the actions observed in the cases.

Comments on table 6.2 Of all the 'list of powers and interactions' (chapter 5) the control of the means of production could not be observed directly in the cases. When looking in more detail, however, the means of production played an indirect role in several cases. Many groups (e.g. the farmers in the Lodz waste disposal case) used their land property rights to start actions which are referred to in the category 'means of coercion', refusing expropriation, farming the expropriated land illegally and using physical power against lorries carrying waste, for instance. Another example can be found in the Dutch DSM-case. Here the national government linked housing subsidies, public finance, to environmental zoning. And the municipality of Geleen tried to develop land in the disputed area within its boundaries.

It is noticeable that 35% of all observations are in the category of the 'means of coercion'. This indicates that the selected cases concern conflicts with a high degree of intensity. The power resources used in the selected cases are directed not only towards conflicts by argument but also to the, sometimes, organised use of force.

The control of the means of coercion seems to be relatively well spread over all cases, Duiven-Westervoort being the only exception. Yet the use of these power resources can easily produce dead-locks (Goverde/Hoeben, 1991). When the administration promotes the use of this type of power resources, it will cause long drawn-out policy-processes.

Table 6.2 Power resources observed in the cases

power resources, control over	operationalisations in the cases	numer of observations
means of production		-
means of coercion	blockade	2
	civil disobedience	1
	directive	4
	formal objection & appeal	18
	obstruction	7
	binding statutory power	36
total		68
means of orientation	expert advice	5
	advisory power	21
	claim for information	1
	investigation/research	13
	claim for investigation	5
	indicative statutory power	22
total		67
means of organisation	demonstration	1
	protest and complaint	19
	claim for directive	2
	claim for expert advice	1
	inter-organisational task force	8
	mobilisation of public opinion or opinion leaders	7
	publicity	11
	claim use statutory power	8
total		57
total power resources observed		192

Strategies, games and dimensions of interactions used

Table 6.3 gives an overview of the 'powers and interactions' observed in relation to step 9 of the 10-steps schedule: that is, the strategies, games and dimensions of inter-actions used by the actors to change the position of the power balance.

Comments on table 6.3

Strategies used Most actors use strategies for maintaining or increasing their power position. Other important strategies are diminishing uncertainties or deliberately running risks.

Competition and open conflicts Many acts and events express competition, but games oriented to co-operation are more often observed than games oriented to open conflict. Conflict-management directed towards co-operation seems to be profitable to most of the actors involved, at least in the long run. Nevertheless, games showing open conflict have a serious social function. In a certain phase of the process, these approaches can create a stronger power position for the actors involved. This especially applies to the Polish cases.

Table 6.3 Strategies, games and dimensions of interactions used to change the power balance in the cases

elements step 9	character + number of observations	number of observations
strategies:		
maintain/ increase power	statutory p.(69);formal objection & appeal(18); directive(4)	91
maintain/ increase certainty	investigation/research(13) claim to use statutory power(8)	21
deliberate running of risks	advisory power(21) obstruction(7)	28
avoidance of power + responsibility	recommendations and advice	1
maintain social constructions + value oriented action	claim for investigation or research(5)	5
total strategies		146
games:		
co-operation	co-operation(8); agreement between opposing parties(5)	13
coalition	coalition of different parties(3)	3
competition	publicity(11); mobilisation of of public opinion(7); demonstration(1)	19
open conflict	formal objection and appeal(18); blockade(3); protest + complaint(19) civil disobedience(1)	41
avoidance	claim for arbitration	-
merger (bureaucratisation)	interorganisational task force(8) institutional arrangement(6)	14
total games		90
dimensions of interactions:		
communication	publicity(11); information (14); mediation(1)	26
negotiation; meeting	opposing parties(13); negotiation(4); claims for compensation(8)	25
exchange	compensation(7)	7
decision-making	arbitration	-
total		58

Conflict-management by co-operation In all cases there were many interactions oriented towards managing the conflict. Patterns of communication, mostly for the transfer of information about different points of view, negotiation starting with meetings between the opposing parties, and exchange, can be discovered in all the cases. In fact, games of co-operation can be observed so often that the following proposition can be argued: opposing parties are ready to keep dead-locks going for a long time, but if a solution becomes urgent they prefer to create it together instead of handing all powers of decision over to an impartial 'outsider'.

Arbitration Although arbitration can be an efficient way of resolving dead-locks, it does not seem to be a popular approach to managing a conflict. Most of the actors seem to be more afraid of losing some of their options than of the uncertainty about what will be finally gained. They seem also to prefer keeping open the opportunity of winning something at some moment in the future.

From the cases studied in this book, and even though objections and appeals are reported frequently, the contention in chapter 3 is not supported, that in the Polish as well as in the Dutch policy-system the intervention of legal institutions is often necessary in order to reach decisions on political and social-economic issues.

Power shifts at two levels

Significant change in power resources used by the actors In almost all cases the opposing actors gained more influence by using the means of orientation, particularly when employing ecological arguments. In this way many citizens and pressure groups in the Polish cases could be organised. These 'green' means of orientation of attitudes and values were important in the Dutch cases as well but they were used mainly by the initiator of the disputed policy. For example, the Dutch national government linked housing subsidies to environmental zoning.

Several conflicts could be resolved after one or several actors were ready to think in terms of exchange and compensation. In this respect, the Lodz-waste case is remarkable, especially because the power resources used were mainly of a coercive type. It is possible to see a relationship with the changing political climate in Poland. The 'Solidarnosc' movement produced a societal context within which farmers refused expropriation, started farming on the expropriated grounds illegally, and used physical force against lorries which wanted to start dumping waste on the fields. The changing political climate produced intense and effective resistance against decisions and plans produced by a regime which had lost its authority. The consequence was that fairly strong coercive means were used and that the opposing actors were not yet ready to look for compromises. A similar development can be observed in the Stara Milosna case.

The changing positions of the dominating actors in the networks The actors' positions can change as a result of their own strategic behaviour or because of the behaviour of other actors. For example, the power position of the ministerial and provincial actors in the Lodz-waste case declined tremendously after the blockade and the civil disobedience of organized citizens.

The context (i.e. the societal situation of the conflict) can also change, influencing the political position of an actor, even though his behaviour does not change at all. The Lodz Polonit case (delay of the relocation of the plant) and the Duiven-Westervoort case (changing demographic forecasts and a policy-change concerning the physical capacities of the 'donor' city) are good examples of this. The changing contexts influenced the position of the dominant actors in the policy networks dramatically.

Lessons from the cases

A general lesson seems to be that the planning and decision-making concerning large scale changes in the physical environment around big cities should be better managed. In order to find ways of managing conflicts in the future, it is necessary to draw practical lessons from the cases.

Advantages and disadvantages of new legal rules
Better management of the ubanisation process should imply a concept of correct action, and a better legal framework as can be learned from the case of Stara Milosna. However, the development of a relevant legal framework should not be perceived as a panacea for all troubles. The DSM-case and the Dutch cases concerning the location of waste disposal sites show that many conflicts are produced simply by the introduction of legal, environmental norms.

The Stara Milosna case also showed that the laws were often used for creating the space within which actors could make decisions. Many errors were the result of informal inter-institutional and personal arrangements. It is not easy to believe that new rules will automatically change this behaviour. On the contrary, it would seem to be realistic to imagine that new rules are mostly the expression and the result of shifts in the power balance-sheet. Those who lost power will try to fight back, and a new conflict life-cycle is born. A lesson from the Lodz-waste disposal case (Palczew) is that the formal policy-network can differ seriously from the actual network of interactions.

As far as legal systems are used in the urban conflicts studied in this book, it is remarkable that all the laws seem mainly to determine procedures. None of these laws forbids anything clearly. When there are norms in the laws it is difficult to maintain them properly, see the case of DSM. The effect of this legal situation is partly that searching for serious alternative technical solutions is avoided and partly that the responsibility of taking decisions is avoided (see Lodz-Polonit case).

Double role played by governmental bodies

Governmental institutions, especially representative councils, often have to play the role of representing the institutions' interest as well as the role either of arbiter or of executor of directives of higher public institutions. The third role is relatively easily accepted. The first and second roles - being both part of the game and being arbiter of the game - are often in conflict. When the political climate is rather unstable, it is almost impossible to play such a double role effectively. The government involved cannot make itself credible enough (see for example the provincial bodies in the case of Lodz-waste disposal site). On the other hand the opposing actors such as the farmers of Palczew could gain a much stronger power position because of this political climate. They could play a more radical role than they ever could have imagined.

New policy instruments reflect and often create conflicts: social technology as a device

The DSM case is interesting for another reason. A new policy instrument was developed in this case. The instrument is called 'environmental zoning' and it covers three different policy fields, environment, physical planning and housing. In all three fields governmental institutions have different competence to intervene. No one party can steer the process alone and, when the parties involved have different interests, co-ordination is difficult. Organizational measures will not always produce a joint approach to the problem. Nevertheless, the lesson is clear, and the management of such a policy process is predominantly a matter of technology in social intervention in an inter-organisational setting, rather than of traditional technology such as goals/means or cost/benefit reasoning or knowledge based decision-making.

A conflict is seldom an autonomous issue

All the policy processes took a long time and some are still not resolved. However, often a conflict is not an autonomous phenomenon. Usually a conflict is part of a complex of ongoing policy issues concerning an area. The resolution of a conflict within such a complex often needs a commitment package about several issues between all the relevant (i.e. powerful) actors involved in a policy-network. This is not easy to realise. The cases of DSM, Lodz Polonit, Stara Milosna, Duiven Westervoort and the Beuningen waste disposal issue illustrate this. In Poland all cases reflect the frustration of the people and organisations with the old regime.

As long as the conflicting interests are not managed by a commitment package ('pacification'), all 'solutions' will be only temporary and provisional. In fact, in such cases an authoritative allocation of goods and values is not possible. No collective rationality is produced.

Control of the management of information: a very strong power resource

Another aspect of the policy processes described is the management of information. As long as relevant information is monopolised and blocked, it is almost impossible for public conflicts to arise. The Polish cases show this quite clearly. Only after the Solidarnosc movement became public (1980) was the relevant information delivered more openly and public conflicts could begin.

However, the Dutch cases are relevant in this respect as well. Who can completely oversee the environmental impact of such a huge chemical plant as DSM? Who has enough information? Who controls this information, if anyone? The Duiven Westervoort case shows very well the effect of a monopoly of information in the hands of experts. The lesson concerning information is that in both policy-systems the urban issues at stake are so complex that information management is a very important power resource for some actors. In fact, unequal power relations are mostly the consequence of unequal distribution of relevant information. The Polish policy system in particular needs much investment in creating institutions ready to express social interests and ready to defend the interests of citizens against state institutions and state owned manufacturing enterprises.

Although the Dutch policy system includes a passive right to information held by the public administration, this does not always work well enough. For example, the municipal council of Beuningen favoured the waste disposal site as long as the local population knew nothing about it. Another important aspect is that the relevant information in private institutions is often strongly protected by privacy or competition and, therefore, not truly available at all.

The management of urban conflicts needs at the very least an attitude of openness to the public by governmental institutions. Otherwise the political price - less democratic decision-making and the administrative price of long drawn out policy processes - will continue to be very high.

The position of inflexible actors

Another lesson from the cases is that any actor who operates completely inflexibly (e.g. the municipality of Borne) will pay the highest price. In a pluralistic regime it is very dangerous to stand alone. The coalition against the actor in opposition is created quickly. On the other hand an inflexible position is often produced by a weakly operating coalition (see the case of Nistelrode). None of the actors in a policy network can produce a definite decision alone. The reverse seem to be true as well, and one actor can resist the other actors only if their behaviour permits it.

Powerful actors

Those actors who can gain control over various sources of power can create a powerful position for themself. The province in the Duiven Westervoort case, for example, not only monopolized the main information (means of orientation) but controled an important means of production (a special former deputy as a power-broker in the policy-network) and a means of organisation (by controlling the planning-procedure). This accumulation of power resources made the province relatively independent from other actors. From this perspective the case of Stara Milosna reflects the other side of the coin. Formal powers are not enough to be effective. Leadership in using powers effectively is very important as well. The arrogant use of power is the worst. Although this is not always punished immediately it is very counterproductive in times of changing political climate.

Performance of the Dutch and Polish political-administrative systems

The political-administrative systems described here are oriented mainly towards conflict-management. In both systems, there are conflicts between individuals, groups and institutions. In the Netherlands conflicting interests are accepted as a quite normal basis for social and political activity. In Poland, however, the existence of different interests and the conflicts related to them had been mostly neglected under the 'old regime'. This can partly explain why the Polish performance in conflict-management was, in general, based on rigidity and therefore not really successful. The performance of the political and administrative systems of Poland and the Netherlands can be analyzed in two ways. Firstly in a summary of the similarities and differences of the systems (cf chapter 3) and secondly by evaluating the roles of the state in both systems, based on general knowledge as well as on an analysis of the cases.

Similarities and differences

In chapter 3 the Polish and Dutch political systems were compared. Some similarities and differences in the performances of these systems were formulated which can be summarised as follows.
Similarities:
- Both policy systems are very complex (legislation, organisation, actors, agencies).
- There is a relative monopoly of public institutions in the fields of physical planning, although the claims and the influence of these institutions decreased over time.
- The effectiveness of comprehensive long-term planning is questioned in both countries.
- In both countries a tendency towards decentralisation and privatisation is to be seen, starting of course from totally different perspectives. In the Netherlands a moderate move towards decentralisation from the central government to provincial and municipal level can be seen. These tendencies are everywhere the same. In the field of environmental policy the involvement of the central government is increasing rapidly. Privatisation has up till now been limited to the delivering of certain kinds of services (engineering, research, consultancy, catering, printing, etc.). In Poland, since March 1989 the round table and the elections for the senate and for president have launched a process of privatisation and decentralisation of which the resulting new equilibrium is impossible to predict.
- In both systems informal networks can be influential. In the Netherlands, for instance, these networks follow political party lines, links between societal organisations and political parties and personal relationships. In Poland the formal and the informal structures include many ideologies, attitudes, approaches, procedures and processes. The roles of administrative bodies are not always clear and often even ambiguous.

Differences:
- Although informal networks are important in both systems, the Polish system is basically a centralised one, whilst the Dutch system is a mixture of centralised and decentralised arrangements.
- In comparison with Polish local authorities, the power of the municipal level in the Netherlands is strong on urban questions although constrained by policies of and subsidies from national and regional governments.
- Although institutionally separated, the Polish physical planning system is, in effect, part of the economic planning system. Physical planning is primarily associated with productive forces and in that way is embedded in social relationships. Therefore many locational, land use and zoning issues are subject to agencies concerned with economic sectoral production as well as to agencies in the field of physical planning. In the Netherlands

physical planning is a planning system as such, with no institutionalised dependency on other fields of planning. In other fields, planning as a vehicle for policy making has been developed recently: traffic and transport, environmental affairs and water management. Economic planning is seen to be the work of government as is global forecasting of private production and of employment. Regional economic planning is very limited in scope and policy instruments.
- The style of government in Poland is legalistic and bureaucratic. In the Netherlands there is a more open and flexible style. The concept of pluralism can help to explain this. In the Dutch system, pluralism can be seen in how other institutional frameworks are embedded in the public administration (intermediate organisations, semi-public bodies with a public task, and pressure and interest groups).
- The gap between formal and informal arrangements is greater in Poland than in the Netherlands. This reflects the exclusive relationship between the communist party and the public administration in Poland, while in the Netherlands the multi-party system, plus the low threshold for the private sector approaching public institutions produces a greater capacity to learn in the decision network. This causes smaller gaps between formal and informal arrangements.
- For the same reason, objections and appeal seem to be more effective in the Netherlands.
- Power is predominantly in the hands of elected bodies in the Netherlands, whereas in Poland this power is concentrated in the hands of public officials as a part of the bureaucratic system.
- The Dutch system has more stability and continuity. It seems that the frequent changes of coalitions in the Netherlands are coupled with less societal changes than are the changes of governments in Poland.

The role of the state: a global evaluation

If the role of the state (chapter 2) is taken into account explicitly, the following general conclusions can be drawn:
- Both political systems fulfil the role of supplier of general facilities and the role of allocator of goods and services. But their effect is different. When the claims made of these systems are taken into account, the Polish system seems to be weaker than the Dutch system.
- The role of safeguarding the interests of the executive administrative institutions is taken seriously in both systems. In Poland, the management of conflicts in which central ministerial offices are involved has to deal with the interests of the buraucracies and of individual officials. Making a career in Poland means being almost completely dependent on those in high positions in governmental offices. In the Netherlands, although central administrative power is very strong, this power is embedded in more decentralized procedures.
- The role of arbitrator and manager of social-political tensions was very difficult to play authoritatively in Poland during the last decade. Nevertheless, the Supreme Administrative Court does play an important role as an arbitrator, especially since 1985. In practice this role of arbitrator is comparable in the countries. In the Netherlands, once again, it seems that these roles are much more part of the system as a whole. Nevertheless, we should realize that in the Netherlands these roles are

also played in constantly changing power-relations between the 'trias politica'. Recently, it has been the courts which take the lead in managing social-political tensions. The executive institutions in particular are so often a serious part of the conflict that the judges have to take over the role of authoritative decision maker. It should be stated, however, that the cases in this book cannot in themselves verify or confirm these observations.

Decision-networks in the Polish and Dutch political-administrative systems

It can be concluded that, in both systems, the decision network approach is indeed used to steer such networks. But both in legislation and in governmental practice, the notion of networks is underdeveloped. The networks differ in structure and in openness to the scrutiny of society. In the Netherlands, interactions between the policy system and societal groups and citizens are more frequent, intensive and influential than in Poland. The same applies to interactions within the governmental system.

A contribution to the theory of urban conflicts

The emphasis of this research project is on how the policy-systems of Poland and the Netherlands perform, especially with respect to managing urban conflicts. The authors make only a modest claim to contribute here to the theory of urban conflicts.

Dimensions of the term 'conflict'

In this cross-national comparative research project, the term 'conflict' has been used in three ways (chapter 1, section 3):
1. conflict as an inevitable characteristic of urban space. Changing the function of the use of urban space always implies the change of property rights and the production of externalities which bring many new actors into the arena and create the need for new political choices;
2. conflict as the actor's strategy for realizing his own interests. Then, the main task of urban management is to promote the use of all types of strategies (e.g. negotiation and forming coalition) apart from the conflict strategy;
3. conflict as the planned or un-planned result of the dynamism of policy-networks. The main focus is to discover and to analyse how conflicts can dominate the actors involved and how co-operation can be brought about in order to tackle the issues.

When looking at the histories of all the cases, all three aspects of the term conflict can easily be seen. The cases were chosen so as to demonstrate conflicting interests in relation to the scarcity of land and its environmental qualities. The second and third aspects were incorporated into the project as the result of a common theoretical approach: the second dimension of conflict is actor-oriented, the third dimension is inter-organizationally oriented.

As a result of this cross-national comparative research-project, the authors claim to have combined usefully these theoretical notions in a common descriptive-analytical framework: the 10-steps-schedule (table 1, chapter 2).

The cases demonstrated important aspects of conflicts. These were: the complexity of the conflict as such, the complexity of the solution-package, its stability over time, the perceptions of the parties involved, the degree of clarity (binding powers in legislation), the course of the conflict, the main interests.

In the cases (chapter 4 and 5) the three ways of looking at conflicts could be observed.

Dimension 1: conflict as an inevitable characteristic of urban space All cases show how parties either already are, or have become aware of, the scarcity of land and try to protect or safeguard the quality of the environment as attached to the place of their prime interest. All conflicts show the clash between a general interest, generally supported or declared by a higher authority or central state body, and a local or private interest. The consequences were often regarded as unacceptable, even when the initial decisions were not questioned at all.

The cases show that problems which can be defined objectively as spatial or physical can easily be translated into terms of social interaction, with all the characteristics involved such as the distribution and redistribution of rights and opportunities between individuals, groups and public administration and the related actions and processes.

It is indisputable that the interests which extend beyond the direct interest of a local community should be served properly, even when the opinion of a local community is not followed. Therefore, institutional arrangements and operational techniques are necessary to accommodate conflicts which can result from the scarcity of land and the environmental quality of space. The cases show that, in practice, the institutional framework, the strategic decision-making, and the operational decision-making are often not very well tuned to each other. These seem to be different domains which act in relative isolation.

Dimension 2: conflict as an actors' strategy to realize his own interest Many of the actors in the cases seem to operate from an attitude which can be characterised as 'not in my backyard' (nimby). Therefore, conflict as a deliberate strategy is apparent in several cases. The most prominent example is in the municipality of Geleen, which opposed the activity on its territory by every means and did so effectively. Taking all the cases together, an extensive arsenal of strategies and techniques can be seen, which can be effective and applicable in conflict situations. It is striking that none of the parties which were the initiators of what turned out to be a conflict policy took the necessary measures in advance to manage the situation properly. The Dutch cases show that it often took a time to find the proper conflict-solving mechanism which was acceptable or reluctantly accepted in the end. Statutory powers, appeal procedures, compensation and open organisational arrangements contributed to bringing disputes to an end.

Dimension 3: conflict as a result of the dynamics in the policy-networks Hardly any initial conflict can be dealt with in an isolated fashion. The number of parties which act as supporters multiply the number of interests, including the hidden interests.

A clear-cut set of responsibilities is no guarantee that a process is developing smoothly. A tentative conclusion can be drawn from the cases that, when the institutional framework (the policy system) is not well accommodated to dealing with such questions, the chance is great that an overt conflict will be the result of dynamism in the policy-network. The Polish cases and, in part two Dutch cases, DSM and Nistelrode, support that conclusion. In such a situation the chance of escalation or dead-lock is real.

Some remarks have been made about the dynamics of both systems. The visually uncontrolled dynamics of the Polish system which reflect both small and fundamental changes in the principles of state, are reflected in the cases, as is the general lack of credibility of the former regime. The main differences between the Polish cases on the one hand and the Dutch ones on the other are the degree of unexpected dynamics and the possibility of transferring experience from similar situations. It has to be stressed, however, that the transfer of more general knowledge and expertise in the Dutch cases was rather limited.

Productive theoretical-analytical framework

The 10 step schedule and the operationalisation of the theoretical basis of this project include a static part (the description of the actors, their goals and means) and a dynamic part (the interdependency between the actors, their strategies to influence each other's position in the network, how these mutual dependencies and interactions work out in the development of the power relations in the policy-network). This theoretical-analytical framework was applied to the cases in Poland and the Netherlands (chapter 4 and 5; the first section of this chapter). This specially developed research tool had several positive functions.

The first function was the creation of a common research language between academics, not only from different countries and cultures but also from different academic disciplines.

The second function was to give a framework for comparison between the selected cases: this too worked out succesfully.

The third function of this approach was the production of a more detailed view of spatial urban conflicts. This third function will now be explained in more detail.

Results concerning the concept of 'spatial urban conflict'

Urban space and scarcity The first characteristic of a spatial conflict is not surprising: it is that it is possible to localize the conflict in a specific territorial area. Such conflicts are related to public policy-making, and this means that governmental institutions are involved. The actions of the government are directed towards public decisions taken to manage the conflict publicly and authoritatively.

The formal decisions in these cases show a high degree of rigidity. This is the result of several things. Physical space is a very scarce good, especially in urban areas, and it is not easy to substitute it. Land has many values for people and not only an economic value. So, in policy-making in spatial conflicts, there are many non-monetary aspects involved. In short, the management of this type of conflict requires political activities based on strong authority. Generally speaking, the physical aspects of urban conflicts demand strong involvement, particularly from local authorities. In the Netherlands these conflicts require different forms of decentralized administration, functionally as well as territorially.

The demands for and the impact of government intervention Actors, such as pressure groups and action groups of citizens, constantly demand the redistribution of development opportunities concerning different urban spaces. More abstractly speaking, their demands on local government include more easier access to better spatial quality. Redistribution of these opportunities by local government means that property rights and land-use rights have to be changed. This implies that the position of the actors in the policy-network will change. So, by re-allocating the access to spatial quality, local authorities constantly produce new externalities, and these will be reflected in the policy-network. Whatever the public decision, it will always touch the interests of social groups. So, theoretically, it will always produce dynamism in the policy-network.

To summarise, spatial urban conflicts can be localized territorially and, as such, they require intervention by governmental institutions, mostly at local level. The management of spatial urban conflicts includes authoritative decision-making, particularly because every resolution will produce new externalities which will have an impact on the interests of other social groups, resulting in a new dynamics in the policy-network.

Managing spatial urban conflicts To manage urban conflicts effectively it is necessary to have the expertise to recognize the problem, to describe it, and to solve it. Knowledge is required of the theories of conflict, the theory of decision-making, and of economic approaches.

We can refer here to Faludi's suggestion of the manipulation of the 'land-regime' (Faludi, 1987, pp. 148-149). More precisely, the land regime has two sides to it. 'From the angle of the individual land decision unit, it is the sum total of all legal barriers protecting it from intrusion and controlling activities on it for the benefit of others. From that of the environmental authority, all land decision units within its jurisdiction form the objects of control' (Faludi, oc, p. 149). So, the land-regime is the total sum of rules which are relevant to a special piece of land and which operate as the framework for decision-making concerning this territory. This decision-making can concern a substantial change in the permitted development of a plot or can be a procedural solution about how to change the function of a piece of land (Faludi, op. cit., chapter 5).

The urban conflict manager needs adequate knowledge concerning the 'land-regime'. Not only that, he ought to know how to manipulate the land-regime according to the dynamism of the policy-network within which he is an actor himself. However, the expert should be realistic as well. For it is an essential characteristic of policy-networks that the actors are so interdependent, that none of them is capable of controlling the process.

Policy-networks: a tool for analysis and steering? The last remark might seem to suggest that the concept of policy-networks cannot be used realistically for steering. Therefore the following question should be put mean: what does the concept of policy-networks mean for the practice of urban conflict management?

From the point of view of the government involved in the conflict, insight into the functioning of policy-networks is important for effective policy-making. If the interdependencies between the relevant actors involved in a conflict are not recognized, there seems to be only a small chance that the policy will be oriented towards the most crucial actors and to their influential, conflict producing actions. Another advantage of a good analysis of the functioning of policy-networks is that the government is primarily seen as an 'insider', i.e. one of the actors in the network and not as an 'outsider', an independent governor or arbitrator, for instance. So, the strategies and interactions of the government are part of the analysis. The analysis can show the limits of steering within the govenment as well as steering by the government. For example, the governmental planning systems relevant to a special spatial conflict are often badly integrated and this makes the implementation of the chosen strategy rather dubious. Spatial urban conflicts in the case-studies of this project often have technical environmental aspects, for example waste disposal by different techniques. If new technologies become available, it is very important to know how these technical instruments can best be employed within the network. Finally, relevant information about the policy network can help in choosing the right policy instruments: which intervention will be the most effective for realizing the synergetic impact which will produce enough co-operation in the network to stop the conflict?

Better analysis of the conflict by using the concept of policy-networks can give more realistic insights into how effective policy can be. To tackle spatial urban conflicts demands governmental managers who know how to operate like the conductors of an orchestra. Their task is to get a harmonious melody out of a cacophony of noise produced by a lot of relatively autonomous actors. To fulfil the task, it is necessary not only to have expertise about the score (the spatial urban conflict), but also about the musicians (the actors), their instruments (the tools or power resources), their approaches to the music as well as to their position in the orchestra.

Of course, this explanation of the usefulness of the policy-network concept can be worked out for every actor in the network. Here we have concentrated on the perspective of a governmental actor, because governmental participation is one of the conditions of the spatial conflicts in this study.

Conclusions

In this last section some observations will be formulated which would seem to be important for the management of urban conflicts in the future.

Acceptance of contextuality as relevant for management and planning

In economics there is a strong theoretical division between macro and micro-economics. It is often discussed in cultural anthropology and sociology how the macro-context should be incorporated into the descriptive analysis of special cases and vice versa, also how knowledge at micro-level can be transferred to general propositions.

The policy network approach claims to be a synthetic tool of social science which supersedes the micro-macro discussion. The macro-context is not only accepted as being important for every case-study, in fact it is an essential part of any issue, conflict or management-process in political and administrative practice. From the point of view of planning and management, every political issue is embedded in a very specific situation. Therefore, the contextuality of all selected cases is assumed throughout this study. This implies that lessons from the cases can be used as a checklist for the management of urban conflicts in the future. However, these lessons can never have the character of recipes for the resolution of spatial, urban conflicts. Because of its specific context, every resolution of a spatial and social conflict needs to be tailor-made. Further, general propositions about averages are not relevant. All solutions are have to be produced for a specific context, under special circumstances. Nevertheless for the future management of social and urban conflicts one slogan is relevant: think global, act local.

The acceptance of conflict in the political system

According to the work of Coser and Simmel, several social functions of conflicts can be distinguished (chapter 2).

The political and administrative culture of the Dutch system does not enjoy social conflicts, whoever the actor is! Yet conflicts exist and an important function of physical planning is the co-ordination between conflicting interests in the field of spatial development. In fact, the main reason that the government assumes the task of producing a physical environment of the highest quality possible, is the acceptance of the reality of conflicts in society.

During the last decade, the 'Solidarnosc' movement changed the political climate in Poland dramatically. The quality of the physical space had been given no priority in Poland until the end of the eighties. During the period of the communist regime, the social conflicts concerning the spatial organisation were ideologically neither recognized nor accepted (see chapter 3). Therefore, social or spatial urban conflicts in the Polish system had never had the positive effects suggested as possible by the sociologists mentioned above.

Generally, the conflicts in the Polish cases became manifest by the increasing use of the means of coercion and they produced severe dead-lock. In the Netherlands the conflicts had more the function of creating consensus, at least of creating a political and administrative atmosphere within which some exchange between conflicting interests became possible.

Types of actors in relation to the character of the conflicts

In the lessons of the cases (see the first section of this chapter) we looked at two types of actors - inflexible actors and powerful actors.

Actors in social conflicts should bear in mind that being inflexible, which means not being ready to work out compromises, is counter-productive to self-interest in the long run. Of course, strategies of obstruction and consistency in arguing can produce a power position in the network. But parties should be aware of the delicacy of this situation and avoid turning to the exchange option too late.

In general, powerful actors neither have enough power resources, nor do they use them to solve a conflict completely by themselves: they are dependent on other actors as well. That may not be so in a specific case or at a specific moment, but they are involved in many issues and they try to keep a long term perspective. They occupy crossroads in the policy-networks. As power-brokers they will try to distribute profits to as many actors as possible and, if they have to harm the interests of some actors, they will attempt to produce an equilibrium between costs and benefits. In fact, power-brokers try to manage conflicts, not by using coercive power resources, but by means of organisation and orientation in order to cause as few political costs as possible. When they meet inflexible actors, power-brokers will prefer a long-term dead-lock to a solution produced by violent, coercive means. As power-brokers they have or can create enough time to wait for a better chance. Only a very urgent problem or a clear distortion of the constitutional state will force them to a decision. The worst attitude people in power can have is to be arrogant. In practice, such an attitude reflects the basic weakness of the basis of their power. In fact they have lost the power-game before it has started.

Roles of the state

In a pluralist, democratic society the roles of the state are difficult to play. In order to make public choices in the general interest, the public policy-making process should have enough democratic credibility for its effective implementation. This is not always easy, as governmental institutions often have their own interest in the policy field. They are more like an actor looking for an effective coalition in the network than an arbitrator, who has enough authority to make a final and acceptable decision. In many conflicts governmental institutions themselves produce the dead-locks because they compete against one another. Whatever the goals the government wants to realise, governmental institutions should recognize the dynamics of the policy-networks in order to create change effectively. Because the courts are getting more involved in arbitration, government should avoid the escalation of conflict, which can preclude it being solved by the government's own institutions. The actions of the court should be employed only in exceptional cases in order to keep credibility and authority within the government.

Resolutions: arsenal of intervention

The total arsenal of intervention is considerable and every policy-situation will need a special combination of intervention, a "policy-mix". In policy-networks every actor can and should create his own scale of interventions. There is no one effective recipe for any actors. Those actors who can produce a new combination of power resources, adapted to the special context of the conflict involved, will gain an advantage. In all the cases studied here the policy-networks are very complex, both in Poland as in the Netherlands. All actors are in some way dependent on one another. The challenge of managing an urban conflict is great. The time at which a resolution to the conflict will be near is, in general, unpredictable.

Steering the network: political choices

Looking at conflict management from the perspective of the policy-network, produces a very realistic picture of complex social and political phenomena and events. Yet, a serious question arises, can there be "good" and "bad" actors?

The policy-network perspective tries to be objective in its description and analysis of the dynamic social facts. Although the selection of the conflicts to be studied can be in itself a political choice, this type of qualitative social scientific research is relatively easy to check. The researcher makes a choice about the good and the bad actors as soon as he decides to whom to give the information about the policy-network. In essence this is a political choice. So, using analytical knowledge for action, the researcher has to make his values and goals explicit. A policy consultant, on the other hand, may manage such choices mainly from motives of expediency.

References

Faludi, Andreas (1987), *A Decision-centred View of Environmental Planning*, Pergamon Press, Oxford

Goverde, Henri and Tom Hoeben (1991), *Netwerken over de landsgrens heen*, Een onderzoek naar Duitse besluitvorming over de afvalstortlocatie Weeze-Wemb en mogelijkheden voor Nederlandse participatie via nieuwe sturingsarrangementen, Nijmegen.

Epilogue

Henri Goverde

In chapter 6 some conclusions and recommendations were presented based on the comparative research described in the chapters 3, 4, and 5. This project was carried out in a very dramatic period, the era when Central- and East-European countries escaped from the Soviet umbrella (1988-1990). Although this international political change was not the subject of the project, it was the setting which influenced the description of the Polish political system as well as the Polish cases. It was clear that such a change would come. But the fact that it happened nevertheless took the research team by surprise and in fact, two of the Polish researchers became under-secretaries of State in the Mazowiecski-cabinet. Because of this unique research context, the authors will try to point out its relevance for developing tools and skills for managing spatial urban conflicts.

Developments in the context of the Polish and Dutch policy systems

At the end of the eighties it became very clear that the planned changes in Poland, as in the Netherlands, were extremely dependent on the global and, particularly, the European context. Both countries are part of the mutually interdependent development of the global network of states and nations and especially of the configuration of all European countries. The actual changes in the interdependencies between the European states are reflected in an increase in the activities of individuals, groups and institutions crossing traditional state borders. This type of economic and social pressure will be reflected in competition for scarce land resources. It will produce extra urban and environmental conflicts which will have to be managed.

International economic and political dependencies It is a truism to say that the developments in the societies of East and Central Europe accelerate faster than anyone could have imagined at the beginning of 1989. Paul Kennedy explained in 1987 how the two main superpowers could get into a spiral of decline [1].

There is no doubt that when some powers decline, others rise. In Europe a newly united Germany will dominate the economy - and probably the politics - of this continent for a long period. Germany will have a strong impact on the Polish and Dutch political and economic systems. It will influence the priorities in these systems, particularly the infrastructure, energy production and the creation of business centres.

Poland and the Netherlands: frontier-states of a united Germany The first impact of the unification of Germany is important not only for Poland and the Netherlands but for the whole of Europe. Nowadays, the impetus of 'Europe 1992' - integration has been lost, because of the recent developments in Central Europe. Some forecasters see that countries like the Netherlands, Belgium and Denmark will be no more than an 'economic zone' of the new Germany. Their sovereignity in practice will be insignificant and only symbolized by their monarchies. Poland's west-border has been confirmed, but it will be a very open one. Perhaps Poland, Hungary, Czechoslovakia and parts of Yugoslavia will soon join the European Community. However, the main reason for such an integration will be political, to stabilise the process of democratisation, and not economic (Lubbers, 1990).

This is not the right place to work out, neither to speculate on, these interdependencies in detail. Nevertheless, it has to be said that the position of the Polish and Dutch political systems is still exceedingly dependent on the 'Great Powers'. If the dominant powers of the USSR and the USA are replaced by the power of Germany it can be expected that the physical environment in both countries will also be greatly influenced by this change. One of the consequence will be a strong pressure to produce housing for emigrants and offices and business districts and to adapt the lines of communication to the higher demand (east-west infrastructure, telecommunication). The physical planners will have a lot of work to do to manage conflicts based on the scarcity of land.

A civil society with countervailing powers

Pluralism demands intermediary and countervailing powers Perhaps the main difference between the Polish and the Dutch political and administrative system is the absence of a balanced system of countervailing powers in Poland and its presence in the Netherlands. The Dutch system is a genuinely pluralistic one and all powers are embedded in other powers. No one agency can control political power processes. In Poland, in contrast, the state is organized in a centralist way. The regional and local government levels are rather weakly developed. This will be the case for the next few years although reforms are continuing. Intermediary powers between the government and the citizens are also weak, if not politically (e.g. church, trade-unions) certainly in institutionalised and formal competences within the political-administrative processes (e.g. advisory boards representing pressure and interest groups). The absence of well embedded intermediary structures gives rise to dead-locks in conflict situations which cannot easily be resolved.

When many demands for scarce space have to be dealt with, dead-locks are very dysfunctional for the development and revitalization of the economic and physical structure of a country.

1989: a civil revolution? From this perspective it is extremely important to find an adequate framework for the historical and cultural interpretation of social-political movements in Central Europe. If T. Garton Ash is right, these movements are more comparable with the revolution of 1848 than with that of 1789. Garton Ash (1990,p.20) stresses that the central concept in opposition thinking during the 1980s was that of a 'civil society' [2]. Even the workers' leader and present President of Poland, Lech Walesa, confirmed in London (1991) that what he wants is a middle-class society. On this, virtually all of Poland's present political leaders agree.

Although the notion of the 'civil society' has not been worked out completely in political theory, it would seem to be very important as a basis for controlled change from a communist to a liberal democratic parliamentary political system. From this perspective, countervailing powers and intermediary institutions can be developed [3]. The neccessity for the creation of countervailing powers should also be an argument for western liberal democracies to offer help to countries in transition in Central Europe.

1991: lack of resolution One year later, however, the political administrative and social situation is not as bright and hopeful as it had been in the beginning of 1990. The political context can be characterized by the change in the slogan from 'there's no liberty without Solidarity' to 'there's no Solidarity in liberty' (T. Garton Ash, 1991, p.46 [4]). Nevertheless, the construction of the 'civil society' as a middle-class society based on the market-economy, political pluralism and intermediary powers, is the accepted goal about which there is certainly consensus. The task can be carried out only if more political stability can be realized. Unfortunately, it could take another lengthy period before this happens. This is tragic, because it prevents fast decision-taking about investments in almost all sectors of society, including the physical environment. Dead-lock in the process of decision-making concerning the development of Granary Island in Gdansk illustrates the powerlessness of the local administration. This lack of a resolution blocks the physical integration of the country into the European network of states, which is an urgent necessity.

Powershifts and predictable conflicts

Prosperity and the political system In his newest book 'Powershift: knowledge, wealth, and violence at the edge of the 21st century'(1990, ch 20), A. Toffler argues that every society needs a certain congruence between the way the people create wealth and the way they govern themselves. If it is true that the world is entering a new phase of economic production from industrial mass-production to an economy based on information, transfering power from multi-national super-firms to the 'flexfirms', in both political systems covered in this book there can be expected fierce conflicts between new actors in the near future. Although Toffler predicts a fundamental and worldwide economic and political powershift which will take several decades at least, he makes his hypothesis plausible with many examples and illustrations of changing economic approaches in many fields throughout the world. If one cannot accept Tofflers' central idea, it still seems realistic to deduce from his analysis a tremendous number of innovations - technological, economic, social and political - which will produce many new claims on the physical environment and, of course, many conflicts between opposing interests.

Conflicts to be expected in local government New technological and social conditions demand that the political system adapt. The trend is not towards a rising scale of organisations and their activities. On the contrary, disintegration of large scale organisations as well as the acceleration of change are the real trends. Therefore the new conditions and developments will cause many conflicts, especially at local and regional level. It is not easy to estimate which of the political systems studied in this book, the decentralized unitary state of the Netherlands or the centralised Polish state, can be most easily adapted to the new challenges.

Conflicts concerning institutional norms Adapting the political system means attacking existing institutional norms. The main problem for local administrations is uncertainty about the dynamism of the new conditions and developments and about how to manage them.
Derksen (1990) distinguished three types of institutional norms:
- norms concerning the recruitment of new public officials (input-norms);
- internal administrative norms concerning behaviour in internal administrative processes (conversion norms);
- norms concerning the way the local community is administered (output-norms).

According to Norbert Elias (1939/1969) the fewer institutional norms, the less civilized the social and political system. Eisenstadt (1987) agrees that the mechanisms of cultural integration may well become more important, but he argues that they become more vulnerable as well. This is the result of the growing complexity of the political system. At the same time, the number of conflicts about these norms will grow. This perspective is congruent with the trends forecast by Toffler mentioned above.

Management of conflicts demands a normative approach by social interaction

Finally, it would be useful to refer once again to Coser (1956). This author stated that 'Social conflict is a mechanism for readjustment of norms adequate to new conditions. A flexible society benefits from conflict because such behavior, by helping to create and modify norms, assures its continuance under changing conditions'. So, conflicts should be approached positively. Yet, this does not mean that if conflicts are socially acceptable phenomena, the management of them is clear and unambiguous. On the contrary, in the last two decades urban planners have usually approached spatial conflicts in an instrumental way. As soon as a conflict was recognized, it was perceived as undesirable. Goals to avoid the situation were formulated and means were developed to realise these goals. Although many alternatives to a linear planning-process have been developed, the goals/means perspective always dominated. This instrumental way of thinking was based on the attitude of engineers perceiving society as a mechanical object.
The policy-network approach accepts conflicts as normal in a society. Of

course, conflicts based on the means of coercion should be avoided as much as possible. The first normative assumption for the attempt to steer the policy-network by conflict-managers should be that destructive violence is not acceptable in a civilized democratic society. The policy-network approach is oriented to intervening in social interactions between actors involved in a conflict. This approach promotes social technology, based on small-group theory, gaming, and simulation (Geurts/Vennix, 1989), in order to let the actors involved discover for themselves what the real chances and real threats are in each other's behaviour.

While the instrumental approach made technicians think for the good of the people, the policy-network approach promotes the creation of situations within which the actors involved can work out the resolution of their conflict in as structured a way as possible.

The authors believe that this approach is flexible enough to be effective in managing spatial urban conflicts, even under the conditions of a 'post-mass-productive economy'.

Notes

1. For the Soviet Union (Kennedy, op.cit, pp. 488-496) the most critical areas are agriculture, industrial efficiency, high-technology and demographics (a steady decline in life expectancy and an increase infant mortality since the 1970s). The United States runs the risk of what might roughly be called 'imperial overstretch': 'the sum total of the United States' global interests and obligations is far larger nowadays than is the country's power to defend them all simultaneously' (Kennedy, oc, pp. 515).
2. According to Garton Ash (February 1990) the year 1989 was the spring of societies which aspired to be "civil" societies. This notion contains at least three basic requirements:
   - there should be forms of association, national, regional, local, professional, that would be voluntary, authentic, democratic, and, first and foremost, not controlled or manipulated by the Party or the Party-state;
   - people should be 'civil': that is polite, tolerant and, above all, non-violent;
   - the idea of citizenship has to be taken seriously.
3. Here is not the place to take sides in the political situation in Poland in the middle of 1990. Yet, this situation illustrates the three major elements that give cause for concern about democracy in East Central Europe (T. Garton Ash, August 1990, p. 56): 1) popular disgruntlement about the processes of parliamentary democracy; 2) the processes of fledgling democracy (a low popular tolerance or understanding of political conflict together with a high level of political conflict inside the new political elites); 3) dislocation and distress associated with the conversion to a market economy.
4. The phenomena in this transition period are not easy to understand. Of course, 'class' and 'class consciousness' played a part in the end as they had in the beginning of Solidarity. But the key to this particular passage of Polish history is to be found not in sociology or economics, but in old-fashioned politics, in the clash of personalities and the competition for power. Not Marx, not Hegel, but Macchiavelli and Thucydides have to be

in our minds, when we write this last, sad chapter in the annals of Solidarity' (T.Garton Ash, 1991, p. 55).

References

Crozier, M. (1970), *La societé bloquée*, Paris.
Coser, L. (1956), *The functions of social conflict*, Glencoe Illinois
Derksen, W. (1990), Institutionele normen in het lokaal bestuur, in: *Bestuurswetenschappen*, nr 4, p. 267-281
Eisenstadt, S.N. and A. Sachar (1987), *Society, Culture and Urbanization*, London
Elias, Norbert (1969), *Uber den Prozess der Zivilisation. Sociogenetische und Psychogenetische Untersuchungen* (1939), Bern
Garton Ash, Timothy (1990), 'Eastern Europe: The Year of Truth', in: *The New York Review of Books*, vol XXXVII, nr 2, February 15, pp. 17-22
Garton Ash, Timothy (1990), 'Eastern Europe: Après Le Déluge, Nous' in: *The New York Review of Books*, vol XXXVII, nr 16, August 16, pp. 51-57
Garton Ash, Timothy (1991), 'Poland after Solidarity', in: *The New York Review of Books*, vol XXXVIII, nr 11, June, 13, pp. 46-58
Geurts, J. en J. Vennix (1989), *Verkenning in Beleidsanalyse*, Zeist
Kennedy, Paul (1987), *The Rise and Fall of the Great Powers. Economic change and military conflict from 1500 to 2000*, Random House, New York
Lubbers, R.F.M. (1990), *'Europa's akkers liggen open'* in: NRC, 2.8.1990
Regulski, J. (1989), 'Polish local government in transition', in: *Environment and Planning C*: Government and Policy, vol 7, pp. 423-444
Toffler, Alvin (1990), *Powershift: knowledge, wealth, and violence at the edge of the 21st century*, New York, Bantam Books

Appendix

Synopsis of the chronological account of the cases in terms of the powers used and the interactions (for abbreviations see Table 5.1)

Lodz waste disposal site

1977
- stat.pow.   Palczew waste disposal site included in the provincial
(strat.bind.)   physical development plan
- stat.pow.   People's Council of Brojce endorses physical plan
(strat.bind.)   including waste disposal
inst.arr   provincial administration becomes the authority in charge
                    of the site
obstr.   prov. administration tries to buy the land; rejection by all
                    the farmers becoming apparent in a meeting of provincial
                    officials and owners

1981
- stat. pow.   introduction of Martial Law, postponement of the conflict,
(strat.bind.)   decision to diminish the area of the site
stat.pow. (op.ind.)
1983
- cl.stat.pow.   request of Lodz authorities to expropriate a small area
(op.bind.)
- stat.pow.   refusal by the People's Council and the farmers; refusal
(op.bind) obstr.   by the local executive to take a decision to change the
                    land use

1985
- cl.comp. resolution by local People's Council setting conditions for co-operation
- meet. meeting between provincial officers and farmers about conditions
- mob. intervention by Patriotic Movement of National Rebirth (PRON) criticising waste treatment in the Lodz area and suggesting villagers claim compensation
- obj. and app. objection of the councils of villagers administrator addressed to the State People's Council and the President of Poland to the location, because of the risk of ground water pollution
- stat. pow. (superv.) reply by the minister of spatial economy confirming the location
- stat. pow (strat./bind) decision by the local executive making change of land use possible for a small area
- meet. and comp. meeting of the President of the province with local residents' committee about a list of compensatory measures; acceptance by the province
- i.o.t. force establishment of a commission for proper realisation by the province
obstr. renewed refusal to sell land by the farmers

1987
- obj. and app. objections by farmers and villagers to a required and accepted by-pass, addressed to the minister of building construction and spatial economy
- stat. pow. (superv.) reply from the minister endorsing the site and indicating the posibility of appeal to the Supreme Administrative Court (SAC)
- obj. and app. several appeals to that court
- info start of using the site, preceeded by press coverage at the request of the president of the province
- block. blockade of the first lorries by the villagers
- meet., i.o.t. force reconciliation meeting of vice-pres. of prov. and villagers: communal representative in the commission for proper realisation
- co-op. acceptance of a group of farmers to sell their land
- obj. and app. appeal against location decision by the council of villagers administrator addressed to the President of Parliament; support of the appeal by many local organisations
- info minister of spatial economy (physical planning) justifies the locational decision to parliament
- cl. stat. pow. minister of the environment claims proper protection for the underground water to the provincial government

1988
- block. blockades of villagers to make development of the site impossible
- invest., obstr. attempt by the provincial government to find other locations; refusal of all other local communities

Waste disposal site Beunigen

1973
- inst.arr.   establishment of body of collaborating municipalities
- co-op   proposal of the mayor of Beuningen to use the Weurtse Polder as a waste disposal site

1975
- adv. pow.   recommendation of body of collaborating municipalities to designate Weurtse Polder, consent of the Municipality of Beuningen
- prot. and compl.   protest by the local residents of Beuningen
- cl. investig   request of the Executive Council of Beuningen to look for other locations
- stat. pow. (op., bind), obstr.   rejection by the Council of Beuningen of the location Weurtse Polder
- stat. pow. (strat., ind.)   designation of the site as "a possible location" in the regional physical plan of the province of Gelderland
- obj. and app.   protest against content of regional physical plan
- investig.   promise by the province to undertake further research
- inst. arr.   disbanding of body of collaborating municipalities

1980
- exp. adv.   result of research: the Weurtse Polder is best site
- cl. stat. pow.   request of the province to make a land use plan accordingly
- stat.pow./obstr.   refusal of the municipality
- dir.   directive of the province to the municipality
- obj. and app.   appeal of the municipality against directive
- stat. pow. (strat. ind.)   publication of waste-disposal plan by the province, indicating Weurtse polder,
- inst. arr.   designation of new body of collaborating municipalities for waste management
- meet./cl. for comp.   negotiations about conditions for co-operation
- co-op, comp   withdrawal of appeal by the municipality
- stat. pow. (op. bind)   publication of a draft land-use plan
- obj. and app.   3,000 objections
- stat. pow (op. bind)   adoption of the plan by the municipal council
- obj. and app.   5,000 appeals to the province
- co-op (stat. pow/op.bind)   shortened land use planning procedure
- obj. and app.   about 11,000 objections

1985
- stat. pow. (jur.)   declaration by the Council of State that all objections are baseless

1988
    site and incineration operational

Waste disposal site Nistelrode

1973
- inst. arr.   body of 9 collaborating municipalities for waste disposal
- invest.   investigation of regional waste disposal site by the body of co-operating municipalities: a number of possible sites.
- prot. and compl. objection from the mun. of Nistelrode to the Hoge Vorssel site (being in use for dumping in contradiction to the land use plan)

1976
- invest.   further research, indicating a clear preference for Hoge Vorssel
- adv. pow.   province preference for another site
- adv. pow.   decision of the board of the body of collaborating municipalities in favour of Hoge Vorssel
- adv. pow.   provincial consent

1979
- co-op/stat.   conditional co-operation of the executive council of
pow (op.)   Nistelrode to revise a land use plan accordingly
- obstr.   refusal of the municipal council of Nistelrode to adopt land use plan
- cl. dir.   request to the province to impose a directive
- inst. arr.   change in the boundaries of collaborating municipalities concerning waste disposal by the province
- cl.invest.   request of the province to the newly established bodies to choose location
- cl. adv. pow.   request of Nistelrode to the national government to check the provinces' choice of site
- adv. pow.   refusal of central government
- adv. pow.   advice by the Provincial Physical Planning Committee in favour of Hoge Vorssel
- neg./cl. comp.   demanding conditions put forward by Nistelrode. interim solutions by the body of collaborating municipalities

1982
- stat. pow   adoption of the provincial waste-disposal plan, together
(strat.ind.)   with connected decisions concerning the provincial
regional
                          physical plan.
- cl. stat. pow.   request by the body of collaborating municipalities to revise the land use plan
- obstr.   refusal of Nistelrode
- dir.   directive of the province
- obj. a. app.   appeal by Nistelrode to the Crown concerning the provincial waste disposal plan
- stat. pow.(jur.)   decision of the Crown in favour of Nistelrode

Waste disposal site Borne

1978
- inst.arr.   establishment of body of collaborating municipalities

	(gewest Twente)
- invest.	research to find sites, commissioned by the gewest Twente
- inf.	publication of a first interim report mentioning 21 possible locations

1980

- obstr.	rejection of Borne location by the council of Borne
- inf.	second interim report mentioning 2 locations with a shift of the Borne location
- obstr.	refusal of Borne to co-operate further, internal debate in Borne
- inf.	final report with a compromise location in Borne
- adv. pow.	adoption of a location plan by the gewest, indicating Elhorst-Vloedbeld in Borne
- cl. stat. pow.	request to the province to incorporate locations in the regional physical plan
- cl. stat. pow.	request to the municipalities to revise land use plans
- obj. and app.	appeal of Borne to the Council of State concerning the gewest decision
- adv. pow.	proposal of an alternative site by Borne
- stat. pow. (ind.)	refusal of the province
- stat. pow. (ind.)	partial review of the provincial regional physical plan of 1966
- obj. and app.	objections of Borne and 400 private objections
- invest. publ.	report issued by a local interest group questioning the
mob.	necessity of two sites: delay of the decision of the Provincial
	Council concerning the review of the regional physical plan

1985

- stat. pow. (ind)	decision by the provincial council concerning the review of the regional physical plan
- cl. dir.	pressure by the municipality of Enschede and Hengelo on the provincial government
- dir.	directive by the provincial executive issued to Borne
- obj. and app.	appeal concerning the directive by the council of Borne
- stat. pow. (jur.)	other location in operation, rejection of the appeal by the Crown
- stat. pow. (strat. bind.)	revision of the land use plan
- obj. and app.	many objections to the draft land use plan
- stat. pow. (op. bind.)	approval by the provincial executive of the land use plan
- stat. pow. (jur.)	rejection of the appeals by the Crown

1990

	technical preparations of the site

Environmental measures around the Polonit plant

1967

- stat. pow. (ind)	in principle a protection zone of 300 m around the plant applicable since 1967

1970
- stat. pow. (ind.)   preliminary decision by the ministry of chemical industry to relocate Polonit

1975
- stat. pow. (op. bind.)   location decision by the dept. of town planning for new housing for the housing co-operative, adjacent to the Polonit plant
- meet.   correspondence between the ministry and the town president indicating uncertainty concerning relocation
- adv. pow.   disapproval of housing by the state sanitary inspector
- stat. pow. (op. bind.)   approval of the plan by the town authorities
- cl. stat. pow.   request of the management of Polonit to stop preparation of the housing location; continuation of construction
- stat. pow. (op. ind.)   cancelling of relocation of the plant; putting the new blocks of flats into service
- neg.   negotiations between town authorities and the ministry about relocation
- cl. stat. pow.   request by Polonit to exceed standards of emission

1980
- stat. pow. (op. bind.)   refusal by the sanitary inspection
- prot. and compl.   start of opposition by residents: letters of complaint to many bodies
- publ. mob.   increasing publicity
- adv. pow.   expectation of relocation in 1985 expressed by the ministry
- prot. and compl.   protest of residents concerning the operation of the plant, environmental measures taken by Polonit, further protest demanding closing down of the plant
- neg.   new negotiations between town authorities and the ministry
- stat. pow (op.)   temporary permits for Poionit issued by environmental agencies
- civ. disob.   refusal of tenants to pay part of the rent
- stat. pow. (op.)   legal action of the housing co-operative against the tenants
- cl. stat. pow.   request by the housing co-operative to stop the operation of the plant addressed to Arbitration Committees of the district and the State

1985
- agr.   agreement about relocation of the Polonit plant by 1992
- prot. and compl.   protest by other groups against new location
- neg.   correspondence about ad hoc measures for the existing plant

Environmental zoning DSM

1977
- stat. pow. (strat/ind)   endorsement by the provincial council of the regional physical plan, indicating a risk zone of 500 m around DSM, to be extended by the provincial executive
- investig.   development of a risk methodology by the national

	agency of the environment (completed in 1984)
- stat. pow. (ind.)	provisional spatial planning policy by the provincial executive

1982

- inf./publ.	publication of a report about the emergency situation concerning housing by the municipality of Geleen
- adv. pow.	plea by the nat. inspector of the environment to add other risk factors to the noise zoning system for industrial areas, which came into force in that period
- investig.	inventory of the noise situation, made by DSM
- i.o.t. force	establishment of a task group by the prov. exec. to make an inventory of spatial problems in Geleen and Stein in relation to DSM plant
- adv. pow.	increasing critical attitude of national officials concerning provisional provincial policy
- meet., cl. co-op.	attempt of the prov. executive to promote flexible attitude by the minister
- stat. pow.(bind.)	decision of the minister to freeze housing subsidies in the area
- inf., adv. pow.	increasing pressure by Geleen on the province and the minister
- meet., agr.	meeting of the prov. executive with the minister; one housing area to be built

1984

- agr.	due to parliamentary pressure, decision by the minister to prepare a comprehensive environmental plan for DSM, asking the province to develop an environmental policy for the area: agreement of the minister, DSM-board and the province about the approach
- inf./publ.	increasingly critical attitude of Geleen concerning progress of task group
- co-op./i.o.t. force establishment	decision of the province to co-operate with the ministry with regard to comprehensive zoning project; of task organisation by the province
- investig.	risk analysis methodology available
- inf./publ.,/prot. and compl.	critical attitude of Geleen concerning comprehensive env. zoning
- investig./ exp. adv.	commission of three research projects to private firms
- prot. and compl.	critical attitude of DSM concerning risk calculation
- prot. and compl.	further criticism by Geleen of comprehensive env. zoning project
- adv. pow.	abandoning of factors other than risk in the task organisation, discussion about the risk factors

1986

- prot. and compl.	activities of Geleen inside and outside task organisation
- coal.	move of provincial opinion in the direction of Geleen
- investig/inf.	publication of a report by the provincial physical planning agency
- cl.stat. pow./ prot. and compl.	address of an environmental interest group to the parliamentary committee

- stat. pow. (bind), cl.inf.	expiration of legal term for establishing the noise zone, request of the minister to the prov. executive for information about delay
- i.o.t. force	establishment of a special. task force by the ministry
1987	
- inf., obstr.	publication of the report of the special task force; withdrawal of provincial official
- mob./prot. and compl.	mobilisation of the population by the municipality of Geleen
- meet.	several meetings between the prov. executive and the municipality of Geleen
- coal.	endorsement by the prov. executive of the opinion of Geleen, municipalities of Stein and Beek took the same stand
- inf.	presentation of draft noise zoning and report of the special task group by the ministry
- obj. and app./ mob.	hearings and objections of 4,500 residents concerning strict risk standards; objections of Geleen and DSM; support of the ministerial view by an environmental organisation
- comp.	change of opinion by the municipality of Stein, environmental subsidies directed at Stein by the ministry
- inf.	visit of the parliamentary committee of the environment to Geleen
- inf.	technical briefing of the parliamentary committee
- meet./mob., adv. pow.	informal contacts between Geleen, provincial bodies, central gov. bodies shift in the position of the minister: the far-reaching risk-standard became a recommendation
- obj. and app.	objection of the province against the view of the minister
- stat. pow. (op; bind./ind)	final decision of the minister (dec 1987)
- stat. pow. (strat., ind.)	elaboration of the regional physical plan concerning env. zoning

Stara Milosna

1983	
- adv. pow.	initiative of Inter-ministerial Group to construct new housing area
1984	
- adv. pow.	proposal from the chief architect of Warsaw for two locations (not included in P.P.D. Plan for the Warsaw Province of 1978)
- stat. pow. (strat./bind), cl. comp.	resolution of people's council of Wesola to change local physical plan; compensation: apartments, technical facilities
- adv. pow.	approval of the team for passing opinions on location
- stat. pow. (strat./bind.)	approval of the people's council of Wesola of an "adjustment plan"
- comp/oth.	letter to the owners with a final offer for the sale of land
- adv. pow.	critical comments of the Warsaw development planning office

1986
- stat. pow.(bind.) approval of the people's council of Wesola of detailed physical plan

1987
- stat. pow. (op.) approval of the mun. office of the city of Warsaw of an action-plan for the housing area
- stat. pow. (strat./bind) decision of the people's council of Wesola to change the local physical plan
- stat. pow. (op./ind.) resolution of the people's council of Warsaw to designate the Mazovian Landscape Park
- prot. and compl. letters of protest bij residents of Anin and Miedzylesie to several government bodies
- prot. and compl. letter of the residents committee to Parliament
- publ./cl.investig. negative report by the Patriotic Movement of National Revival (PRON), demand for assessment
- adv. pow. positive reaction to the location by the nat. chief san. inspector and the state insp. of env. and the min. of health
- cl. invest. letter of the Polish Ecological Association to the min. of physical planning, asking for assessment by the Chief Comm. for Urbanism and Architecture
- publ., inf. note of the Inter-ministerial Group about the progress of the project

1988
- obj. and app. meeting of residents of Anin, fostering legal steps concerning the breach of the law
- prot. and compl. negative reactions by the children's hospital and other institutions of Anin and Miedzylesie
- prot. and compl. complaint of the League for the Preservation of Nature to the Gov. Comm. for Law
- prot. and compl. second letter by P.R.O.N.
- stat. pow. (jur.) case before the District Court, declaring the residents committee incapable of opposing
- stat. pow. (jur.) opinion of the General Prosecutor's Office:
  a. no breaches of the law
  b. irregularities in proceedings
- mob. letter of representatives of Warsaw authorities to the president of the Council of State Gen. Jaruzelski in favor of housing project
- stat. pow. (jur.) session of the consultative council (Council of State) committed the matter to the Chief Board of Supervision
- exp. adv. cl. investig. Chief Board of Supervision supported the residents' view proposing further expert assessment of several topics
- dir./investig. order of the Council of State to the Office of the City of Warsaw to make the Board's recommendations effective
- stat. pow. (op./bind) decision to stop construction of sewage treatment plant and development in protected zones by the president of the town of Wesola
- obj. and app. Inter-ministrial Group starts construction again and appealed against the decision to stop construction
- dem. protest march organised by resident committees and simultaneous picnic by Interministerial Group

- stat. pow. (op.)	decision of the chief architect of Warsaw cancelling the decision to stop the construction
- exp. adv.	promise made by a vice-president of Warsaw to appoint an independent team of experts, appointment in Nov. 1988
- i.o.t. group	resolution of Warsaw's people's council to appoint a Special Commission
- publ.	statement by the First Secretary of Warsaw's Communist Party about first positive results of experts' work
- mob., cl. exp. adv.	discussion during the Round Table talks, decision to let the Chief Committee for Urbanism and Architecture examine the case
- mob./publ.	open letter of residents of 10 Warsaw residential areas
- exp. adv.	preliminary activities by the Chief Comm. for Urbanism and Architecture and the Special Committee
- stat. pow. (op. bind.)	resolution by the people's council of Warsaw to partially stop the construction

Duiven-Westervoort

1967

- stat. pow. (strat./ind.), co-op.	designation of the Duiven-Westervoort area as a possible reception area for urban development by the nat. gov.; consent of the province and the municipalities
- stat. pow. (strat./ind.)	municipalities start a joint preparation of a physical development plan (structure plan)
- inst. arr.	merger of the two physical planning agencies of the municipalities

1970

- adv. pow.,obj.	proposal of the province to prepare a merger of the 2 municipalities, strong opposition of the 2 municipalities
- adv. pow./cl. i.o. task force	advice of the provincial physical planning committee to create a consultative body between all layers of government

1973

i.o.t. force	establishment of an intergov. steering committee chaired by a member of the prov. executive council
- meet.	discussion within steering committee concerning size and conception of new town
- stat. pow. (strat./ind.)	revision procedure of the provincial regional physical plan, differences in opinion between parties involved about alternatives

1976

- stat. pow. (ind.)	designation of Westervoort as a "growth town" by nat. government giving the opportunity to apply financial instruments of nat. government
- stat. pow. (strat. ind.)	draft of the regional physical plan indicating a new concept and postulating the necessity of administrative reform
- obj., cl. comp	objections by Duiven and Westervoort, claim for compensation because of changing policies

- adv. power	provincial council rejects administrative reform
1978	
- meet.	negotiation in the steering committee about compensation
- stat. pow. (ind.)	formal designation of the area as a growth town
- agr.	financial deal prepared in the steering committee
- inst. arr.	disbanding of the merger of physical planning agencies
1980	
- oth.	appointment of a former minister as project co-ordinator
- meet./neg.	negotiations about the application of growth town instruments
- invest./oth.	new population forecasts and new concept of the development of the inner city of Arnhem
- adv. pow.	cut down of the targets for the Duiven-Westervoort area by the province and the national government
1984	
- i.o.t. force	establishment of a working group to define new targets
- meet.	discussions about the financial implications of new policies, discussion in the parliament committee of housing and physical planning
- cl. comp.	claims especially that of Duiven, for compensation
- med.	attempt by the Queen's Commissioner of the province to prepare an agreement,
- cl. comp.	claim for compensation by the provincial electricity company because of cancellation of a central heating system
- stat. pow. (strat./ind.)	national report on urbanisation indicating loss of growth city status of Duiven
- comp.	financial compensation for Duiven and Westervoort paid by Arnhem and the ministry; electricity company gets compensation "in natura" (in kind)
1987	
agr.	agreement signed by all parties

List of abbreviations

CBD: Central Business District
CEZ: Comprehensive Environmental Zoning
CUP: Central Planning Bureau/Office/Commission
DSM: Dutch State Mines
EAP: Environmental Action Programme
HPPE: (Ministry of) Housing Physical Planning and Environment
MCE: Municipal Cleaning Enterprise
MD: Municipal Developer
MUPP: City or District Urban Office
NIK: Supreme Chamber of Control
PGEM: Provincial Electricity Company of Gelderland
PKPG: State Committee for Economic Planning
PONECOS: Poland - Netherlands Comparative Study

PPC:	Provincial Physical Planning Committee
PRON:	Patriotic Movement for National Rebirth
PZPR:	Polish United Workers Party
RDPP:	Regional Planning Directorate
STF:	Special Task Force
TF:	Task Force
VAM:	Waste Transport and Processing Company
VNG:	Association of Dutch Municipalities
VROM:	see HPPE

About the authors

Professor Ir. Arie Dekker teaches physical planning at the Catholic University of Nijmegen in the Netherlands. He has a special interest in the administrative aspects of physical planning. He is at the same time head of the department for regional physical planning of the provincie of Overijssel.

Dr. Henri J.M. Goverde is senior lecturer at the department of administrative and policy sciences of the Catholic University of Nijmegen in the Netherlands. His main field of activities is related to administrative and organisational aspects of the public sector, especially of infrastructure planning and environmental policy.

Professor Dr. Aleksandra Jewtuchowicz teaches at the department of urban economics of the University of Lodz, Poland. Her special interest is industrial policies and externalities.

Dr. Adam Kowalewski has been director of the City Planning Office of Warsaw and UN expert. He was senior researcher at the department of regional economy of the Polish Academy of Science in Warsaw in the first stage of the project. He was appointed Deputy Minister for Spatial Economy and Architecture in November 1989.

Professor Dr. Tadeusz Markowski teaches urban economics at the University of Lodz. He is head of the department of urban economics and deputy director of the Institute of Regional Policies of the same University.

Drs. Leo P.W. van der Meer is senior official at the department of regional physical planning of the province of Gelderland.

Dr. Barrie Needham is senior lecturer at the department of physical planning of the Catholic University in Nijmegen, the Netherlands. He has a special interest in the implementation of physical planning.

Dr. Maria Ptaszynska-Woloczkowicz was senior researcher at the department of regional economy of the Polish Academy of Science in Warsaw. In 1990 she was appointed director of the Foundation in Support of Local Democracy in Warsaw.